Good Times, Bad Times

Good Times, Bad Times

Soap Operas and Society in Western Europe

Hugh O'Donnell

Leicester University Press
London and New York

Leicester University Press
A Cassell imprint
Wellington House, 125 Strand, London, WC2R 0BB
370 Lexington Avenue, New York, NY 10017–6550

First published 1999
© Hugh O'Donnell 1999

British Library Cataloguing-in-Publication Data
A catalogue record for this book is available from the British Library.

ISBN 0-7185-0045-8 (hardback)
   0-7185-0046-6 (paperback)

Library of Congress Cataloging-in-Publication Data
O'Donnell, Hugh, 1949–
  Good times, bad times: soap operas and society in western Europe/Hugh O'Donnell.
    p.   cm.
  Includes bibliographical references and index.
  ISBN 0-7185-0045-8 (hardcover). — ISBN 0-7185-0046-6 (pbk.)
  1. Soap operas—Europe—History and criticism. 2. Soap operas—Social aspects—Europe.
  I. Title.
PN 1992.8.S4026 1998
791.45'6—dc21   97-51601
                                            CIP

Typeset by York House Typographic Ltd, London
Printed and bound in Great Britain by Biddles Ltd, Guildford and King's Lynn

Contents

Acknowledgements

Some of the material appearing in the chapters on Spain and Portugal, and also in the Introduction, appeared in an earlier form in 'From a Manichean universe to the kitchen sink: the *telenovela* in the Iberian peninsula', in the *International Journal of Iberian Studies*, vol. 8, no. 1, 1996.

Some of the material appearing in the chapter on Sweden, and also in the Introduction, appeared in an earlier form in 'From "People's Home" to "Home and Away": the growth and development of soap opera in Sweden', in *Irish Communication Review*, no. 6, 1996.

A general overview of a number of the productions studied here appeared in 'The rise and rise of soap operas in Europe' (with Paul Mohr), in *Scottish Communication Association Journal*, vol. 2, 1996.

I would like to thank the following staff of various European television and production companies for their help in providing me with tapes and other material in the course of this project: Paul de Borger (BRTN), Fernando José Correia Filipe (RTP), Christina Ferneklint (SVT), Truus Genbrugge (VT4), Jacqueline Glencorse (Scottish), Mónica Jiménez (Tele-cinco), Alacoque Kealy (RTÉ), Remco Kobus (Joop van den Ende Produkties), Lene Nedergaard (DR), Ed Prelinski (Grundy Worldwide), Fernando Rodríguez (TVG), Anna Vicent (Retequattro), Stephan Wiese-höfer (ZDF) and Ilonka von Wisotzky (GFF). In particular I would like to thank Anne Birte Brunvold Tørstad (NRK) for taking the time to speak to me at some length during a visit to Oslo in January 1995. Many others working in press offices and drama departments throughout Europe sup-plied me with information without my ever discovering who they were: to these anonymous colleagues a collective 'thank you'.

I would also like to take this opportunity to thank the following Catalan scriptwriters who so generously gave me of their time during a trip to

Barcelona in May 1997: Jaume Cabré (*Estació d'enllaç*), Josep Maria Benet i Jornet (*Poble Nou, La Rosa, Nissaga de Poder*) and Maria Mercè Roca (*Secrets de família, Vidas cruzadas*). I am particularly indebted to Salvador Cardús of the Universitat Autònoma de Barcelona who arranged these meetings on my behalf.

I am also much indebted to the following colleagues who either supplied me with tapes and/or a wide range of material relating to the productions analysed in this book, or encouraged me to look into areas I might otherwise have neglected: Cristina Água-Mel (Dublin University), Lars Åhlander (Svenska Filminstitutet), Hilde Arnsten (Bergen University), Harald Bjerregård (Hellerud Videregående Skole), Jan Blommaert (Antwerp University), Raymond Boyle (Stirling University), Rinella Cere (Sheffield Hallam University), Peter Dahlén (Gothenburg University), Joep Debeij (Hogeschool van Utrecht), Siân Jones (Cardiff University), Tamar Liebes (Jerusalem University), Sonia Livingstone (London School of Economics), Aonghas MacNeacail (Sabhal Mòr Ostaig), Cláudia Monteiro (Leicester University), Barbara O'Connor (Dublin City University), Roel Puijk (Høgskolen i Lillehammer), Sven Ross (Stockholm University), Iiris Ruoho (Tampere University), Helena Sheehan (Dublin City University), Isabel Simões Ferreira (Instituto Politécnico de Lisboa), Bernadette Vriamont (Brussels University) and Lieve van der Walle (Hogeschool Limburg).

The following students at Glasgow Caledonian University also provided me with much very valuable taped and other material: Nacho Burrull, Sara Ceusters, Judith Dijkstra, Svend Larsen, Jaume Marín, Mairi Thomson, Stephen Tierney, Alexandra Trindade Paulo, Tuuli Pokki and Anita Tuomainen.

Among my own colleagues and research students at Glasgow Caledonian University I want to thank, in particular, Carolyn Carr for her technical expertise in relation to production aspects of some of the soaps analysed, Josune Etxebeste for her help with the Basque soaps, David Hutchison for the use of his materials on the UK soaps, Katerina Mantouvalou for providing me with tapes of and material relating to the Greek soaps, Fernando León Solís for organizing tapes of a whole range of Spanish *telenovelas*, Mark Meredith for his help in consulting electronic databases in relation to the UK soaps, Paul Mohr for making available to me a mountainous supply of material in connection with the German soaps, Myra Macdonald and Margaret Ross for their extremely helpful comments on the UK soaps, Roz Smith for her material on the Welsh soaps, and finally Neil Blain for his (as ever) highly insightful observations on various sections of the manuscript, and Bill Scott, not only for his penetrating comments on the Introduction, but also for his unfailing support, both intellectual and financial, in this and other projects.

For
Joanne, Karen and Alison

Introduction

The project

This book is the result of a project into which I stumbled almost by chance. In December 1992 I asked a colleague who had just had a dish aerial installed to record whatever programmes happened to be showing that evening on the commercial Dutch channel RTL4. When I watched the tape the following day, I realized that one of the programmes it contained was a soap. It was entitled *Goede Tijden, Slechte Tijden* (Good Times, Bad Times) and featured Dutch actors playing Dutch characters speaking Dutch. I was rather surprised by this since I had not been aware of the fact that there were any domestic Dutch soap operas. A few weeks later, on viewing an evening's programmes from the German commercial channel RTLPlus (taped by the same obliging colleague), I was even more surprised to find a German soap, featuring German actors, and entitled *Gute Zeiten, Schlechte Zeiten* (Good Times, Bad Times). But what surprised me most of all was that, despite having the same title and sharing what were essentially the same characters – although the names did not necessarily coincide in each case – these two soaps were very different from each other. The Dutch soap was sombre and moody, while the German version was youthful, energetic and up-beat.

Some initial research quickly established the common genealogy of these two soaps. Each was based on the now long-defunct Australian soap *The Restless Years*, a Grundy production of the late 1970s, and in each case the domestic Dutch and German producers had simply translated the original scripts for about a year, making such changes as were required to adapt them to local conditions. In their initial stages both soaps were, therefore, very close to each other, as would also be the case later with *Verbotene Liebe* (Forbidden Love) in Germany and *Skilda världar* (Separate Worlds) in

Sweden, also both Grundy rewrites, based on the earlier *Sons and Daughters*. However, once the domestic scriptwriters began to write their own scripts, a stage was very quickly reached – certainly by around mid-1993 – when these soaps had diverged so much that it would have been genuinely difficult to know they had ever had anything in common. What, I asked myself, was it about Dutch culture on the one hand and German culture on the other that had caused such an amazing transformation to take place. I resolved to investigate why this might be the case, and to establish what other domestic soaps there might be in Europe, and what connections they might have with their domestic cultures. This book is the result. It analyses all new domestic soaps and *telenovelas* which have emerged in Europe since 1990.

Some terms defined

In this book I will deal with soap operas and *telenovelas*. Both the soap opera and the *telenovela* are forms of seriality (Oltean, 1993). In principle, the difference between serial and series is a simple one. While the narratives in a serial roll seamlessly across episodes and the characters may (and indeed often do) change over time, the characters in a series remain relatively stable while each episode contains its own independent, completed storyline. And while the episodes of a serial must be shown in strict chronological order, the episodes of a series could, at least in theory, be shown in any order at all. However obvious these kinds of differences might seem now, there is nothing in any way automatic about them, and both broadcasters and viewers require the appropriate cultural competences in order to deal successfully with the serial form. Jostein Gripsrud (1995: 205) describes in some detail the original difficulties experienced by Norwegian audiences watching *Dynasty* in the early 1980s since they initially expected it to come to an end in the way a traditional narrative would, while Milly Buonanno recounts how, when *Dallas* was originally shown in Italy by the public service broadcaster RAI, the episodes were not shown in the correct order since the broadcasters believed it to be a series which they could show in any order whatsoever (1994: 129).

There is little doubt that the difference *in practice* between series and serial is now being increasingly blurred in a number of European productions, in particular hospital dramas (*Casualty* in the UK, *Stadtklinik* and others in Germany, *Medisch Centrum West* in the Netherlands, *Hospital* in Spain and so on), where completed narratives in each episode are often combined with much longer-running narratives which not only continue from one episode to the next, but sometimes even from one season to the next. Despite this, the difference between serial and series remains an important one, since the *télévision-fleuve* nature of the serial generates a different relationship between product and viewer than that which accompanies a series, even one with longer-running narratives embedded beneath the shorter ones.

Though sharing certain technical similarities, the soap opera and the *telenovela* are really rather different forms of serial, and I will attempt to outline their main differences below.

The *telenovela*

Though in this book I will deal in detail only with those *telenovelas* currently being produced in Portugal and Spain, the *telenovela* itself is originally a Latin American product. It is in fact the successor to the *radionovela* which originated on radio in Cuba in the 1940s (González, 1995: 106), and it has now spread as the major televisual form throughout Latin America as a whole.

The popularity of the *telenovela* in Latin America is beyond question. *Telenovelas* can attract audience shares of over 90 per cent (Lopez, 1995: 263) – indeed, in a recent interview in the Portuguese magazine *Expresso* (7 December 1996), Brazilian *telenovela* author Lauro César Muniz claimed that the final episode of the production *A Próxima Vítima* (The Next Victim) had an audience share of 100 per cent – and up to 40 million people watch them daily in Brazil alone (Allen, 1995: 2). Latin American *telenovelas* also currently enjoy very considerable popularity as an imported product in many southern European countries, and their success in the countries of the former Soviet Union has been remarkable. Over 200 million people regularly watched *Los ricos también lloran* (The Rich Also Cry) when it was screened there in 1992: indeed, it had to be rescheduled from its original afternoon slot to the evening since the levels of absenteeism caused were damaging an already weakened economy. Latin American *telenovelas* are now the most exported television products in the world: Delia Fiallo, the veteran Cuban *telenovela* author whose many works include the enormously successful *Cristal* and *Alejandra*, claimed recently that her productions had been seen by over 1600 million people worldwide (*Cambio 16*, 8 August 1994), which would make them surely the most viewed televisual fiction programmes of all time. Due, no doubt, to the influence of the Latin American products, the currently dominant form of domestic serial in both Spain and Portugal is the *telenovela* rather than the soap, and a number of domestic *telenovelas* have also been produced in Italy and Greece.

As the term suggests, the *telenovela* (i.e. television novel) is essentially a *story*. Though it can have a very large number of episodes – the average is around 170, though the highly popular Venezuelan production, *Cristal*, for example, had 250, while *Simplemente María* (Simply María) had 500 – the *telenovela* has a beginning, a middle and an end, and, to that extent, conforms to the classic definition of narrative. It is, therefore, a form of *non-continuous* serial: part of its agreement with its viewers is that it will, indeed, come to an end.

The Spanish analyst López-Pumarejo plays down this difference between soap and *telenovela*. He posits a single all-inclusive *telenovela* genre which he sub-divides into 'classic *telenovela*' (the American daytime soaps), 'transnational *telenovela*' (the American supersoaps) and 'Latin American *telenovela*', suggesting that 'closure is optional for the *telenovela*' (1987: 71). I would find it very difficult to sustain such a point of view. No Latin American *telenovela* has the option of continuing endlessly *à la Coronation Street*, any more than any European, Australian or American soap has the option of coming to a pre-programmed end. Following a *telenovela* to its climax is a very different cultural (and indeed emotional) experience to watching a soap, and the approaching end is often accompanied by what, to the outsider at least, looks like something approaching hysteria in the press of the country in question, particularly the specialized television press. Although moments of high tension can occur in soaps, seasoned soap viewers know that the narratives will continue to roll on once the crisis is (at least temporarily) over. The end of a *telenovela* is, by contrast, 'The End', with neither storylines nor characters reappearing (other than in the form of reruns or remakes, both of which occur) and leads to all kinds of techniques to ensure viewer loyalty during the changeover: in the final week of a *telenovela* it is not unusual for each of the last five episodes to be immediately followed by the corresponding opening episode of the new *telenovela*.

While soaps have no obvious heroes or heroines, the narrative in a *telenovela* almost always centres on a main character whose name may also be used as the title of the serial: Kassandra, Micaela, Joana, etc. (these characters are usually, though not invariably, female). There are always other simultaneous narrative lines, but they tend to be secondary to, rather than parallel with, the main narrative. The presence of a main character combined with the discreteness of each product has also led to a highly developed star system surrounding *telenovelas* in Latin America. Since the star, by definition, transcends his or her role (Butler, 1995: 146–7), soap actors find it difficult to become stars given that they remain fixed in the same role indefinitely: at best they can become celebrities or become stars once they leave the soap (by and large, stars figure in soaps only as guest appearances or because they were already stars before accepting the role in the soap). The leading actors of the *telenovelas* are, by contrast, *the* great stars of Latin America, genuine household names throughout the continent, and their appearance in new productions is eagerly awaited by their audiences. It also seems clear that a (perhaps more modest) *telenovela* star system is now forming in Portugal, though not yet in Spain.

Thematically *telenovelas* fall into two large groups. The first group –

stereotypically the Mexican and Venezuelan products – concentrates heavily on stories dealing primarily with emotions, and routinely present a very Manichean view of the world. The second group – consisting mostly of the Brazilian and, to a lesser extent, the Columbian *telenovelas* – engages much more openly with issues of the day. For more information on this divide see Lopez (1995), Martín-Barbero (1995) and O'Donnell (1996a).

Telenovelas belonging to this second group can be extremely topical. Martín-Barbero describes how, for example, a Peruvian film crew going to shoot on location were unable to reach their destination because of a taxi drivers' strike, so they simply included it in the narrative (1987: 246). *Telenovelas* can also often be highly political, much more overtly political than any soap. The Venezuelan production *Por estas calles* is believed to have contributed to the downfall of former president Carlos Andrés Pérez by exposing corruption on his part (*L'Unità*, 17 January 1994), while Lauro César Muniz was forced by political pressures to change the ending of his 1989 production, *Sassá Mutema*, since it was based on the candidate standing against Fernando Collor de Melo in the Brazilian presidential elections. Later, *O Marajá*, covering the actual presidency of Fernando Collor de Melo, was prevented from being screened by the latter's lawyers (*L'Unità*, 17 January 1994; *El País*, 4 February 1994). *Telenovelas* can also have important agenda-setting functions. When the leading character in the Venezuelan production *Cristal* contracted breast cancer, this led, according to the actress Mariela Alcalá, who interpreted the role, to a huge increase in the number of women asking for screenings in that country. The Brazilian *Barriga de Aluguel* (Womb for Hire) dealt with the question of surrogate motherhood, which, again according to its leading actress Cassia Kiss, led to increased public debate when first screened in Brazil (both reports from *Semana*, 3 October 1991).

Structurally, *telenovelas* also fall into two large groups. Among those involved in their production these are known respectively as 'open' and 'closed' *telenovelas*. A 'closed' *telenovela* is one which has already been filmed in its entirety before it goes on the air, while an 'open' *telenovela* is still being shot while earlier episodes are being screened. The open *telenovela* – which was a Brazilian invention – is, therefore, able to change its direction in mid-stream, either because it is losing its audience – as was the case with the Mexican production *Valentina*, for example (Lopez, 1995: 269) – or due to straightforward political pressures, as in the case of *Sassá Mutema* mentioned above. As far as European *telenovelas* are concerned, Spanish *telenovelas* are open, while the Portuguese ones are closed.

The soap opera

The origins of the soap opera in 1930s America have been well studied and well documented. Anyone wishing further information on this should consult, in the first instance, Allen (1985). There is now widespread critical agreement concerning the specificities of soap opera as a form of *continuous serial* (Allen, 1985, 1995; Ang, 1985; Buckman, 1984; Buonanno, 1994; Fiske, 1987; Geraghty, 1981, 1991; Gripsrud, 1995). In terms of structure, the key element is the inherent absence of any prospect of *final* narrative closure (though of course local closure of individual plot lines does occur). As González Requena puts it (1992: 121):

the soap opera ... proclaims its desire never to end, to continue indefinitely ... it is a narrative whose aim is never to finish – the fact that some actual soap operas do come to an end, do stop reproducing themselves indefinitely, must be seen as an epiphenomenon, as a more or less arbitrary act of violence by the real world attacking the very essence of its formal structure.

This narrative endlessness is combined with a multiplicity of simultaneous, overlapping story lines and a large number of characters, meaning that protagonism tends to be shared out – a situation Milly Buonanno describes as 'polycentric protagonism' (1994: 130). In terms of content, a soap is also characterized by the relative priority it accords to relationships and dialogue over action, though this does not mean, of course, that action is entirely absent. Regarding mode of address, there has also been a traditional tendency (noticeably reduced in more recent times) for soaps to address a mainly female audience.

Concerning the definition of a soap, there are three points to note. First, soaps cannot reasonably be described as 'never-ending stories' – a description used quite literally (in the appropriate language) by Italian analyst Milly Buonanno (1994: 131) and by German analyst Joan Kirstin Bleicher (1995: 41) ('una storia infinita' and 'unendliche Geschichten' respectively). This description is inappropriate not because soaps are not 'never-ending', which they manifestly are, but because they are not stories. A *telenovela* is a story; a soap is a narrative structure which allows a never-ending *series* of stories to be told, usually featuring the same characters and, by and large, set in the same location, but it is not itself a story.

Secondly, I am unable to agree with suggestions that in a soap the ending is somehow subject to 'continual postponement' (Geraghty, 1981: 11) or 'endless deferment' (Fiske, 1987: 183). The ending of a soap cannot be described as 'postponed' or 'deferred' since it is not possible to postpone or defer something which is not on the agenda. Only someone who has never sat through the 150- or 200-plus episodes of a *telenovela* as it inches its way agonizingly towards a conclusion could ever talk of the ending of a soap opera as being 'postponed'.

Thirdly, I am unable to agree with the view that because a soap lacks an end it therefore lacks finality, or, to use Buonanno's terminology, that it is somehow 'a-teleological' (1994: 131). This is a point I return to in greater depth below when I look at narrative closure and ideology.

A shared characteristic: industrialized production

On one or two occasions in the course of this study I came across productions which fulfilled all the criteria given above for a soap, but which I was unwilling to classify unproblematically as soaps. The reason was that they were too short. But it was not their shortness as such which ruled them out as soaps; instead it was the fact that, being short, their production never achieved the industrialized methods which characterize both soaps and *telenovelas* as a whole. I have not been able, for reasons of space, to go into the production aspect of soaps in this book. A small number of studies do exist (Hobson, 1983; Gustafsson and Lovén, 1993; Jurga, 1995), but beyond these there is a great deal of information available in the press of the various European countries concerned, and programmes of the *The Making of . . .* variety, of which I have seen perhaps half a dozen, are becoming more and more common. All of these sources make it quite clear what is involved: terms such as 'factory techniques', 'assembly-line production', 'mass production' and so on abound, and there are even references to 'taylorization'. Particularly in the case of the daily soaps the pace of production is frenetic, and large numbers of people are involved at every stage. In the midst of these industrialized processes all notions of authorship are lost. According to the Swedish soap writer Ola Höglund (*Dagens Nyheter*, 26 September 1996), the editorial office of the Swedish soap *Rederiet* (High Seas) has a plaque outside saying 'No auteurs beyond this point', while the final product is on occasions so unrecognizable for some writers that they prefer a pseudonym to appear in the credits rather than their own name (apparently Lazlo Bentsson is a favourite for Sweden's other weekly soap, *Tre Kronor*).

This is a characteristic shared by the *telenovela*, both in its Latin American and in its European variants. Unlike most soaps, each *telenovela* tends to have an identifiable author or authors, but their relationship with the final product is often very distant indeed. While they produce the broad outline of the story – sometimes referred to as the Bible – the processes by which this is transformed into concrete scenes with concrete dialogues is very complex and large- and small-scale changes are routinely made at all steps in the process: even the actors get their oar in at times, ad libbing, making unexpected changes, refusing to go along with the script. The changes can be structural. In the case of the Catalan *telenovela Secrets de família* (Family Secrets), the incident which was used to open the first

episode had originally appeared in the seventh chapter of the Bible (information supplied by the author, Maria Mercè Roca). Despite the name of the
author(s) appearing in the credits, *telenovelas* are every bit as much collective products as soaps. As Renato Ortiz says of the Brazilian products in
particular: 'You end up with a creative world ... without an identifiable
author where the role of each participant is entirely circumstantial' (1995:
129). Indeed, according to Lauro César Muniz in the interview mentioned
earlier, the loss of a sense of authorship is currently a source of much
frustration among certain Brazilian *telenovela* writers.

Both soap operas and *telenovelas* routinely receive very negative coverage
from the highbrow press of the countries where they are produced, the (at
least proposed) object of such criticism being their perceived lack of quality.
This is a very complex issue, since quality is an ideological concept, not an
aesthetic one, a point I will return to on a number of occasions in the course
of this book. However, whatever one might think of soaps and *telenovelas*, it
is worthwhile bearing in mind that they are produced by real people –
writers, storyliners, actors, directors, technicians and so on – who, given the
budgetary and resource constraints all European producers are currently
operating under, are working close to or at the limits of the televisually
possible.

Narrative closure and ideology

As mentioned earlier, the presence or absence of narrative closure is the
primary differentiating feature between *telenovelas* and soaps. Narrative
closure is often seen as a mechanism whereby ideological closure is attempted by the text. The final ideological focus of a *telenovela* is, in fact, often
clear. For example, Portugal's best-selling TV magazine *TVMais* (31
December 1993) described the Brazilian production *Vale Tudo* (Anything
Goes) as a '*telenovela* ... inspired by the lack of ethics which has become
standard in Brazil', and went on to sum up – in advance! – what it called the
'inevitable denouement' of the likewise Brazilian production *O Dono do
Mundo* (Master of the World). Talking of the two main characters, Karen
and Felipe Barretos, it wrote:

The solution found for Karen brings to an end her career of scheming and
skulduggery, with a moral which is typical for Brazil: while people are busy trying
to eliminate society's small blemishes, the large evils continue to proliferate. And
the Felipe Barretos of this world continue on their way unpunished, in the
telenovela as in life.

Since soaps are, by contrast, endless, it has on occasions been argued that a
fundamental element of the genre is its refusal of ideological closure. As
Feuer, for example, suggests (1984: 15):

serial form and multiple plot structure appear to give TV melodrama a greater potential for multiple and aberrant readings than do other forms of popular narrative. Since no action is irreversible, every ideological position may be countered by its opposite.

Indeed, this position has to some extent assumed the proportions of an orthodoxy in relation to soaps.

Although I would not wish to challenge this orthodoxy completely – there is clearly a relationship between narrative closure and at least the possibility of attempted ideological closure – I would not wish to make any unproblematizing assumptions either that a text without an ending cannot have a consistent ideological position beyond the ups and downs of individual narratives, or that the overall ideological position of a text must necessarily coincide with that attempted by the narrative closure where there is one. I would agree here with the arguments put forward by Jostein Gripsrud in his study of the *Dynasty* phenomenon in Norway (1995: 238–9), themselves to some extent a development of theoretical perspectives advanced by Umberto Eco (1981) and of Barthes's earlier distinction between 'readable' and 'writable' text (1970: 10). Gripsrud argues that 'openness' and 'closedness' are not simply (or even primarily) a technical feature of the macrostructure of the narrative, but are more fundamentally a feature of the *fabric* of the text. Thus a narrative which is structurally closed, i.e. has an ending, may be open to a variety of meanings, and a narrative which is structurally open – in other words is endless – may offer little scope for multiple meanings to emerge. In short, the ideological *burden* of a text is not dependent on technical closure, and where closure occurs, need not necessarily coincide with the apparent ideological closure attempted by the ending.

Thus a number of researchers – Feuer included – have seen the American supersoaps of the 1980s as concise expressions of a Reaganite ideology for all their structural openness (an interpretation with which, incidentally, I do not necessarily agree). López-Pumarejo, for example, sees them as 'the narrative functionalisation of the Republican worldview of the eighties, that is to say of the Reagan era' (1987: 126), while Feuer sees these programmes as 'bearing what appears to be a right-wing ideology by means of a potentially progressive narrative form' (1984: 16). And when endings do occur, they can, as Gripsrud rightly points out, be 'logically satisfactory or unsatisfactory' (1995: 249): in other words, they can contradict the ideological burden of the preceding text. Buonanno argues cogently, for example, that the ending of the 1992 Italian serial *La storia spezzata* (The Broken Story) runs counter to the world view developed by everything that went before.

Or again, the text can allow more than one possible ending. When the Brazilian production *Roque Santeiro* was drawing to a close, two endings were prepared and the public invited to vote for the one they preferred. Despite the very different ideological message of each ending, neither appears to have been rejected as 'impossible' by those interviewed (Allen, 1995: 23). That two such opposite endings could have been considered acceptable by viewers in itself testifies to the at least potential openness of the preceding text. A similar technique was used again with *A Próxima Vítima*, and, rather fascinatingly, the Brazilian audience chose a different ending from the Portuguese audience when it was shown there. There have also been occasions where the proposed ending of a *telenovela* has been changed half-way through the production, as was the case with *Poble Nou* (see page 163) and with Telemundo's production *Valentina* (Lopez, 1995: 269).

Moreover, although a final narrative closure is always eventually reached in a *telenovela*, the ending is not always *perceived* as the most important part of the production by the viewers. As Assumpta Roura points out in her interesting study of the Latin-American *telenovela* in Spain, for the viewers, 'the denouement . . . is never the main attraction. What gets the audience hooked are precisely those desperate situations in which Destiny has placed each of the characters' (1993: 19). Indeed, the end of a *telenovela* sometimes seems to be accompanied by a sense of dissatisfaction and even disappointment among viewers. It may well be the case that there is an unresolvable structural tension between televisual narratives of such prodigious length and effective ideological closure, a tension which is not to be found in shorter productions such as films, or even mini-series.

The analytical model

The analytical model followed in this book is represented diagrammatically in Figure 1. I should perhaps point out that I did not set out on this project with this model already in mind. It was very much a model which developed as the project proceeded, and it is no doubt capable of considerable further refinement.

My approach to the soaps and *telenovelas* analysed here could perhaps best be described as, broadly speaking, neo-Gramscian. I do not view these serials as texts in themselves, but see them rather as sites of a complex ongoing process of negotiation between producers and consumers, itself taking place within a much larger framework. This is the framework represented by Figure 1. Areas of the diagram which have been filled in represent what are in my view particularly important boundaries within the framework: the darker the filling the more hermetic the boundary, though in general terms these boundaries are much more permeable working from the periphery in, than they are working from the centre out. However, although this diagram provides a two-dimensional representation of the

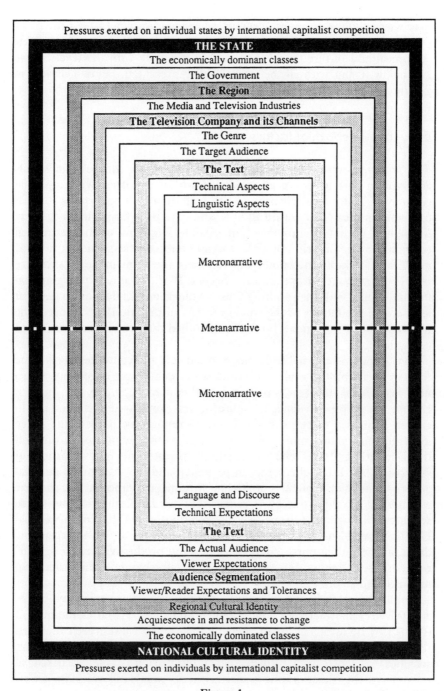

Figure 1

processes involved, a more accurate representation would be a three- or even multidimensional one. In particular, each level of the diagram has reciprocal and bi-directional relationships not only with the levels above and below it, but with all the other levels represented. Below I outline in greater detail what is meant by each level.

Extra- and intertextual factors

The pressures exerted by international capitalist competition. The serials analysed in this book are all produced within countries with capitalist economies. Long-term changes in the patterns of international capitalist competition mean that we are all now, and have been for some time, living through a period of prolonged internal realignment within individual economies. The oil crisis of 1973 was no doubt a catalyst in this realignment, but attempts to contain and roll back the gains made by ordinary people throughout Europe after the Second World War had been going on for some time, with the resulting sense of blockage and disillusion being at least one of the factors in the student unrest of the late 1960s: indeed, the failure of those movements no doubt smoothed the way for the subsequent realignment.

In Europe this internal realignment has taken, and continues to take, the form of an attempt to replace a former social-democratic hegemony with a new neo-liberal one (the situation is rather more complex in southern Europe given the existence of more or less long-lived dictatorships in certain countries there), the aim being to reduce social costs and make individual economies more competitive internationally, primarily through the dismantling of the welfare state and the privatization of a wide range of services. The Maastricht Treaty in particular and the attempts of national governments to implement it are part of this ongoing process. The rhetoric engendered by this strategy is remarkably similar from one country to another. Throughout Europe 'we' are being informed that 'our' National Health Service costs too much, 'our' state pensions are an unacceptable drain on the public purse, 'our' efficiency and productivity are low, 'our' economy is uncompetitive, 'we' are pricing ourselves out of international markets, and so on.

In most western European countries (there are a few exceptions) soaps and *telenovelas* attract very large, popular audiences. As far as the bulk of (though by no means all) soap opera and *telenovela* viewers are concerned the increasing penetration of neo-liberal practices in western European societies has led to much greater economic insecurity, increased risk of unemployment, deteriorating social services, worsening working conditions, all combined with sustained attempts – on occasions carried out through their domestic soaps – to reposition them as individual post-modern consumers enjoying increased choice and enhanced lifestyle opportunities.

The state. All the serials analysed in this book are produced within the framework of individual states, and are primarily consumed within the framework of that state (there are *very* few exceptions to this). They are therefore both produced and consumed within long political and cultural traditions inside and outside the television industry. Particularly large-scale upheavals, such as the restoration of democracy in Greece, Portugal and Spain (leading to an internal reorganization of the country in the latter case), have all exerted powerful influences on the television industries in these countries and, either directly or indirectly, on the serials produced.

Despite all the talk about Television Without Frontiers, state frontiers remain remarkably impermeable boundaries as far as domestic European soap operas and *telenovelas* are concerned. Transnational television is undoubtedly a technological reality (which I have eagerly exploited in the preparation of this book) but is not yet in any meaningful sense a cultural one.

Social classes. All the serials analysed in this book are produced within countries divided internally along class lines. The definition of class I follow is essentially the Marxist – and to that extent a material – one, in other words that class is primarily defined by relationship to (ownership of or control over) the means of production. Even allowing for differences arising from the very different histories of different European states – which can at times be quite substantial – all western European countries have, following this definition, a relatively small, economically dominant (or ruling) class which exercises enormous, and to a very large extent, unaccountable control over the economy as a whole; a very large working class which consists of a shrinking industrial proletariat, and a much larger 'new' working class employed mainly in the tertiary sector; and various middle-class groups in between: the traditional petite bourgeoisie (owners of small businesses and the like), an older middle class consisting largely of the liberal professions, and a newer middle class made up of individuals who exercise decisive control of various kinds over small but significant portions of the social product (managers, financiers, stockbrokers and so on). The class-composition of its audience is a crucial factor in understanding any soap or *telenovela*.

A fundamental difference between the former social-democratic hegemony and the new neo-liberal one which is attempting to impose itself lies in the dominant discourse of social class. The social-democratic hegemony – which was by and large followed, with local variations of course, by European political parties of both the Left and the Right between the end of the Second World War and the late 1970s/early 1980s – recognized the existence of social classes: this was a basic principle behind the Scandinavian *folkhem*, the *Sozialpartnerschaft* of the German-speaking

countries, even the One Nation ideology of the old-style British Conservatives. Systems and structures were then put in place – at times on the
basis of very concrete agreements, as, for example, the Saltsjöbad Agreement in Sweden, or the historic *rapprochement* between employers' and
workers' organization in Finland during the Winter War – whereby the
different classes could contribute usefully to a stable and prosperous
society, all accompanied by a variety of discourses based on the general
principle of 'pulling together'. The dominant discourse of the neo-liberal
hegemony – of which Margaret Thatcher was Europe's first official representative – is predicated on the abolition of the notion of class, and, in
extreme forms, even of society itself. Everyone is redefined as an individual,
wealth is a reward for personal effort and risk, the unemployed are
encouraged to 'get on their bikes'. The conflict between these two discourses – and the practices which they simultaneously accompany and
legitimate – saturates contemporary European societies at all levels.

A clear element of the neo-liberal thrust has also been concerted attempts
– quite successful in many countries – to reduce the power of the trade
unions, thereby atomizing and individualizing the members of the working-
classes more effectively.

The government. Europe has seen a number of dramatic changes of
government as the 1990s have progressed. The 1997 victories of the British
Labour Party and the Parti Socialiste Français are the most spectacular so
far, but the 1996 victory of the right-wing Partido Popular in Spain was also
a significant turning point in that country, as was the resignation of Cavaco
Silva in Portugal in January 1995 and the defeat of his party in October of
the same year after ten years of government there. This lurching from Left
to Right or Right to Left is not in any sense a sign of political schizophrenia
among European electorates. We are in a situation of prolonged tension
between the economically dominant classes in Europe, among whom the
neo-liberal ideology is now widely (though by no means universally)
accepted, and the economically dominated classes who simply refuse to
swallow it unquestioningly (as the slowing down of the Maastricht process
due to popular resistance makes clear). The function of the contemporary
'political classes' in western Europe is to find a workable degree of fit
between the dominant ideology of their ruling classes and the expectations,
tolerances and resistances of the economically disenfranchised (by which I
do not mean poor) sections of their population. The outcome of this process
is by no means yet clear: indeed, it is not even certain that anything stable
enough will ever be reached to be reasonably described as an 'outcome'.

I am not suggesting here that changes of government are irrelevant. The
UK has, in small, but at least in some cases, important ways (increased
spending on secondary education, some commitment, however qualified, to
a minimum wage), become a more agreeable place to live for some of its
inhabitants since the Labour victory, even though it has been made

absolutely clear that many of the major planks of Thatcherism – in particular its often aggressive anti-trade-union legislation – will be left in place. For a significant proportion of its population Spain has become a less agreeable place to be since the victory of the Partido Popular, as the 'flexibilization' of the labour market (in other words, making it easier to dismiss workers) and the year-long freeze on public sector wages clearly demonstrate. But whatever differences of approach these changes might bring, they are in no sense 'revolutions': the British electorate is already being softened up for the 'hard choices' ahead. In much the same way as the former social-democratic hegemony was maintained with different empha-ses and priorities by previous governments of both Left and Right, the new neo-liberal hegemony is now actively being pursued with different empha-ses and priorities by governments of both Right and Left. The Parti Socialiste Français was one of the first traditional left-wing parties in Europe to undergo this change in the early 1980s, followed quickly by the PSOE in Spain, and the remaining dominoes have all fallen since. These changes of government are the successive phases of a prolonged period of negotiation between opposing classes mediated by the politicians.

An area where the population of most European countries has been prepared to accept larger doses of liberalization has been, specifically, the television industry. One of the great cultural failings of the social-democratic hegemony was that it largely gave up on the idea of 'fun': it was a serious business, aimed at educating the individual into responsible citizenship. The emergence of private commercial stations has, beyond any doubt, provided channels of expression for popular views, tastes and experiences which had been ignored by the public service channels, and this has been probably the most successful 'populist' strand of the new ideology (tax cuts have been another rather less successful 'populist' tactic). This has resulted in the relatively easy – and from many points of view quite remarkable – appropriation of notions such as 'fun' and 'glamour' by neo-liberalism, which is not in any sense a fun-oriented or glamorous ideology (this has been one of the greatest ideological 'steals' of recent times).

The new commercial channels which have arisen with the increasing liberalization of western European economies have been a crucial factor in the growth of domestic soaps in Europe and, in a number of cases, changes in government have been important in allowing the legislation to proceed which made the operation of these commercial channels easier (Greece and Sweden are cases in point).

The region. I use the term 'Region' here in a purely technical sense to indicate subdivisions of existing state structures with powerfully developed cultural identities and in most cases institutions which allow region-specific practices to flourish and region-specific discourses to circulate. The term therefore applies to 'regions' as disparate as Scotland, Catalonia and Flanders. Some of these 'regions' also have their own language, or a very distinctive dialect of the state language. The establishment of regional television stations, the endeavour to find a form of expression for the regional identity, and material support from regional authorities in that endeavour have been crucial factors in a number of the soaps analysed here.

These regions also include some where the majority – in some cases the vast majority – of the population believe that they constitute a separate nation. This is, for example, the case in Scotland and, perhaps to a somewhat lesser extent, Catalonia. In these cases the question of National Cultural Identity, which is normally restricted to the state level, is either supplemented or to some extent supplanted by a similar phenomenon at the regional level.

The media and television industries. In all countries the media are an important meeting point for the myriad discourses which saturate our societies. Competing ideologies are seldom explicated in any way. Instead they find expression through a vast range of discourses covering all areas of social and personal life: the family, work, the role of women in society, unemployment, the welfare state, fashions and so on. The mix of discourses acknowledged, reworked and reproduced by any media varies enormously as a function of its clientèle. Thus newspapers whose readership is primarily among the economically dominant will often circulate neo-liberal discourses in a technicist and almost 'taken-as-read' way through their political and, in particular, economic analyses; middle-brow newspapers addressing the economically privileged who identify with the economically dominant can on occasions carry very aggressive neo-liberal discourses (the unemployed and lone parents as scroungers, the National Health Service as an expression of 'the nanny state' and so on); while newspapers with a popular readership – which do not exist in all European countries – will often challenge these discourses and counter them with others deriving from the former social-democratic hegemony. (There is nothing automatic about this pattern, of course, since there are 'quality' newspapers which champion social democracy and popular ones which champion forms of neo-liberalism, as the British *Sun* did for many years.)

The media – both press and television – are an important and acknowledged source of ideas for those involved in writing soaps and *telenovelas*, as well as for others involved in writing series with highly topical storylines. To give a simple example, when Swedish scriptwriters Peter Emmanuel Falck and Christian Wikander agreed to write the Norwegian soap *De syv søstre* for Norway's TV2, they spent six months reading Norwegian newspapers every day in order to know what kind of storylines to include (see page 139). And when in a personal conversation with Jaume Cabré, chief writer for Catalonia's longest-running weekly serial *Estació d'enllaç* (Main Station), I asked him where he got ideas for his storylines, his immediate answer was 'the press'. As a result the issues and discourses of the press and news and current affairs services invariably make their way into the serials, but chosen and reworked in such a way as to meet the audience expectations for the genre. Soaps and *telenovelas* in their turn also feed heavily into other media, particularly the press. Coverage in popular newspapers in particular can be extremely intense.

The television company and its channels. The expansion of the number of television companies and channels has been a central factor in the growth of soap operas and *telenovelas* in western Europe, and has been a direct result of the processes of liberalization mentioned above. In the case of many television companies – in particular, though by no means exclusively, the commercial ones – soap operas are often an important point of contact between the station, advertisers and sponsors, as a number of cases analysed later will show. The emergence of regional television stations has also been important in some cases, but the new commercial companies have played a leading role, and they have been responsible for the bulk of the new serials which have appeared. In most cases this has eventually meant a response (not always immediate) from the public service broadcasters in the form of their own soap.

An important point to mention here is the increasing extent to which the production of soaps is 'contracted out' to independent producers, even by some public service stations. Over half the serials analysed here are not produced in-house. A major player in this field has been Grundy World-wide, the international arm of the Australian production company of the same name (which is in fact now owned by the British-based multinational Pearson), which is now co-producing eight soaps in different European countries (four in Germany, and one each in Italy, the Netherlands, Sweden and the UK). As I will demonstrate in the various country-by-country analyses, what Grundy contributes is basic storylines and production expertise: in all other respects each of these soaps is very much a product of the culture of the country within which it is screened.

As well as helping to define the company and, in particular, signal its relationship with what it sees as its audience, soaps are occasionally used to emphasize the different identity of channels belonging to the same company. This has been the case, for example, with RTL2 in Germany and RaiTre in Italy (see pages 74 and 115). The proliferation of channels has helped to lead to an increasing segmentation of the viewing public, to such an extent that the leading soap opera in Germany, for example, a country with a population of 80 million, can only hope to attract some eight to ten million viewers.

It is important to stress that the production of a soap or *telenovela* is not necessarily something around which the station rallies with a common will. In fact, the multifarious nature of the production of such serials and their importance for the station more or less guarantees ongoing tensions and conflicts of all kinds. In her analysis of the Irish public service broadcaster

RTÉ Helena Sheehan describes in some detail its internal conflicts regarding the production of drama in the early 1980s and the strong feelings held by many that the company was not producing the kind of drama they wanted to make and that it should be making (1987: 408–26). There can also be powerful tensions between the company and outside producers when the production is not screened at the time it was supposed to be screened (this has happened to some Portuguese *telenovelas* for example (see pp. 150 and 155)), or where pressures are exerted not to include certain issues among the storylines (see page 170 for the case of *Goenkale* in the Basque Country), or there can be unresolvable financial conflicts which can result in the removal of the production from one channel to another (see page 186 for the case of *Vänner och fiender* in Sweden).

The genre. The Colombian analyst Jesús Martín-Barbero describes the relationship between viewer and genre as follows: 'Being speakers of the language of "genre", the viewers, as natives of a textualised culture, "do not know the rules" of its grammar but are able to speak it' (1987: 242). Genre is, indeed, dynamic and changing like language and, as Allen points out, it is essential not to reify it: it is not a thing, or even a fixed set of rules, it is an ongoing agreement between producers and consumers regarding their reciprocal expectations in relation to the product, 'a dynamic relationship between texts and interpretative communities' (Allen, 1989: 45). Like any agreement, it is capable of particular inflexions to suit specific situations, and is also open to change over time.

The clearest example of the influence of genre is the dominance of the *telenovela* format rather than the soap opera in Spain and Portugal, but everywhere there is interpenetration between soap opera and/or *telenovela* and other aspects of the national/regional culture, in particular earlier and contemporaneous forms of television drama. This is one of the many factors which help to explain the poor exportability of European soaps, even where there is no language barrier (I return to this point in the Conclusion).

The audience. The penetration of soaps varies enormously. Some, like the main UK soaps, aim at and achieve a truly mass audience, while others bump along with at times only a few hundred thousand viewers. The definition of the audience for a soap is extremely important for the channel screening it, and mistakes can be enormously costly, as a number of cases covered in this book will show. Both soaps and *telenovelas* are the subject of unrelenting audience studies by the television stations: characters found to be unpopular will be ruthlessly ditched, storylines will be abandoned or changed, endings will be rewritten. Since different audiences are available at different times of the day, the timing of a soap is also an important part of its relationship with an audience.

It is quite common in the high-brow press throughout western Europe (and indeed beyond) for soap opera and *telenovela* viewers to be dismissed as entirely passive, undiscriminating and uncritical. The programmes are frequently described as working like drugs to dull the senses, and viewers are often exhorted to 'get a life'. Throughout this book I will propose an active and dynamic viewer, one who is indeed very critical of the product she/he is watching, and one who will not think twice about condemning any serial which does not live up to expectations, no matter how much money was invested in its production or how much effort went in to making it 'look good'. Television executives for their part are acutely aware of the devastating power of the viewer.

The text

I will follow here a variation on the distinction suggested by Barthes (1986) between 'work' and 'text'. The 'work' is the serial as a concrete product which can, for example, be copied, distributed, sold to another television channel or even sold abroad. The text is the symbolic dimension of the serial, the complex range of potential meanings generated by the soap or *telenovela* through its multiple contacts with the institutions, practices and people which have brought it into being and through the teeming discourses which traverse it. While the work can be lifted out of this network – this is what happens in the case of exports – the text cannot. A work which is exported is re-energized as a (different) text by being placed within a new set of relationships similar to those outlined in Figure 1 as they apply to the receiving country.

Though it is not my intention to pursue this point here, it follows from the argumentation above that an exported soap opera or *telenovela* can never generate the same range of potential meanings in the receiving culture as it was able to generate in its 'native' culture, since the network of relationships established will necessarily be different. In fact, any change beyond the boundary of the text will alter its meaning potential, and the further from the text the change occurs, the greater the effect will be. A change at the level of the state will lead to potentially large changes of meaning the more the national cultural identity of the receiving state differs from that of the exporting state. The work of Katz and Liebes (1990) as well as that of Miller (1995) shows a number of such cases in operation with specific reference to soaps. A change of 'region' will likewise affect the ability of the serial to generate meanings, and there are, again, a number of such cases mentioned later. A change of channel can also have the effect of 'repositioning' a serial semiotically, if on a smaller scale: those involved in *Brookside*, in the UK, for example, have long believed it would attract much greater audiences if it was shown on ITV rather than Channel 4: this is, no doubt, correct, though if this were to happen *Brookside* itself would undoubtedly have to change to some extent to accommodate its expanded audience. The Italian soap *Un posto al sole* (A Place in the Sun) went out on a different channel from the one originally planned (see page 115), and it will be interesting to see how the forthcoming change of channel for the Swedish soap *Vänner och fiender* (Friends and Enemies) will affect its relationship with its viewers (see page 186). Even a change in the actual audience can lead to a new range of potential meanings. It can occur that a particular programme is appropriated by an audience which is quite different from the one at which it was originally targeted. In the UK, for example, the 1995 Channel 4 programme *Soap Queens* examined how members of Britain's gay community viewed *Coronation Street*, deriving meanings from this soap which were in various ways different from those derived by the mainstream audience. And complex, multiple displacements can occur, as, for example, outlined by Gillespie (1995: 95–8) in her study of how young Asians living in Southall in London watched the Australian soap *Neighbours*.

Technical aspects of the text. What I have in mind here are elements such as the presence of location shots, their frequency in relation to studio shots, the general *mise-en-scène*, the directing, the acting and so forth. This is of course related to the television company and how much resources it is able and willing to make available for the production, which is in turn related to the size of the country and its economic performance. I would simply want to make the point here that in the course of my researches I have found nothing to suggest that there is any *necessary* relationship between the lavishness of the production values of a serial and its likelihood of success. Some of the cheapest-to-produce serials in western Europe are among the most successful, while some of the most expensive productions have failed catastrophically.

An interesting element of this aspect of the text which I am unable to develop at any length here is the use of extra-diegetic or background music. This varies from none in the British and Irish soaps, to relatively little in the Scandinavian soaps, a fair amount in the German, and almost constant music in the Greek soaps. These are important differences in the definition of the genre in the countries in question.

Linguistic aspects of the text. In some cases, the language of the soap is a key element in its general make-up. This is most obviously the case in the Catalan, Basque and Gaelic soaps analysed here, but is also important in a different way in the Flemish soaps. Beyond that, the use of dialect can also be important. Only the UK soaps (and to a lesser extent the Norwegian soaps) use dialects consistently as a source of signification, though the incidental use of dialect forms also crops up rather infrequently elsewhere. By and large, continental European soaps are havens of the standard forms of the language in question, something which has important consequences for the meanings generated by the serial as a whole.

As far as sociolectal considerations are concerned, the increasing frequency with which teenage characters now appear in soaps has brought with it a corresponding increase in the use of teenage jargons (however, although swearing is very commonplace among teenagers in all European countries, it only ever surfaces in its mildest forms in soaps and *telenovelas*). This again can be an important part of a soap or *telenovela*'s relationship with its target audience.

Language is, however, central to the meaning potential of the serial in a much more fundamental way than that. On one occasion I found myself watching a production whose language I could not understand at all – the Basque soap *Goenkale*. I could, of course, make some very obvious observations about it. I could see that it was set in a fishing town and that the characters were neither particularly rich nor particularly poor. Beyond these very superficial observations, however, I would not have been able to say anything of any real interest about this production, and had to search for supplementary information about it elsewhere for the analysis which features later in this book.

The dialogues in soaps and *telenovelas* are frequently criticized as being trivial and banal. However, no matter how trivial or banal they might be (and this is open to debate) they are the main door into the entire edifice of meaning constructed by the serial. There is, of course, nothing surprising about this. Discourse, by definition, saturates language even in its most trivial and everyday manifestations, and the most complicated discourses can be carried by the most threadbare exchanges. In fact, nothing as developed as an exchange is always needed. On occasions complex and powerful discourses can be carried by the fact that a single vowel is pronounced one way rather than another.

Levels of narrative

In the analyses which follow I will propose three levels of narrative. Although I believe that these three levels can in fact be very easily identified in any soap or *telenovela*, I am not suggesting that they are in any way discrete. On the contrary, each level simultaneously sustains and is sustained by the other two, and a change to any one of them will automatically involve changes to the others.

The micronarrative. The micronarrative level is the level of individual storylines based on the relationships between the various characters of the serial. It answers such hermeneutic enigmas as: Who is falling in love with who? Who is falling out of love with who? Who is cheating on who? Who is having whose baby?, and so on. Given that most serials now have some kind of business interest, this level can also be replicated there: Who is allying with who? Who is competing with who? Who is stabbing who in the back? This level is the most obvious and enduring aspect of soaps and *telenovelas* – for example, both the official handbook of the German soap *Lindenstraße* (Linden Street) (Lotze, 1995) and the commemorative *Rederiet* brochure of

1996 (see page 182) carry long lists of the number of marriages, divorces, pregnancies, miscarriages, illnesses, imprisonments and so on – and it is what gives them their feeling of circularity and repetition. Eco (1978: v) points out that popular culture is dominated by the 'already known', by the constant iteration of commonplaces with which the reader is already familiar. This endless recycling of stories based on relationships is the most obvious inheritance of both soap opera and *telenovela* from melodrama.

The metanarrative. However, this does not alter the fact that all soaps and many *telenovelas* incorporate, as mentioned earlier, narrative lines dealing with highly topical issues: throughout Europe and beyond many currently feature storylines dealing with racial discrimination, homosexuality, AIDS, HIV, drug abuse, rape, domestic violence and so on. It would, in fact, be quite possible to classify these themes in terms of the frequency of their appearance. I would suggest three categories:

1. Well-established, almost obligatory themes (homosexuality, racism, rape, drugs)
2. Clearly emergent themes (AIDS, lesbianism, euthanasia, incest)
3. More or less taboo themes (poverty, long-term unemployment)

(It is not that characters in soaps or *telenovelas* are never unemployed, but they are seldom unemployed for long, and finding work can often be remarkably easy: in the space of two weeks in September 1996 five characters in UK soaps found jobs by simply walking off the street into cafés, pubs and bars and asking if there were any jobs available.)

It is this level of narrative which allows us to account for the fact that endless products such as soaps appear to be simultaneously repetitive and new. Of course, the relationship between any cultural product and the society within which it is produced is a very complex one. At times soaps can lag behind social trends, at others they can be ahead of them, and the link is always highly mediated and subject to a range of pressures of varying force. A simple example of this complex relationship was the kiss between two homosexual males which was shown on screen in episode 107 of the Swedish soap *Rederiet* towards the end of February 1996. This particular episode was preceded by heavy coverage in the press, particularly in the two tabloids *Expressen* and *Aftonbladet*, complete with interviews with the two actors involved, statements from official bodies and so on. This hype was all the more surprising since Sweden is a country where there is, and has been for a long time, a high level of social acceptance of homosexuality. In a sense the Swedish tabloids were – as well as hyping the programme and providing good copy for themselves – celebrating the fact that Swedish soaps were finally getting up to date on this issue (public reaction to the kiss was minimal). It is the metanarrative which transforms the apparent circularity of soaps into 'spirality', a three-dimensional coiling of thematic repetition and millimetric temporal advance. An abortion in 1985 is not the same as an abortion in 1990; a homosexual kiss in 1990 is not the same as a homosexual kiss in 1995.

The metanarrative is partly a feature of the narrative requirements of soaps. While *telenovelas* are renewed automatically by the ending of one and the beginning of another, the need for a constantly updated set of storylines in even the slowest-moving soap is immense – much greater than in any other kind of fiction, televisual or otherwise. And since soaps are also almost invariably among the most popular programmes in their own country, they need to find a style and a thematic content which are broadly in tune with the expectations of their mass audience. Soaps do, therefore, through the issues which are imbricated in their constantly recurring plots, tell their own story about their society at a level which transcends the factual detail of individual storylines and which rolls forward as inexorably as the soap or soaps themselves. A similar point is argued by Michael Forsman in a long article on *Rederiet* in the Swedish broadsheet *Svenska Dagbladet* of 7 May 1996: 'In this way "Rederiet" operates as a kind of explanatory meta-narrative in relation to the moral, personal and existential questions which arise in our daily lives and in public debate.' At the level of the meta-narrative soaps and *telenovelas* champion almost exclusively progressive views, coming out clearly against discrimination or narrow-mindedness of any kind, and often adopting courageous stances in relation to highly controversial issues.

The macronarrative. The macronarrative relates to the kind of (mini-) society constructed by the soap or *telenovela*. Is it a working-class community, a middle-class one or an upper-class one? Does it have characters from a range of classes? What kind of values does it defend? Does it celebrate community or individualism, solidarity or self-aggrandizement, sharing or consumption? On whom is moral protagonism bestowed? As I will argue throughout this book this is, from the viewer's point of view, the key narrative level of the soap.

Dimensions of narrative

Beyond these three levels of narrative, which are inherent in the text at any given time, I will propose a further two levels – or, more precisely, dimensions – of narrative which are not represented in Figure 1. These are the transnarrative and the hypernarrative.

The transnarrative. Most European countries nowadays have more than one domestic soap. In cases such as this each individual soap can be seen as part of an even greater, overarching narrative created simultaneously by all the soaps, a dimension which I will refer to as the transnarrative. Typically, the various soaps in a given country will either cluster around a particular centre – the case of the UK soaps and to some extent the Norwegian soaps – or follow two main divergent lines as they attempt to appeal to very different audiences, these two lines broadly representing a discourse of continuity as opposed to a discourse of change. The most striking example of this kind of dichotomy is provided by the German soaps, though something similar can also be found to varying degrees in Flanders, the Netherlands and Sweden. The transnarrative can be highly revealing of both the distribution and evolution of values within the country in question.

The hypernarrative. If the transnarrative is the synchronic dimension of soaps and *telenovelas*, the second dimension is their diachronic dimension and consists of the story told by the various productions as they stretch out over time. This I will term the hypernarrative. While the internal levels of narrative are at any given moment, broadly speaking, under the control of those involved in producing the soaps – even allowing for the tensions and conflicts mentioned earlier – the hypernarrative is not. No soap or *telenovela* – particularly the 'open' variety – is planned even a year in advance, never mind four or five years in advance. Changes occurring at this level also tell their own complex story of the society in which the serial is being produced, the developing relationship between the serial and its audience, and so on. This dimension of narrative can be carried by such apparently secondary elements as the opening credits, or the theme tune or song: there have been startling changes to a number of the opening sequences or title songs of a number of European soaps, all of which have heralded important changes of direction in the hypernarrative.

The hypernarrative is, in my view, the ultimately defining element of soaps and to a lesser extent of *telenovelas*. It is what makes them absolutely different from any other kind of televisual output, even long-running series. There is a very real sense in which soaps in particular are 'alive': they have an almost organic existence as they squirm and coil their way forward unpredictably through time, moving this way and that as the range of pressures exerted on them vary in intensity, sometimes carrying their audiences with them, sometimes alienating them, sometimes expiring through fatigue or dying a spectacular death. They are unique. This book attempts to unravel at least part of that uniqueness.

Structure of the country-by-country analyses

Each of the following chapters begins with a brief outline of the television systems currently operating in the country in question, concentrating on the major developments since the late 1980s. It goes without saying that entire volumes have been written on what is condensed here into a page or even less. The sole aim of this section is to sketch the main developments which have occurred and, in particular, the new stations which have emerged.

This is followed, where appropriate, by a very brief indication of any tradition of soap operas or *telenovelas* in the country in question prior to the 1990s. I restrict myself here to domestic production. I do not in any way analyse the American soaps of the 1980s, though I may occasionally make reference to them where appropriate.

There then follows a description and explanation of each of the domestic soaps or *telenovelas* either currently showing or which appeared earlier in the 1990s. This in turn is followed by an analysis in which I attempt to place these soaps within the broader frameworks outlined in Figure 1 as they apply to the country in question. These analyses vary greatly in length, partly because some countries have many more soaps than others (eight in Germany as opposed to one each in Italy and Denmark, for example), partly because some soaps are 'meatier' than others and require much more to be said about them, and partly because, in the final analysis, I simply know more about some countries than others.

The viewer's perspective

What is entirely absent from this book is any attempt at reception analysis. This is partly due to the fact that the scale of the project simply made any such analysis impossible, but it is also due to the inherent difficulties involved in finding a methodology which produces genuinely usable results. While the old 'intentional fallacy' now appears completely discredited (the idea that the meaning of a text is the meaning the author claims to have put in it), what might be called the 'interpretational fallacy' seems to be getting a much easier ride (in other words, the idea that the meaning which viewers derive from a text is the one they say they derive from it). It is difficult at first glance to see why this should be the case. The outcomes of interviews, focus groups, discussion groups and the like are themselves *texts*, and an analytical model of some considerable complexity is required to establish exactly what range of meanings might reasonably be extracted from them.

The various theorizings which have arisen in the last decade or so relating to 'dominant', 'subversive' and 'aberrant' readings of texts (Morley, 1980; Fiske, 1987) clearly represent a considerable advance on the former view that a text had a canonical meaning which it was up to the reader to identify, and the references to 'negotiation' and 'dialogue' are very much to be welcomed. However, my residual sense of unease with these theorizings derives essentially from the fact they appear to pay little attention to the production side of the equation. They posit a relationship between a variable reader on the one hand and, on the other, a text with, so to speak, enough 'semiotic slack' for multiple readings to emerge. In the case of long-running serials such as soap operas and *telenovelas*, however, the negotiation is between the reader and the producers *through* the text and as a result the text itself is subject to change.

My own position is perhaps closest to that argued by Umberto Eco when he talks of the *intentio operis* (the intention of the work) as a site of convergence between the *intentio auctoris* (the author's intention) and the *intentio lectoris* (the reader's intention). He defines the *intentio operis* as follows (1992: 64):

A text is a device conceived in order to produce its model reader . . . The empirical reader is only an actor who makes conjectures about the kind of model reader postulated by the text. Since the intention of the text is basically to produce a model reader able to make conjectures about it, the initiative of the model reader consists in figuring out a model author that is not the empirical one and that, in the end, coincides with the intention of the text.

My own view is that, particularly in the case of long-running serials such as soaps and *telenovelas*, it is more focused to attempt to derive the model reader from the text (an entirely feasible proposition), since, if the real readers do not coincide closely enough with the model reader in sufficient numbers the serial will either fail (a number of such cases are analysed) or will attempt to alter its model reader in order to achieve a greater degree of fit with the actual ones (a number of such cases are also analysed). This, I believe, is simultaneously more fruitful, more economic and more 'doable' than reception analysis as normally understood, and it is, by and large, the direction I have taken in the following chapters (in saying this, however, I am not in any sense denying the value of a number of reception analyses which have in fact been carried out).

As far as actual reception analyses are concerned, a certain amount has been done on the UK and Irish soaps, though relatively little has been done so far on the continental European soaps (Swedish researchers have been the most active in this field). Where I am aware of any such work, I mention it at the appropriate point.

Countries not included

There are currently only four western European countries not producing (to the best of my knowledge) their own soaps or *telenovelas*. These are Luxemburg, Switzerland, Austria and France. Switzerland and Austria have in common the fact that there are no domestic commercial television channels (the recent launch of W1 in Austria, distributed by cable to 800,000 inhabitants of Vienna's suburbs, has done little to alter this situation). As will become clear in the following analyses, the emergence of commercial channels has been a crucial factor in the appearance of domestic soaps in most countries. The only country with no commercial channels which produces its own soaps is Ireland, and its situation is somewhat unique in the sense that the UK channels – both PSB and commercial – to some extent fulfil the function carried out elsewhere by domestic commercial channels (though it might be argued that the German channels, in particular recent developments such as SAT1 Österreich, also carry out this function in relation to Austria and German-speaking Switzerland: see, for example, Murschetz, 1996). To this we might add that Luxemburg's small size and the internal fragmentation of the Swiss market make the prospect of a domestic soap a somewhat unlikely one.

France is *the* great exception to the current trend, despite the success of *Châteauvallon* in the 1980s. Short-run summer serials (*'feuilletons d'été'*) are shown in France, but they never reach the kind of industrialized levels of production given earlier on as part of the definition of a soap. Other productions are occasionally referred to as soaps – *Beaumanoir, Le château des oliviers* – but they also appear to have been relatively short-lived (I am not, in fact, familiar with either of them) and they are certainly no longer on the air.

As far as I am able to ascertain, there has only been one attempt at an out-and-out domestic soap in France, and this was *Voisin, voisine* (Boy Next Door, Girl Next Door), begun in 1989 and shown for a few hundred episodes on the ill-fated channel La Cinq which foundered in 1992. *Voisin, voisine* was a very low-cost production produced at the truly astonishing rate of three episodes per day and generally viewed as a somewhat cynical mechanism to meet the regulations regarding percentages of French-language production rather than being a serious contribution to the genre (Chanian, 1994: 52). I do not consider the 260-episode *Riviera*, shown from July 1991 onwards, to be a genuinely domestic French soap. Despite being shot in France it was a co-production between TF1, Granada (UK), Studio Hamburg (Germany) and FORTA (Spain), and though TF1 provided half the investment, it was always seen as a 'European' soap and was even shot in English. In any case, despite the truly enormous amounts of money invested in the programme, it was stopped in March 1992 after achieving very low viewing figures (Jenny, 1992). The early-evening slot filled in some countries by soaps is now filled in France by daily sit-coms such as *Hélène et les garçons, Premiers baisers, Le miel et les abeilles* and *Les filles d'à côté* (these very whimsical programmes make many European soaps look like heavyweights).

There are also a number of factors which make the French case somewhat different. The emergence of commercial channels there was fundamentally different in that, unlike anywhere else in Europe, the first PSB channel TF1 was simply privatized, giving it a quite different tradition and relationship with its viewers from the other commercial channels which emerged more 'spontaneously', so to speak, elsewhere. But over and above that, France remains the European country where official opposition to the supposed 'Americanization of culture' remains highest – as its position during the much-protracted Uruguay round of the GATT negotiations made very clear – and the soap opera as a genre appears to be viewed as a form of capitulation to that culture (an idea which the heavy American influence on *Riviera* no doubt did little to dispel). Whatever the reasons, there seems very little prospect of a domestic soap appearing in France even in the medium term.

Postscript

In mid-1989 there were eight domestic soaps in production in Europe, six in the United Kingdom, one in the Republic of Ireland and one in Germany. By mid-1994 when I began this project in earnest that number had edged its way up to around twenty. By mid-1997, as I bring this manuscript to a close, the number has increased to over 40. It has simply not been possible for me to keep up to date with all these productions all the time. On occasions on 'returning' to a country after an absence of only two or three months, I would discover that one or even two new soaps had appeared.

If I have discovered anything of any particular importance which was not included in the analysis of any particular country when I closed my chapter on it, I have added a postscript to give brief details of that new development. No doubt, however, yet more products will have come on stream in the time it takes this manuscript to be transformed into a book.

Belgium

Television in Belgium

Belgium is a country with two major, but separate, media systems reflecting its two main language groups, the Dutch-speaking Flemings and the French-speaking Walloons (there is also a small German-speaking minority with its own much less developed media). Between the introduction of television in 1953 and 1987 only public service television channels broadcast in Belgium, two French-speaking channels in Wallonie – RTBF1 and RTBF2, now known as La Une and La Deux – and two Dutch-speaking channels in Flanders – BRT1 and BRT2, now known as TV1 and TV2. In 1987 the Luxembourg-based RTL group launched the commercial station RTL-TVi in Wallonie, and this was followed two years later by VTM (Vlaamse Televisie Maatschappij, or Flemish Television Company) in Flanders, a company owned mostly by Flemish press interests. In 1994 the commercial channel VT4, which broadcasts from London, also came on stream, though it currently attracts only around a 6 per cent audience share, and in 1995 VTM introduced its second channel, Kanaal 2, which broadcasts mainly American series. VTM has quickly become the most popular channel in Flanders, and can often claim six or more of the ten most viewed programmes in any week.

Domestic soaps in Flanders

The only domestic soaps to have been produced so far in Belgium have been in Flanders. The only relatively long-running serial in the 1980s was BRTN's *Het Pleintje* (The Square), screened in 27 episodes in 1986–87. It was immensely popular, attracting average audiences of 2.5 million viewers per episode in its first season. The producer of *Het Pleintje*, Winnie Enghien, is also currently the producer of *Thuis* (see below).

A civilized soap: Familie

Familie (Family) was launched in December 1992 by VTM and, apart from a summer break, is screened from Monday to Saturday every week, making it the only six-day-a-week soap in western Europe. It passed its 1000th episode in September 1996. It was originally shown from 20.00 to 20.30, was then brought forward to 19.30 to 20.00, and since early 1997 has undergone a further scheduling change (of which more below). It is very popular, usually figuring among the top three programmes when it is on the air, and has audience shares of around 27 per cent, averaging some one million viewers.

Familie's style is sober, with limited camera movement and only very occasional use of techniques such as fades and the like, and it is characterized by relatively long shot and sequence times, a feature of Flemish fiction in general (Biltereyst, 1994: 15 ff). Though the location shooting is done in Mechelen, the setting itself – as was the case in *Het Pleintje* – is never actually identified: we are simply aware of the fact that it is a large town somewhere inland, and probably to the north-east of Brussels. The Dutch spoken throughout, though conforming entirely to the norms of Standard Educated Dutch – is spoken with a recognizably Flemish accent, with the strong dialects which are often acceptable in other Flemish programmes (Biltereyst, 1991: 476) – notably sit-coms – being entirely absent. The characters read real Flemish newspapers such as *Het Laatste Nieuws* and *De Gazet van Antwerpen*.

Familie is based, as its title confidently announces, on a family: the Van Den Bossches. Three generations of the family are represented: the elderly parents, Anna and Albert; their three children, Guido, Jan and Rita; and their various grandchildren. Other important characters include Anna's brother Walter, who is a priest, making *Familie* one of a relatively small number of European soaps to feature members of the clergy prominently. The age range of the characters when the serial started was approximately fifteen or sixteen to 70 (Anna celebrated her seventieth birthday in an episode towards the end of 1995). The family of the title is in fact highly fissile. As the opening lines of the title song put it: 'The strong bond of a family / is pure but brittle and oh so fragile'.

Most of the narrative complications concern the middle-aged group with both Jan and Guido divorcing and forming new relationships, and their former partners in turn also forming new relationships while staying in the soap. As well as the inevitable personal relationships, *Familie* also maintains a strong business interest, since Guido is the director of the Van Den Bossche electronics company, while his former wife (and also for a time his daughter) ran the Maison Marie-Rose, a small fashion design company. Business intrigue is provided by the rival electronics company FAIC, whose owner, Didier de Kunst, not only buys up some of the shares of Van Den Bossche Systems (having in the meantime married Jan's former wife Monique and moved in with her and her children) but also eventually persuades Jan to go and work for him briefly too. The business side of the soap has been the mainspring of its most dramatic storylines, one of which was a high-octane narrative centred around Guido's kidnap in Canada, his detention on his return to Flanders following his escape, and the arrest of his secretary Babette for complicity in industrial espionage and international fraud (a storyline whose narrative treatment, with its rapid cutting, point-of-view shots, frantic music and so on, contrasted strongly with that of the soap as a whole). A more recent storyline involved the murder of Guido's second wife Claire while they were setting up a new company in Malta.

Despite this strong business interest, it has to be said that remarkably little work ever appears to be done in the various business premises. All the viewer ever sees of Van Den Bossche Electronics is the offices of the management. During a debate over a possible restructuring of the company in 1994, the workforce was mentioned, the possibility of trade union resistance was mooted, and the need to avoid getting into a 'clinch' with a particularly difficult shop steward was stressed. Despite this, no workers ever appeared: in fact the workers in the company's Maltese branch have figured more in the soap than any Flemish workers ever have (and even they have figured only very minimally). The only manual work ever to be shown on screen – unloading computer equipment from a lorry – was carried out by the office staff (mostly the secretaries) with the help of other family members and friends. In fact, the only Flemish 'workers' to have made any kind of appearance in the programme were the 'creative' types from the Maison Marie Rose, whose only male member, Maxim, was deliberately portrayed as effeminate. (But while 'workers' in the traditional sense are nowhere to be seen, the lumpenproletariat did make a stylized appearance in the form of Micheline, a woman who had befriended Rita during the latter's brief spell in prison.)

The sector of society which figures most prominently in *Familie* is, by and large (with the exception of the Greek soaps (see pp. 88–9)), rather different from most other European soaps: it is more firmly bourgeois, a factor which may at least partly explain the absence of dialect forms, since these are associated on Flemish television with working-class or uneducated characters. The decors are plush and comfortable: the house originally owned by Guido and Marie-Rose had its own swimming pool and a full-time housekeeper who was the only person ever seen carrying out such menial tasks as hoovering, for example. As well as being well-off, the characters are also mostly well-educated. These are not the super-rich of the American or Greek soaps, but nor are they the lower-middle-class characters of the British soaps, nor do we find anywhere the kind of social mix present in Swedish soaps such as *Varuhuset* or *Rederiet*.

Familie is also one of a very few European soaps to feature overseas locations on a fairly regular basis. At the beginning of 1995 a storyline centred on Rita involved scenes shot in London while another centred on Guido had scenes shot in Canada (mostly Montreal). More recent storylines have also taken place in Italy and Malta, and a 1997 storyline again involving Rita not only took place in but was also clearly at least partly filmed in and around Benidorm, where Rita earns a living as a singer on the tourist circuit (a role already essayed by Trish Valentine in the UK soap *Eldorado* (see pp. 194–6)). But over and above that, travel is an ongoing theme. As the head of Van Den Bossche Electronics Guido goes to Venezuela, Canada, Korea and so on, and sets up a company in Malta. Phone calls and faxes arrive from him from around the globe, Jan and Bart talk in English on the phone to Joe Bonduano, the manager of the plant in Malta, and when he comes to Flanders a whole string of people have long conversations with him in English. And when François and his new wife Mia discussed at length their forthcoming grand trip, the questions they asked themselves were: Will it be Mexico, the South Pole, Alaska or Asia? If it is Asia, will it be Turkey, a cruise around the Greek Islands, a trip on the Orient Express? In this sense, *Familie* is without any doubt the most cosmopolitan of European soaps.

At the beginning of 1997 something rather remarkable happened in *Familie*; something which, to the best of my knowledge, had never happened in a soap opera before. It was referred to in Dutch as the 'tijdsprong', which translates into English as the 'time leap', and concerned the age of the characters. Between the first Friday of the year and the following Monday all of them, without exception, aged by seven years. Large chronological leaps are not uncommon in *telenovelas*: in the Portuguese production *Roseira Brava*, for example (see page 151), eight years pass between the first three minutes and the rest of the narrative, and a caption appears on screen apprising us of this fact. But since these are closed narratives in the traditional sense with complete mastery over their internal time-frames, this never seems surprising. However, for such a leap to occur in an ongoing serial is, to the best of my knowledge, unprecedented.

The *tijdsprong* was carefully prepared in the weeks leading up to the end of 1996. In the week between Christmas and New Year the grandchildren Bart and Mieke had 'visions' of themselves in the future, either in the form of daydreams or in recounting dreams dreamt during the night: he saw himself negotiating with the members of the Maltese workforce, for example, while she saw herself treating the wounded in a war zone in Africa. Other pointed references to the future were made. In a clash between

Veronique and Bart while she was the caretaker director of Van Den Bossche Systems following an accident in which Guido broke his back, he announced threateningly 'OK, I'm going, but I'll be back in a couple of years'. Each episode was followed by a trailer of the new-style production announcing '*Familie* will be completely new'. After the *tijdsprong* other references to the amount of time elapsed were made in reverse ('Don't tell me this has come up again after all these years').

The ageing of the characters was done in different ways. For example, the new 25-year-old Bart was played by a different actor, while the new Mieke was not. By and large the convention employed was simply to make the men's hair greyer and the women's hair shorter (in itself a socio-semiotically interesting distinction). Other narrative devices contributed as well. Thus at the end of 1996 Jan and Lene discussed having a second child whom they would call Martin. After the *tijdsprong* he duly appeared, seven years old. And the mystery of the murder of Claire with which the 'old' narrative ended has resurfaced with the original investigating policemen also looking suitably older. The whole thing has also been accompanied by a new opening sequence. The old theme tune has been given a much trendier and pacier reworking with much 'woa-ing' and 'waa-ing' in the background (while keeping its old words), the presentation of the characters is much more energetic as they stride towards or look directly at the camera, and the former-twentysomethings-now-thirtysomethings smile and hug and pose for the camera generally whooping it up in a way not unreminiscent of *Unter uns* in Germany (see page 68) and in keeping with a broad representational shift visible throughout European and American television whereby people in this age range continue to behave like teenagers. The proportion of location shots per episode has increased and the length of each episode has been reduced by around five minutes.

There are two things in particular to be said about the *tijdsprong*. The first is that it has not in any way altered the characters' relationship with 'real time' (*Familie* is a 'real-time' soap in the British tradition: when it's Christmas outside it's Christmas in the soap). The story was not set in the past before the *tijdsprong* and is, of course, not set in the future after it. The characters continue to read today's newspapers now as then. The 'leap' has taken place only within the narrative world. Secondly, the group which has been removed by this 'time leap' is very precisely the teenage group. A small pre-teen group has appeared, as has a pensioners' group living in an old people's home, but the teenage sector has been evacuated completely. The group who have disappeared are precisely the group which *Familie* always had difficulty attracting in the first place – an audience which has tradition-ally preferred programmes such as *Wittekerke* (see below) and the summer season, daily teen 'swimsuit serial' *Wat nu weer!?* (Whatever Next!?) – 'swimsuit serial' is the term routinely used by the television magazine *Humo* to describe this production – the latter attracting audiences of around

600,000. This is an extreme example of how producers will, if they feel it is necessary, alter their model viewer to fit their actual viewer more closely. For despite its title, *Familie* is not a family soap; it is an older person's soap. It is not a soap for those who are searching for the way, but for those who have already got there, and the teen problems Bart and Mieke would have brought with them had they followed a normal course would have been singularly out of place. The solution opted for by the producers was breathtaking in its audacity, but, going by current viewing figures, appears to have worked.

A village soap: Thuis

BRT's response to the success of *Familie* took some time to materialize. An experimental serial entitled *Het Park* (The Park) was dropped after a relatively short period of time due to poor viewing figures, and a fully-fledged five-day-a-week soap finally emerged on 23 December 1995 in the form of *Thuis* (At Home), shot in wide format with support from the EU's 16:9 Action Plan. It goes out on TV1 at 19.00–19.30 and clocked up 265 episodes over two seasons, with the third season beginning in September 1997. *Thuis* attracts just over 500,000 viewers, a 24 per cent audience share.

Unlike *Familie*, *Thuis* does have one non-standard speaker, the plumber Frank Bomans who speaks a noticeable Antwerp dialect. In a long interview published in the television magazine *Humo* (4 March 1997) the actor who plays this part, Pol Goossens, explained that this had been his decision rather than that of the producers:

In the first episode Frank spoke Standard Dutch like everyone else but I didn't think that was right. A plumber doesn't speak the same way as a doctor, that would be completely unbelievable. So I adapted his way of speaking a bit. If the script contains words or puns which go over his head, I make special Frank-versions of them.

Like its commercial rival, *Thuis* is noticeably 'British' in its production style. In fact the producer, Winnie Enghien, stated clearly that 'The English serials are the standard we go by. Perhaps we won't manage it, that might be the case, but we are trying to achieve that kind of quality' (*Ratel*, Autumn 1995). There are, however, some notable differences in terms of the narrative universe it creates and that of *Familie*. First, it is set in a small village as opposed to a large city. Much of it is, in fact, positively down-on-the-farm, with a fair amount of the action taking place in a traditional rectangular farmstead. This not only houses the local hostelry but also riding stables which are the scene of much mucking out of horses and crowing of cocks. Between them the pub and the stables employ a large group of characters, most of whom are in their mid-to-late twenties or early thirties. Secondly, the social level of the characters is markedly lower. The peak of village society is represented by the doctor, Walter De Decker, and his family. Entrepreneurial capitalism, on the other hand, culminates in the local heating and plumbing installation firm run by Vercammen and his daughter Leontien. Thirdly, the drama is relatively low-key by soap standards, and certainly compared with *Familie*. In fact, the atmosphere is generally cosy and reassuring, with threats and danger usually coming from outside. As the opening verse of the theme song (sung in a squeaky voice by well-known Flemish singer Isabelle A.) puts it: 'No more trusted house than home / Nowhere so safe / From night till morning / Always home.'

Thuis also displays sizeable doses of humour as snooty ladies are thrown from horses and end up with dung all over their clothes, the local doctor shocks village society by leaving a valuable necklace in his will to the local hairdresser, and even Vercammen being knocked down and dying as a result appears to have its funny side, with Frank bursting into uncontrollable laughter when he learns how it happened (he did owe Vercammen a large sum of money by way of compensation for an earlier set-to between the two). Felicienne, who 'does' for the doctor and for Harry, is also by and large a figure of some fun. In this respect *Thuis* appears to owe little to its commercial rival, and to continue a tradition exemplified by *Het Pleintje* and its predecessors. Despite the differences, however, what it does share with *Familie* is – despite the inevitable conflicts which all soap operas share – the general sense of conviviality, of people getting on reasonably well with each other despite the frictions and tensions of collective life, of a society which is by and large civilized and well-behaved.

A teen soap: Vennebos

On 20 January 1997 VT4 started a twice-a-week soap entitled *Vennebos*, going out on Mondays and Wednesdays at 20.30. It attracts around 200,000 viewers, and is one of VT4's more successful programmes. *Vennebos* is the only Flemish soap to continue broadcasting over the summer. As channel spokesman Roland Rentmeesters put it in the magazine *Dag Allemaal* (17 June 1997):

This is a deliberate choice. We are still a young channel, and we have to win our viewers one by one. If we were to disappear from the screen for two or three months the risk would be too great that we would have to start again from scratch in September. That would be stupid.

I learned of the existence of this soap rather late and have been able to view only a small number of episodes. It is in some respects reminiscent of the early *Hollyoaks* in the UK (Vennebos is the name of a leafy residential suburb, just as Hollyoaks is: see page 199), and the opening sequence suggests an affluent lifestyle of golf courses, horse-riding, swimming-pools, souped-up motorbikes and expensive soft-top cars, all accompanied by much larking about and jolly grinning or winking at the camera. It has to be said that the production itself does not quite live up to this glamorous and devil-may-care introduction. The interiors are understated, the fashions are unremarkable and everyday, the storylines are slow and at times rather grim, with a notable criminal undercurrent involving kidnap, murder, rape and so on (one of the characters is a detective). *Vennebos* centres mostly on a group of six youngsters who, when the serial started, were in the final year of their Modern Languages course at a very good school (a situation reminiscent of *Goudkust* in the Netherlands – see page 131 – a soap with which *Vennebos* has a number of things in common). With the exception of Jeroen De Voghelaere, whose widowed mother works as the concierge at the school, all the youngsters come from very wealthy backgrounds: Sandra's parents, for example, are European civil servants who spend 90 per cent of their time in Strasbourg, while Marco's father is the owner of three sports complexes. Despite this focus on the six teenagers (who feature in VT4's postcard accompanying the soap), the adult characters could not reasonably be described as secondary, and they figure in a number of storylines, combining their relationships with other dramatic events. The world of *Vennebos* is, if anything, a rather more unsettling one than those of its more popular competitors.

A re-versioned soap: Wittekerke

However, the most popular soap opera in Flanders is, at the time of writing, none of the above, but the twice-a-week *Wittekerke* (the title is the name of a small coastal town), which goes out on VTM at 20.45 and regularly attracts audiences of over one million, thereby fractionally outperforming *Familie* (it just as frequently tops the ratings for Flanders as a whole). However, I do not intend to include this soap opera in my analysis because, despite appearances, it is not in my opinion, properly speaking, a Flemish soap. It is, in fact, like the German soap *Westerdeich* (see page 81), a reversioning of the Australian soap *E-Street* (though it has proved to be much more successful than its German counterpart) and has remained entirely faithful to the Australian originals, even when this means writing out characters who have proved popular with the domestic audience. For example, the Flemish newspaper *Het Laatste Nieuws* (5 August 1996) explained the imminent departure of the character Bart as follows:

Wittekerke is based on the Australian *E-Street*. That means that the storylines are already set and that the original Australian scripts are reworked following Flemish norms. The script requires Bart, played by Werner De Smedt, to disappear from the serial.

In view of this, I am not able to classify *Wittekerke* as a truly domestic Flemish product, since the freedom to develop independent storylines and respond quickly to viewers' preferences – as *Familie* and *Thuis* have been able to do – is a fundamental part of my minimum definition of a genuinely domestic production.

Analysis

In general – despite the *ex officio* conflicts and tensions of the genre – there is a much greater sense of harmony in the two major Flemish soaps than one would associate with the bulk of European serials. In the case of *Familie*, the family of the title is in fact extremely fissile – only Anna and Albert are a stable couple, and between early 1994 and late 1995 both of their sons changed their partners (in the case of Jan, more than once) – but these genre-specific moves (Bleicher, 1995: 45) cannot cancel out the overall sensation of solidarity and interest in the well-being of others. The group of people invested with moral protagonism in this highly successful soap are very precisely those who featured in the *failed* British soaps *Eldorado* and *Castles*: independent businessmen and (though to a much lesser extent) ex-pats living in Spain. But whereas the British characters embodied a 'winner' philosophy left over from the neo-liberal thrust of the 1980s (see pp. 210–11), there is no such smugness and self-congratulation to be found among the protagonists of this Flemish soap.

On the business level, Van Den Bossche Electronics has been described on several occasions as a very fair and socially responsible employer committed to treating its workforce well even if this means going against current management trends. And more recently the 'new' Bart's appeal to his Maltese workforce in late 1996 (it took the form of a flash-forward) was strongly reminiscent of, for example, a very similar situation in the Italian soap *Un posto al sole*, involving the young Alessandro's negotiations with his workforce (see page 122). Like Alessandro, Bart asks the workforce for their trust (though he does not go so far as offering them any kind of control), assuring them that the management are working to win orders in order to ensure their future. It is based on a philosophy of employer responsibility, not on the neo-liberal notion of 'hire and fire'. And while youngsters in the German soaps come back from America with a personal commitment to the consumerist ethic (see page 84), and characters in the Catalan soaps bring back illness and death from the same country (see page 177), what Bart brings back from his studies at the Harvard Business School is an understanding of 'conflict management' – this is specifically the title of a text book he was studying at the end of 1996 – and he puts this knowledge to use in his relationship with the Maltese workforce.

And this sense of responsibility and consideration is not restricted to the characters' immediate surroundings or contacts. As they prepare for their trip abroad, Mia informs François that, wherever they go, she wants to be fully up-to-date on that country's customs, traditions, standards of politeness and so on, and in general to 'respect its culture'. And, in a recent storyline, Mieke and her boyfriend Michel went, at great personal danger, to help in a war situation in Africa under the aegis of Médecins sans Frontières (the actual footage was shot on location in Toubacouta in Senegal).

Perhaps the word which most readily springs to mind on viewing *Familie* is 'civilized'. The characters misbehave constantly of course – an essential ingredient of any soap opera – they can be petulant, churlish, truculent, scheming, even unethical and scoundrelish – but there are no out-and-out villains: even the slippery and manipulative Didier has his soft and vulnerable side. The divorced characters not only maintain reasonably friendly relationships with their former spouses, but also positive and even supportive relationships with their spouses' subsequent partners, with whom they sometimes work: in fact Monique recently employed Babette in her restaurant, despite the fact that the latter had been involved in her original break-up with Jan ('That's all so long ago,' she says, 'forgotten and forgiven'). Crankiness of all kinds is met with patience, tolerance, understanding, even good humour. Characters apologize constantly for speaking out of turn, for being suspicious without good reason, or for having caused offence without actually having meant to. Even Micheline (whose lumpenness was signalled primarily by a lack of social graces, which strikes an immediately jarring note in the well-mannered world of *Familie*) is, despite an initially very frosty reception from Anna, eventually accepted into the parental home, invited out to restaurants and so on. Albert, in particular, is quite unique in this respect, in that he is the only truly socially competent man of his age group to figure anywhere in a European soap. The granddaughter Veronique's gradual mutation from merely hard-bitten businesswoman into 'bitch' – in December 1996 Bart twice described her as this (he actually used the English word) – has been accompanied by the progressive adoption of a hectoring and bullying tone (helped, no doubt, by the role being taken over in 1996 by a different actress), but her aggressiveness has been met by indulgent winks and nudges by everyone else.

For the bulk of the post-war period, Belgium was well known, both internally and abroad, for what was called quite literally its 'compromise politics' (*compromispolitiek* in Dutch). This 'compromise' existed not only at the level of party politics, where the large number of parties has made coalitions of one kind or another a more or less permanent feature of government, but in a broader sense on a social level as well, with a commitment among employers' organizations to maintain the Welfare State and accept the various costs which that implied. This compromise *is* now under threat. It is threatened at the level of party politics by, for example, the emergence of the Vlaams Blok, a party with overtly racist views and extremely unpalatable Nazi undertones which has become a small but nonetheless non-ignorable part of Flemish political life. But it is also under threat in the broader social sense as well as the highly developed Belgian Welfare State comes under increasingly close political scrutiny and employers call for the reduction or even removal of benefits for the unemployed. Seen against this historical background *Familie*'s representation of Flemish society is undoubtedly socially and economically skewed, but it nonetheless narrativizes the values its viewers want to see defended.

The Flanders which *Familie* symbolically defends is the affluent and dynamic region which has, over the past 30 years or so, moved from a position of economic (and consequently political) inferiority within Belgium to one of superiority and much greater political power (the move from post-war poverty to present affluence is mentioned on more than one occasion by various characters), producing in the process a cohesive society based on consensus politics. It is one which is confident of its own identity and its own place in the world, and indeed of its own ability to count for something in that world. *Familie* constructs a society with established values where adolescent angst can be skipped over in the rainy weekend of a *tijdsprong*. In its own more downbeat, good-natured and less spectacular way *Thuis* constructs a similar symbolic universe seen from the middle rather than from above (and certainly not from below, since, despite Flanders' well-developed industrial base, there are still no industrial workers anywhere). Ghastly things can happen from time to time, of course – in *Familie* Rita recently learned that she has leukaemia, in *Thuis* Bianca is raped by the psychopathic Neil, Ann attempts to commit suicide, and so on – but it will all be sorted out in the end. Only *Vennebos* appears to offer an at least partly alternative world view, which its 200,000 viewers no doubt enjoy.

It is almost certainly not coincidental that *Familie* emerged roughly simultaneously with the processes which have led to Flanders' new federal status within Belgium and its now much greater ability to project itself on an international level (a phenomenon rather similar in many respects to what has happened in Catalonia (see pp. 161–8)). *Familie* constructs a society which is both more than capable of surviving on its own physical resources (even if how such resources might actually be converted into wealth is conveniently overlooked) and which simultaneously has the collective cultural resources – in the broadest possible sense – needed to deal with the inevitable stresses and strains of social life. An elegant vision, if an idealized one, and one which clearly appeals to wide sections of Flemish society at large.

Denmark

Television in Denmark

Television was introduced in Denmark in 1953 when the public service channel Danmarks Radio (DR-TV) first came on air. It was not until 35 years later that DR's monopoly was broken on a national level, with the launch of the second channel TV2 in 1988. TV2 has eight regional stations which both opt out from and feed into its national network, and, despite a clearly commercial orientation – TV2 is financed mostly, but not entirely, from advertising – it is also subject to a number of requirements regarding programme mix, quality and the like (Petersen and Siune, 1992: 39). DR's second channel, DR2, which begins broadcasting at 18.00, came on stream in 1996.

Until very recently there were no 'purely' commercial domestic national channels in Denmark. TV3, the Scandinavian satellite channel broadcast from the UK, has been available since the late 1980s, but take-up appears to be limited, its most popular programmes attracting about half a million viewers, as opposed to, at times, well over a million in the case of DR1 and TV2. In April 1997, however, the commercial nationwide channel TV-Danmark was launched. It emerged from the structures of the former local channel Kanal 2, which, in conjunction with a number of other local channels, went through a brief interim period of calling itself Kanal Danmark. TV-Danmark is a heavily entertainment-oriented channel with many American imports, though it also gives considerable space to local news, with an hour-long broadcast every evening. Other smaller players are 3[+], which only begins broadcasting in the mid-afternoon, and DK4, and there is also a new sports channel, TVS.

Danish soaps in the 1990s

A forerunner: Ugeavisen

There was no tradition of domestic serial production in Denmark until the early 1990s (Pedersen, 1993: 25). The first long-running series to appear was DR's *Ugeavisen* (The Weekly Newspaper), broadcast in 52 episodes in 1991–92. The action in *Ugeavisen* took place in the (fictitious) town of Holby, and it displayed a feature which will reappear in the analysis of *Landsbyen* below: a mixture of the fictional and the real. Thus the editor of the local newspaper worked formerly for *Politiken*, an actual Danish newspaper. The photographer played in his youth for an actual football team, Copenhagen B1903. The characters also have political beliefs allied to current Danish political parties. One was a communist during the war – when he was a member of the Danish resistance – but now has a position somewhere between the Socialist Party and the SF (Sosialistisk Folkeparti). This is in stark contrast to virtually all soaps currently showing in western Europe, which studiously avoid any kind of reference to actual politics at all (indeed in some cases – that of the Basque soap *Goenkale* for example – this is a stated part of their overall approach (see page 170)).

An eventual soap: Landsbyen

The longest-running domestic serial to be produced in Denmark so far has been *Landsbyen* (The Village), which was also first launched in 1991. *Landsbyen*'s progress towards full 'soap-hood' was slow and somewhat faltering. The first six episodes were shown in August and September 1991, and were a co-production between DR, the eastern region of the TV2 network, TV2 Øst, and the film company Nordisk Film, with a further six being screened in 1992, and yet another set of six in 1994. *Landsbyen*'s serial format at this time was quite clear. The third set of six episodes shown in 1994 were preceded by a special programme – *Landsbyen: en portræt* (Landsbyen: A Portrait) – in which the authors and director talked at length of what the serial meant for them, and the writers were careful to leave the last episode of each set of six open so that the story could be continued. For example, the following is an extract from DR's own press release in relation to episode twelve:

So the question is now – what will Astrid do to escape the grasp of the police and get Bo [her son] home again – what will Eva do to get her stolen money back – what will Frank do to get Karen back – what has in fact become of cousin Mille – and how will Ingeborg respond to her resolute suitor, Johannes?

Despite this, however, *Landsbyen* was not yet a soap at this stage because it had not entered into the kind of industrialized production rhythms and patterns characteristic of soap opera output.

It was not until Autumn 1995 that *Landsbyen* achieved real soap opera status. At this point a fourth season of 25 episodes went on air. The first of these was also preceded by a special programme, *Nyt fra Landsbyen* (News from *Landsbyen*), in which a number of the actors were interviewed, as well as those involved in the production of the serial. In this programme it was explained that the production routines had changed completely, and that these had been revised to meet the needs not only of producing such a large number of episodes, but also of being in the process of filming while writing was still taking place. The specific changes were the drafting in of additional writers, and the use of four directors instead of just one. For example, Stig Thorsboe who, along with his brother Peter had written the scripts for the early episodes, explained the need to call in extra writers as follows:

The fact that we had to involve outside/guest writers was actually a question of necessity. Peter and I simply weren't able to write so many episodes in such a short time. There is a special discipline involved when production is taking place while writing is continuing. Even if it started out of necessity it has turned out to be incredibly exciting for us getting guest writers to relate to our characters.

And one of the new directors, Anders Reen, spoke at length of the introduction of the new team of directors:

There are four directors involved in these 28 episodes. Before we started on them we spoke about how we would go about it. It's a lot to bite off to have to put together 28 episodes. You have to keep the characters alive in your head and you jump around in the material when it's being shot, you don't shoot continuously the way it appears on the screen, you jump around – you do a bit at the beginning, a bit from the end, a bit in the middle. So it is, in fact, exhausting to produce an hour's worth of drama. It's fun to have four different directors who each do their own episodes and colour them in their own way with their particular temperament.

At this point in its existence, *Landsbyen* moved from being a proto-soap to being a full-blown soap, although, as we shall see below, it remains different from other European soaps in a number of ways. It attracted an audience of around 900,000, a 44 per cent audience share.

The action in *Landsbyen* takes place in the (again fictitious) small village of Østerby. Just before the fourth season went on air in October 1995, the television magazine *Se og hør* described it as follows:

One of Denmark's best known villages, Østerby, can't be found on any map. No one has ever driven through it, but many know almost all the names of the village's inhabitants. Its size is minimal, but the village is extremely famous throughout the land.

However, since the characters read the *Næstved Tidende*, it can be located in the region around Næstved, some 60 kilometres south-west of Copenhagen.

Landsbyen is primarily a family-based soap, with only one family centrally involved – the Andersens. It is dominated by the 70-year-old Ingeborg (she was 65 when the serial started) and its main characters are her two sons Axel and Frank, the various women in their lives, and Axel and Eva's daughter from their earlier relationship, Astrid. Of the two sons, Axel remains tied to the village, working his land and running the local sawmill, while Frank is constantly involved in (not always entirely honest) business dealings which frequently take him away not just from the village but, on occasions, from Denmark. During episodes 26 and 27 he was in Germany on business, and a number of scenes in these two episodes were actually shot in Berlin. The brothers are also very different in character, with Axel being taciturn, cautious, perhaps even a little unsophisticated, but honest, while Frank is loquacious, ambitious, self-centred, and dishonest to the point of not thinking twice about deceiving the other members of his family. Other important characters include Ingeborg's much younger lover, Johannes, and her niece Mille.

Analysis

In one of its own descriptions of the serial in 1992, DR suggested that Østerby was a 'Danish mini-society which reflects the customs and conditions of Denmark in the nineties with its breaks with the past and its reforms, its new times and new styles'. This is a view which gained a certain currency in the Danish press, and appeared in a short article on *Landsbyen* in the quality newspaper *Politiken* in October 1995, which described the serial as a 'saga about life in a Danish mini-society in the 1990s'. It is not immediately clear in what sense *Landsbyen* is meant to represent Danish society in miniature (if this is the drift of these quotes). The bulk of the Danish population now lives in medium-sized towns (not to mention the over 600,000 inhabitants of the capital Copenhagen), and in this sense the group of people and the lifestyles represented in *Ugeavisen* could make a much better claim to being a version of contemporary Danish society in miniature. Nonetheless, *Landsbyen* is often presented as quintessentially Danish – the issue of *Se og hør* mentioned earlier even described it as an 'arch-Danish TV-series'.

What *Landsbyen* constructs, in fact – and, in its own terms, very successfully – is not so much a 'Denmark in miniature' but rather a 'Denmark of the past in the present'; a Denmark which no longer quite exists but which is still seen by many as the real Denmark. In *Nyt fra Landsbyen* some of those involved in the programme made this point quite explicitly. The director Lotte Tarp's view was as follows:

Landsbyen is first and foremost an image of Denmark as I see it ... The rural Denmark which is disappearing and being industrialised away. So it is also, of course, a romantic vision of what the country once was. In between there's a lot of material for conflict in the story. Shopping centres get built, the land is sprayed with toxic substances, and there are discussions about environmentally-friendly agriculture. At the same time there are quarrels over who will inherit from whom, who is whose father, who is whose mother. There is a lot of good material for conflicts here which is typically Danish.

While Stig Thorsboe added:

Landsbyen ... gives, at least this is what we are trying to achieve, an image of Denmark as we approach the new century. We focus on the land where we somewhere or other all come from if we just go back a generation or two. It's a very compact world, and we can choose to take a very nostalgic look and a romantic look at it. But it is also very real, it's about agriculture, it's about pollution, it's about money. I think people should watch *Landsbyen* to see which way the two brothers go, since each of them chooses his own way. The two ways they choose say a lot about Denmark today.

Landsbyen is, in fact, very much a mixture of the romantic and the modern. The images of modern Denmark are in themselves quite noteworthy. The building site on which Frank and his business partner, Matisen, are building the shopping centre gives much more detail than is normal in soaps: workers in blue overalls and hard hats tramp around in the mud amidst piles of concrete pipes and walk in front of the camera carrying huge lengths of plastic ducting, earth-moving equipment of all kinds trundles past with its caterpillar tracks churning up the ground even more, and so on (all of which contrasts strongly with the very nominal building sites in the UK soap *Hollyoaks*, for example, or the Swedish soap *Skilda världar*). The only business actually established in the village – the Tømmegården sawmill – is populated by workers sawing up actual lengths of wood amidst piles of sawdust. This kind of detail is extremely rare in European soaps, where, at the very most, a mechanic might be glimpsed under the bonnet of a car (although something rather similar can be found in the Norwegian soaps *I de beste familier* and *Offshore* (see page 137)).

As far as agricultural activity is concerned, Axel is often seen trudging through muddy fields in his wellingtons or driving his tractor or pick-up. He and Johannes hammer stakes into the ground to set up a fence to keep in Johannes' new 'eco-friendly' pigs (eco-friendliness being a clearly emergent signifier in European soaps of social solidarity (see also page 175)). The depiction of agricultural activities is less developed than those of construction and light industry, but it is still quite unusual by European standards, despite the large numbers of rural soaps currently being screened in various countries.

The local supermarket, the Brugsen, where Eva works, is one of the most convincing supermarkets in any European soap (and there are many). In terms of local politics, the councillor who halts the building of the shopping centre isn't the kind of anonymous politician so common in European soaps, nor is he that other soap favourite, an 'independent': he is a member of the Social Democratic Party, and gets into trouble with his party for voting against the project. The journalist who comes to cover the incident works for *Ekstra Bladet*, Denmark's best-selling tabloid. On a more domestic level, Ingeborg at home frequently wears a very unglamorous, full-length apron, and can at times be seen ironing, baking, washing dishes or mending clothes. Some of the scenes of *Landsbyen* are actually difficult to watch. When the heavily pregnant Eva goes into premature labour after being knocked down in episode 28, the blood she loses is seen dripping to the ground. While miscarriage is a fairly common theme in soaps – although in this case Eva successfully gives birth to a baby daughter – nowhere is it shown as graphically as this.

Despite this, the predominant impression of *Landsbyen* is not so much one of 'realism'. On the contrary, perhaps the most striking aspect of *Landsbyen* is its lyrical qualities: it is surely the most lyrical of all European soaps. This is due to a very large extent to Bo Holten's theme tune, played out over sepia-coloured images of geese slowly taking flight above the village's duck pond, and snatches of which recur insistently throughout every episode. This is one of the most haunting theme tunes of any European soap, melancholy and romantic in style, perhaps even a little Wagnerian (its only possible rival is the theme tune of the Gaelic soap *Machair* in Scotland), and played by the Danish Radio Entertainment Orchestra. And the filming techniques also differ greatly from the European norm. *Landsbyen* will often linger on shots of empty fields or courtyards in the twilight, dimly lit by the farmsteads' outside lamps. Small and apparently insignificant details can become the centre of focus. The camera will stay with a character for several seconds while all he does is slowly put on his coat and leave his office, putting out the light behind him. As Axel and Eva get ready to go out, the camera lingers not on their faces, but on Axel's hands as he slowly knots his tie. In another scene, during a lengthy conversation between Frank and Karen the camera stays not on them, but on Mille: this breaks an almost universal soap tradition whereby the speaker is virtually always the centre of focus (this is not to say that others cannot be seen reacting to what the speaker is saying, but these are usually brief shots cut into scenes dominated by a focus on the speaker). There can be long silences. In episode 28, in which Karen looks for the little Kurdish boy Baran who has gone missing in the village, there is a first period of 1 minute 15 seconds in which not a single word is said, and a second sequence of 2 minutes 30 seconds in which the only word spoken is the young boy's name. This is unthinkable for most European soaps, and for the genre in general where dialogue is the main mechanism through which the narrative is carried forward. At the same time, the cutting can be extremely rapid in moments of high drama. When Eva is run over by a hit-and-run driver in episode 28, causing her to go into premature labour, there are seven shots within the space of seven seconds, several of them deliberately out of focus.

Landsbyen is, in fact, in a certain (admittedly restricted) sense one of the most 'domestic' of all western European soaps. As pointed out earlier, Denmark is a country in which out-and-out commercial competition to the public service sector is still relatively limited. It is a matter of simple observation that countries where this kind of situation obtains either have no soaps at all – for example, Austria or Switzerland – or have soaps which are rather more *sui generis*, as in the case of Ireland. Many soaps currently showing in western Europe show, at least in their production techniques, the marks of external influences of one kind or another – British in the case of *Lindenstraße* in Germany, *Thuis* in Flanders and *Poble Nou* and *Goenkale* in Spain, American in the case of the Greek soaps, Australian in a whole range of Dutch, Swedish and German soaps – but *Landsbyen* shows traces of none of these. If anything, it in fact links in with longer-standing Danish (and even Scandinavian) traditions.

Among *Landsbyen*'s many other unusual features is an almost complete absence of teenage characters, a feature it shares with *Ugeavisen*. At the start of the 1995–96 season, the average age of its main characters was well over 40, the youngest being the 30-year-old Astrid. Moreover, the relationship between this dominant generation and the following ones is highly prob-lematic: Frank and Karen have no children, and she considers artificial insemination without asking for his consent. Astrid was brought up believ-ing that Axel was her brother, not her father, and only learned at the age of 25 who her actual parents were. Her son is the child of a drug addict who commits suicide while in prison. *Landsbyen* is in some sense the story of a generation which feels it is dying out.

Landsbyen makes no recognizable pitch at a younger audience, a feature reflected by the age-breakdown of its audience. DR's own audience research shows that the great bulk of its audience – just under 75 per cent – is over 35, with the greatest single segment – almost 40 per cent – being over 55. None of this is surprising. *Landsbyen* is very much an 'educated' older person's soap – thoughtful, unhurried, philosophical, literate – and the mini-society it develops is not so much the inhabitants of Østerby as the society of viewers constructed by its complex appeal. This is no doubt the sector of Danish society for whom the romantic recollection of country life – itself primarily a culturally maintained memory rather than necessarily a 'lived experience' – still makes sense, but who realize – in contrast to the Finnish soap *Metsolat*, for example (see page 52) – that history cannot be put into reverse. If the paths chosen by the two brothers really do say anything about contemporary Denmark, it is that people in this age-group prefer the values of the past to those of the future, at least so far as these are represented respectively by Axel and Frank. In the narrative universe of *Landsbyen* the values of a disappearing Denmark upheld by the gruff but sensitive and caring Axel easily win the symbolic battles against those embodied by his flash and superficial brother, but while the childless Frank offers no possibility of continuation, Axel at least offers some hope for the future through his grandson Bo.

Postscript

DR is currently planning a new long-running serial to be entitled *Taxa* (Taxi). At the moment I have no further details regarding its content.

Finland

Television in Finland

National broadcasting was launched in Finland by the state broadcasting company Suomen Yleisradio (YLE) in 1957, its second channel TV2 beginning in 1964 (Tapper, 1992: 48). Finland's first commercial station, MTV, also began broadcasting in 1957, giving Finland the longest-established duopoly in western Europe outside the United Kingdom. However, this did not initially result in the appearance of a new channel, as in the case of the UK, since for many years MTV's programmes were in fact transmitted on YLE's channels at agreed times of the day. A separate third commercial channel, TV3, began transmissions in the mid-1980s, and has now been taken over by MTV. Since 1993 the latter's programmes have moved out of YLE's channels altogether, and are now broadcast in their entirety on TV3, which has been renamed MTV3.

Beyond these national channels, the cable channel PTV (now PTV4) was established in 1990 by the cable companies of Helsinki, Tampere and Turku, while Swedish Television broadcasts TV4, a Swedish-language service consisting of a variety of programmes from its first and second channels, to Finland's Swedish-speaking minority, some 6 per cent of the population, living in areas along the shores of the Baltic.

Domestic Finnish television serials

Finland's earliest television serials date back to the early 1970s with *Oi kallis kaupunki* (My Dear Town) shown by TV2 and *Naapurilähiö* (The Neighbourhood) shown by MTV. Despite their success, no such serials were produced in the 1980s. The 1990s, however, have seen a tremendous resurgence of the television serial, with audiences reaching record proportions. None of these productions is, properly speaking, a soap, since they usually present a self-contained narrative.

Productions in the early 1990s were *Ruusun aika* (The Time of the Rose), screened by MTV in 1990–91 and dealing with a well-to-do suburban family, *Hyvien ihmisten kylä* (The Village of Decent People), which ran for nine episodes on TV2 in 1993–94 and attracted audiences of up to 800,000, and *Puhtaat valkeat lakanat* (The Pure White Linen), an MTV production running in 1993–94 and tracing the rise of the Finnish Welfare State in the 1960s and 1970s through the fortunes of the Raikas, a family of clothing manufacturers. According to the scriptwriter Raija Oranen (who had also scripted *Ruusun aika*) it was aimed at least partly at redressing what was seen as a one-sided view of how the Welfare State came about: 'The leftist radicalism of the era is preserved in popular collective memory, but seldom are the actual makers of prosperity, i.e. entrepreneurs and industrialists, given the credit or even a voice' (Hietala, 1994: 106). While it is clear that the Finnish Welfare State – like all contemporary welfare states – arose from an agreement between capital and labour, Raija Oranen's view is, needless to say, a somewhat tendentious interpretation of how the wealth used to produce the Finnish Welfare State was generated in the first place.

The most successful Finnish serial of the 1990s, however, has been without any doubt *Metsolat* (The Metsolas), a rural saga of a family running a small farm at the end of the 1980s which ran for 40 episodes on TV2 in 1993. It was the most popular programme in the history of Finnish television, attracting audiences of almost two million: an astonishing achievement in a country of some five million inhabitants. Two special episodes were added for Christmas 1994 and 1996. I return to *Metsolat* in a little more depth later.

Blondi tuli taloon (The Blonde Came to the House) ran on a twice-a-week basis in 1994–95 and dealt with the daughter of a poor family going to work as a housekeeper for a widower and his children, the latter belonging to the new middle classes. Though sometimes referred to as a soap, it was more of a long-running sit-com. Its cast of characters was very low by soap standards – only half a dozen in the episodes I saw – and it lacked the overlapping narratives characteristic of proper soaps. It was, however, a reasonably popular production, and was on occasions able to attract over one million viewers.

In 1994–95 *Kohtaamiset ja erot* (Meetings and Separations) appeared on TV2. This was a 21-episode production set in the small rural community of Kärttämä in Karelia (on the border between Finland and Russia). It was very rustic indeed: one episode I saw featured a boar emerging from the woods and terrorizing one of the villagers. It was also a reasonably successful production, attracting 640,000 viewers in January 1995, being on that occasion TV2's seventh most popular programme (*Katso!*, 30 January 1995).

If anything, the pace, in terms of serial production, has quickened in the second half of the 1990s. Notable recent productions have included TV1's 1995 offering *Kotikatu* (Home Street) dealing with two city families, one well-to-do and one working-class; *Elämän suola* (The Salt of Life), the saga of a well-to-do city family; *Shampanjaa ja vaahtokarkkeja* (Champagne and Candies), a soap dealing with young, single city people; and *Ihmeidentekijät* (The Miracle Workers), set in that favourite location of the 1990s, the city hospital, and again dealing with relatively affluent, single people.

It may be worthwhile pointing out the very considerable success of the American day-time soap *The Bold and the Beautiful* in Finland during this period. Under the title *Kauniit ja rohkeat* (The Beautiful and the Bold) it has been one of the most popular programmes in Finland throughout the 1990s, on occasions attracting over one million viewers. For example, in the week that *Kohtaamiset ja erot* attracted 640,000 viewers, *The Bold and the Beautiful* had 1,225,000, and was the third most popular programme in Finland overall.

A mythical soap: Metsolat

Way Home is the title with which YLE has put *Metsolat* on the international market. Its description of the serial for potential customers was as follows:

A serial drama of a Finnish family living on a farm in the northeast of the country, taking place during the worst economic depression in Finland when the rural way of life was facing major challenges and changes. The 1990s audiences perceived the farm as the archetypal home, and identified wholeheartedly with the ups and downs of the sons and daughters of the family, returning to the mother's coffee table after failures in the outside world. Described by an expert as 'a drama of breathtakingly ordinary life', the series became a mega-hit reflecting the way the recent past can quickly acquire mythical rose-tinted attributes in the mind of the audience.

The analyst referred to in this summary is Veijo Hietala, whose article 'Finnish Television Today' examines the major Finnish television serials of the 1990s. He used the phrase 'a drama of breathtakingly ordinary life' in a subsection entitled 'The white linen of the Metsola family – the return of the past'. His summary of the serial is as follows (1994: 108–9):

The Metsola saga was produced, quite accidentally, at a time when there was an exceptional number of threats and crises concerning 'Finnishness'. Consequently the producers unintentionally happened to deal with many burning issues which they probably had not even considered. Primarily the serial was meant to address the agricultural crisis, living conditions in the country. The events – and partly the production – of the serial took place at a time when Finland saw the fastest economic rise in its history – i.e. the latter half of the 1980s, or the 'casino game years' as it was later known. The media, both at home and abroad, even talked about the 'Japan of the North'. Finland's economy was going through a major structural change which implied that the small farms in middle and northern Finland in particular were rapidly losing their significance in the new order. Will there be life in the Finnish countryside after the change?

At the beginning of the Metsola serial this crisis was symbolically manifested by the heart attack of the old master of the Leppävaara farm, which forced the family to discuss seriously the future of the farm. The old lifestyle of agriculture and cattle-breeding was to give way – to what? The serial offered a comforting solution, and actually concrete instructions. It suggested that even the notorious 'casino players' still want to spend their leisure time in the countryside, if only someone organizes leisure activities for them. Erkki Metsola, unemployed alcoholic and former cross-country champion, accepts the challenge and constructs a modern skiing centre almost single-handedly, thereby employing the rest of the family as well. Even the old Metsolas find the new way of earning a living – by renting parking space to visitors – much easier than toiling in the field and cowshed.

There can be little doubt that the production and screening of *Metsolat* did indeed coincide with a crucial period of change in Finland – crucial not just for the reasons given above, but also because the collapse of the Soviet Union and the disintegration of its previously complex relationship with its Scandinavian neighbour (formalized in the so-called Friendship, Co-operation and Support Agreement, which was finally ended in 1991) has had powerful repercussions at many levels and in many quarters of Finnish society. It has led to the perfectly visible rewriting and reinterpreting – both official and unofficial – of a number of elements of post-war Finnish history, of which the erection in 1994 of a statue to the formerly disgraced president Risto Ryti (imprisoned in 1946 for acts of aggression against the Soviet Union) is only one of the more obvious signs. Indeed, this rewriting of history has to some extent assumed the proportions of a national project.

Analysis

Unfortunately, my knowledge of Finnish is not yet entirely up to speed, and I am not, therefore, able to analyse the productions listed earlier in the same depth as those of other European countries, or trace their broader links with other discourses within Finnish society at large. Nonetheless, my own impression of *Metsolat* on the basis of the episodes I was able to see was not so much of the return of the past, but of history actually being put into rewind, of a return *to* the past. As Hietala points out in his article, there have been a number of productions in western European countries dealing with social and political developments in the second half of the twentieth century. He mentions *Heimat* and *Zweite Heimat* in Germany, but other examples much closer to home would include *Vestavind* in Norway (see page 136) and *Det var då* and *Tre kärleker* in Sweden (see page 180). The Scandinavian productions in particular are attempts – as to some extent *Puhtaat valkeat lakanat* also was, though from a rather different angle – to come to terms with the end of the long period of social-democratic hegemony in those countries, and to face up to the much rawer climate which the fast-advancing neo-liberal hegemony would bring. But the main difference between the Swedish and Norwegian productions and *Metsolat* is that they traced a forward chronology in the past, whereas *Metsolat* appears to trace a reverse chronology in the present. What I mean by this is that the movement of people in *Metsolat* is from the city – Tampere – to the countryside and from dispersed nuclear families to a localized extended one, at a time when *actual* trends are very much in the opposite directions (giving rise, for example, to the well known 'ruuhka-Suomi' or 'congestion-Finland' where one-fifth of the entire population now lives in a relatively small area in the southernmost part of the country). But they do not cling stubbornly to the values of this past as they do in the Portuguese *telenovelas* (see page 158), nor do they attempt to modernize them on their own terms as, for example, Johannes does in the Danish soap *Landsbyen* (see page 44) by updating his agricultural methods; they replace them with the new free-market values of a particular version of the present. In fact, simultaneously with the move from new to old social patterns, the characters move from various petit bourgeois or old middle-class positions at the beginning of the serial (when the children of the Metsola family were variously bank managers, doctors or skilled craftsmen) to new entrepreneurial ones at the end. In other words, the past is not just being revisited, it is being rewritten – a feature which *Metsolat* therefore shares, though in a rather different way, with *Puhtaat valkeat lakanat*. This rewriting coincides broadly not just with the official redefinition of Finland's relationship with Russia, as mentioned above, and the replacement of the old agreement with a more even-handed Neighbourhood Agreement, but also with the landslide victory of the conservative Centre Party in the 1991 Finnish general elections.

In a passage which has striking points of contact with official descriptions of *Landsbyen* (see page 43), Hietala suggests that 'the Metsola family and the Leppävaara farm were a unique micromodel of the whole of Finland – mythical Finland, that is'. There is a clear sense in which this serial does rework the concept of 'mummola', or 'granny's place' (almost invariably in the country for older Finns), and this concept has indeed acquired a mythical (in the Barthesian sense (see Barthes, 1973)) status in Finland as it has also done in other recently urbanized societies such as Denmark, where Ingeborg in *Landsbyen* also connects, though in a somewhat different manner, with this myth (see page 43). However, *Metsolat* is also mythical in the sense that Finland, like so many other countries in so many other serials, is being reduced to its middle classes. Hietala points out that the serial was screened during Finland's worst economic crisis ever – the 'bust' of the 1990s following the 'boom' of the 1980s – and during heated debates on whether entry into the EU really was in the 'country's' best interests. But the economic crisis did not just produce bankruptcies among Finland's entrepreneurial middle classes; it produced structural unemployment among the Finnish working class, who are neither present in this production nor invited to join its pilgrimage into myth: Erkki makes the leap from lumpenproletarian to entrepreneur without ever coming into contact with the working class. The 'optimism and faith in a more prosperous future' which Hietala sees in this production (1994: 108) is for those already owning or able to generate enough capital to live on the fringes of the new society.

The frequency with which contemporary Finnish serials use rural settings is also part of a much wider trend. But these programmes do not return the viewer to 'the roots of the nation' via 'a retreat into the innocence of the agrarian life-style' (Hietala, 1994: 109) – indeed, there is very little 'innocence' in the lives depicted in these serials – they valorize the countryside at a time when, given the dramatic collapse of agricultural employment throughout Europe since the end of the Second World War, rural 'escape' is a retreat available only to those with sufficient income or capital to be already self-sufficient.

While the theoretical framework within which I work certainly allows for cases where the producers of popular cultural products 'unintentionally happen to deal with many burning issues which they probably had not even considered' (see above) – since discourse, like ideology, operates most efficiently below the level of consciousness – it is much less accommodating of the suggestion that this might have happened 'accidentally'. It is almost certainly no coincidence that the much less glamorous – indeed, rather dingy – *Kohtaamiset ja erot* attracted only a third of the audience of *Metsolat*. The rewriting of history which, in my interpretation at least, *Metsolat* realizes will be connected with, and ultimately derives from the same sources as, other related discourses in Finnish society, as outlined above. What more specific forms these might take I am at this moment unable to say in greater detail, but I am in no doubt that they are there.

Germany

Television in Germany

The public service television system currently operating in Germany consists of three channels. The oldest of these is the Arbeitsgemeinschaft der Rundfunksanstalten Deutschlands (ARD), a single nationwide channel run jointly by a number of regional channel television companies, and also known as the First Channel (das Erste Programm). Since reunification, a further two regional stations have joined the ARD, covering the territory of the former East Germany. The second channel, Zweites Deutsches Fernsehen (ZDF), was set up in 1961 in order to prevent the ARD from occupying a monopoly position (Hellack, 1996: 19). As well as jointly producing the First Channel, the various members of the ARD each also run their own regional channels, which are known collectively as the Third Channel (das Dritte Programm). Limited advertising has been available on these three PSB channels more or less from the outset (Hoffman, 1992: 533–4).

Since the mid-1980s, the growth of private television stations in Germany has been quite spectacular. First to arrive, on 1 January 1984, was Radio Luxembourg, illegally broadcasting four hours of programming per day to the area between Saarbrücken and Mainz. This station was part of the Luxembourg-based CLT group, though the powerful German Bertelsmann media group is also now a major shareholder. It would eventually rename itself RTLplus, and broadcast throughout Germany. It was followed exactly one year later by SAT1, which is part of the Kirch media group, Bertelsmann's main rival within Germany. Tele 5, launched in 1988, eventually disappeared in 1992, its frequency being taken over by the dedicated sports channel Deutsches Sportfernsehen (DSF). Other smaller stations to arrive in the late 1980s and early 1990s were Pro 7, a film and series channel popular with younger audiences, and Vox, a middle-brow channel showing a large number of British and French quality series in the evening. With the exception of Pro 7, which has an average audience share of around 10 per cent, these are relatively small players in the German television market. Other smaller players still are Kabel 1 (like DSF and Pro 7 also part of the Kirch group), the women's channel TM3 and the 24-hour news channel N-TV. There are also two German music channels, Viva and Viva II.

Both SAT1 and RTLplus quickly became very popular. The latter in particular has now expanded its operations considerably: a second, mainly youth-oriented station called RTL2 was introduced in March 1993 (at which point RTLplus changed its name to RTL), followed by SuperRTL, a channel which specializes in rerunning older programmes. Bearing in mind that a number of the regional ARD channels are available nationwide via satellite and cable, Germany now has the greatest range of domestic television channels available nationally anywhere in Europe – more than twenty. There has also been increasing differentiation and even fragmentation of audiences, with older viewers clearly favouring the long-established PSB channels, and younger viewers favouring the more recent channels, in particular RTL. Competition between RTL and SAT1 on the one hand, and between these two and the PSB stations on the other, is intense, and there are frequent high-profile clashes between their directors in newspaper and magazine interviews. Audience shares for the leading channels in 1995 were: RTL, 17.6 per cent; SAT1, 14.7 per cent; ZDF, 14.7 per cent; ARD, 14.6 per cent; Third Channel stations, 9.7 per cent (Hellack, 1996: 27). These figures are still broadly correct, with a slight fall for ZDF and a slight rise for the Third Channels and Pro 7.

Domestic German soaps

The only German soap to pre-date the 1990s was *Lindenstraße* (Linden Street). Initially inspired by the UK soap *Coronation Street*, it first went on air on 8 December 1985 at 18.40, and has run continuously ever since on a once-a-week basis, having now logged up over 600 half-hour episodes. It is shown on Sundays on ARD's Erstes Program, and then at different days of the following week on the various Third Channels. Average viewing figures now are in the region of seven and a half million for the Sunday screening (Frey-Vor, 1995: 145).

Though filmed in Cologne, *Lindenstraße* is set in Munich, and the central characters all live in the same block of flats. Of all the European soap operas I have viewed, it is by far the most overtly campaigning, and in that sense the most overtly political. It is notable not just for its campaigning style, but for the directness with which it *nominates* the issues with which it is dealing.

This is a radical departure from normal soap opera style: many soaps tackle what are ultimately political issues, but tend to do so indirectly through their narrative without explicitly nominating them. But no one can ever be in any doubt about what is being targeted in a *Lindenstraße* campaign. Some information in English is available on the early years of this serial in Silj (1988).

The anguish which is easily visible in many of *Lindenstraße*'s storylines is reinforced by the overall style of the soap, which is, as a whole, ridden with angst. This is where *Lindenstraße* most deviates from its English inspirers, and the reason for this is quite clear: the characters in *Lindenstraße* 'own' Germany in a way in which no character in any UK soap could ever be said to 'own' Britain. *Lindenstraße*'s characters claim Germany as their own and take responsibility for its defects and its shortcomings. The result is a striking mixture of incongruous capers, grand melodramatic gestures and the stentorian defence of civilized values.

Despite its array of teenage and even pre-school characters, *Lindenstraße* is essentially an older person's soap (Frey-Vor, 1995: 149). While the arrival of the new commercial channels has caused viewing figures for individual programmes on the PSB networks to fall, *Lindenstraße*'s audience figures have remained relatively good (Frey-Vor, 1995: 145) precisely because the largest part of its audience is exactly that sector of German society which has remained most faithful to the public service channels: the over-fifties. *Lindenstraße* provides a narrative vehicle for the working through of the responsibility they continue to feel for their country as a whole, an agreement with its viewers which will keep this soap going for many years yet.

The new soaps

A postmodern soap: Gute Zeiten, Schlechte Zeiten

Germany's first five-day-a-week soap started on 11 May 1992. Entitled *Gute Zeiten, Schlechte Zeiten* (Good Times, Bad Times), it was launched by the then RTLplus, and continues to run on RTL today, having now clocked up well over 1000 episodes. The similarity of its title with the Dutch soap *Goede Tijden, Slechte Tijden* (also Good Times, Bad Times) is of course no coincidence. Like RTL4's soap (see page 125), this German production is also a descendant of the Australian soap *The Restless Years* of the late 1970s, and it is also a co-production with Grundy International, the German partner in this case being Ufa, the film and TV branch of the Bertelsmann publishing group which is also the major shareholder in RTL. *Gute Zeiten, Schlechte Zeiten* had a somewhat slow start, and was originally the target of much critical hostility: *Der Spiegel*, for example (34/1993), described it as a 'daily embarrassment . . . with less dramatic technique than a mail-order catalogue'. However, it not only managed to establish itself, but has in fact achieved almost cult status, particularly among the youth audience, with viewing figures of sometimes over five million (typically about 4.5 million or 17 per cent of actual viewers) in a time-slot where it is up against stiff competition in the very fragmented German TV landscape of the 1990s, and it is usually among the top five programmes on RTL. It costs around DM4500 per minute or DM80,000 per episode (Cunningham and Jacka, 1996: 156) – less than one-quarter of the cost of an episode of *Lindenstraße*. *Gute Zeiten, Schlechte Zeiten* is currently one of RTL's largest advertising revenue earners. Together with the daily soft-news magazine *Explosiv*, which immediately precedes it, it brings in 80 million marks per year, four times as much as all RTL's other programmes taken together (*Der Spiegel*, 2/1996).

Like its Dutch counterpart, for just over a year *Gute Zeiten, Schlechte Zeiten* closely followed the scripts of its Australian model (specifically for the first 231 episodes), with the same characters and the same storylines (see Stern, 1978). However, the Germanifying effort was already clear in the use of German settings, German names, German fashions and so on. Although actually filmed in Berlin (first in the Tempelhof studios, later in Babelsberg), *Gute Zeiten, Schlechte Zeiten* shares with its Dutch counterpart a deliberate avoidance of naming the narrative setting: in fact, the producers even went so far as to invent fictitious licence-plates for cars appearing in the programme, and the characters read the non-existent newspaper *Morgenecho*. Without exception everyone speaks a very polished High German, which geographically places the setting somewhere in the north, but this is in fact part of a fairly long-standing tradition on German television representing basically 'somewhere in Germany': it is a deliberate choice, since many other German television genres – notably detective programmes – are often characterized by regional accents of one kind or another. But it is not in fact just 'anywhere' in Germany: the Germany portrayed in *Gute Zeiten, Schlechte Zeiten* is an affluent society of enthusiastic consumers. As a long (and rather critical) article in the German weekly magazine *Der Spiegel* (22/1996) put it, referring to Germany's 'new regions' (i.e. the former East Germany), 'Settings and decors make one thing clear: soaps are definitely not set in the new regions . . . the soap cities are situated in the Somewhere and Everywhere of the shopping centre aesthetic.'

After the first year, a team of German scriptwriters (sometimes working in conjunction with Australian scriptwriters from Grundy International) took over, and *Gute Zeiten, Schlechte Zeiten* became a 100 per cent German product, a change which coincided with a notable increase in popularity. Within a few months the differences between it and its Dutch cousin had become very noticeable. For example, on a quite simple level, *Gute Zeiten, Schlechte Zeiten* is, unlike its Dutch cousin, which is shot almost entirely in the studio, positively expansive in its locations. Outside shots are absolutely routine, occurring in every episode, and they are not just confined to city streets, often taking place in parks, woods, the school playground, on lakes and so on. Even in the case of inside shots genuine (or at least apparently genuine) cityscapes can sometimes be seen through the windows, giving the whole production an outward-looking feel which contrasts strongly with the heavy claustrophobia of its Dutch counterpart (in fact, they are probably the well-known Babelsberg painted backdrops). To some extent the difference in mood between the two productions can be seen simply by comparing their title songs. While the Dutch title song is sombre and apprehensive (see page 128), *Gute Zeiten, Schlechte Zeiten*'s is enthusiastic and forward-looking, beginning as follows: 'You have lots of dreams / You know exactly where you're going / You're always searching / Until you satisfy your longing'.

The main family in *Gute Zeiten, Schlechte Zeiten* are the Richters – the parents Vera and Clemens and, until mid-1996, their son Heiko. They live amidst abundant affluence, first in their leafy-suburban house, later in their well-appointed flat, their tables invariably groaning with the riches of economic success, and their abode never too small to turn away yet another visitor arriving for an indefinitely extended stay. Other central characters include Heiko's former schoolteacher Elisabeth Meinhart. The early story-lines centred around these and various of Heiko's former schoolmates. However, while the turnover in cast in *Goede Tijden, Slechte Tijden* has been relatively slow, in *Gute Zeiten, Schlechte Zeiten* it has proceeded at a truly vertiginous rate. Within a relatively short period of time a whole new set of characters arrived, most of whom have also now been replaced by yet another new wave, and at the time of writing, of the original group of young people only one now remains. In fact speed of change is one of the key defining elements of *Gute Zeiten, Schlechte Zeiten* as a whole. People change their jobs at a dizzying rate, setting up companies and dissolving them, opening shops and health clubs, starting up motorcycle repair businesses, reopening factories which have closed, launching magazines, inventing new designs for fashions and toys, with the necessary skills and expertise somehow or other always being miraculously available to them. Even the decors change at a disorientating speed. For example, the café where the young people meet was originally called the 'à propos', then 'Das Bistro', then 'Siggy's Bar' and is now known as 'Daniel's'. Even as 'Daniel's' it has gone through a number of radical changes to its interior decor, to such an extent that it is no longer recognizable as having any relationship with its earlier self.

In the early part of the life of *Gute Zeiten, Schlechte Zeiten* there were a number of storylines which dealt with what might broadly be called social issues, or even points of political principle. The social issues clustered mostly around the figure of Peter Becker (and in fact derived from his model in *The Restless Years*, Peter Beckett), and occasionally pointed to a rather different Germany lurking beneath *Gute Zeiten, Schlechte Zeiten*'s

affluent and frivolous surface. Peter was the adopted son of a lumpenproletarian family where the alcoholic father was given to regularly beating his
wife and children. His conflicts with his father culminated in him finally
striking him back, and walking out to begin a life on his own. Part of this
involved him working in a refuge for homeless youngsters where some of
the early characters came from. This storyline involved some criticism of
the funding policies of local councils as financial support for the refuge
came to an end. In 1993 the storyline of his family resurfaced when Peter's
adoptive sister Karen came to live with him fleeing from her father, and a
number of uncomfortable flashbacks – some with very dramatic point-of-
view shots – suggested overwhelmingly that she had been consistently
abused by him. In 1993 statements of political belief could also still be
found. Vera Richter's decision to return to work, ending up in the same
advertising agency as Clemens (and in fact taking over his office), caused
some earnest lecturing on the theme of the emancipation of women. In the
'save our park' story described in more detail below, while the demonstrations themselves were fun events, a parallel subplot involved a serious clash
between Heiko and Clemens, since Heiko was leading the resistance to a
project being carried out by Clemens's employer's wife, and Clemens was
coming under considerable pressure at work as a result. Having at first tried
to persuade Heiko to give up his involvement in the protest, and having
been accused of 'hypocrisy' by his son, Clemens eventually decided to stand
by his principles and made a speech on the values of freedom and
democracy which would not have been out of place in *Lindenstraße*. These
days have gone, however, and it is now a very long time since any serious
social or political issues were directly raised in *Gute Zeiten, Schlechte Zeiten*.
As the article in *Der Spiegel* put it (22/1996): 'particularly in German
productions, being German means basically not being unemployed. Only in
exceptional cases do German television productions show any awareness of
the country's economic crisis ... the ratings killers here are "the ugly, the
socially disadvantaged, losers"'.

If characters and decors change relentlessly, speed of turnover is also the
hallmark of the storylines in *Gute Zeiten, Schlechte Zeiten*. While storylines
in the Dutch programme can run on occasions for months, in *Gute Zeiten,
Schlechte Zeiten* they seldom last more than a few weeks and in some
extreme cases have lasted only two days. *Gute Zeiten, Schlechte Zeiten*
simply devours storylines. Everything is thrown in but nothing is treated in
depth. For example a story with a mild ecological slant – a 'save our park'
demonstration against the villainous Claudia Löpelmann – was a source of
much enjoyment for the characters as they painted their slogans on banners,
rehearsed their chants and decided what they would wear as they lined up
against the earth-moving equipment. The dominant note in this demonstration was fun, with relaxed characters laughing and smiling as they made
their ecological-cum-fashion statement. The frivolity of this entire episode

becomes immediately apparent when it is compared with the 'save our square' movement in the UK soap *EastEnders* in 1996, a much grimmer and at times quite bitter conflict pitting the inhabitants of Albert Square against the local council in the defence of a play area for their children. There are stories about drugs which are not really about drugs and stories about politics which are not really about politics. The storylines pile up in a truly chaotic manner, mixing the trivial and the fantastic with the awful. One day Flo discovers she is really a Ruritanian princess; on another Harumi declares her lesbian love for Saskia; on yet another Diana's jealous rival Anya pushes her from a ladder causing her to lose the child she is expecting with Tommy.

This kaleidoscopic mixing of storylines and styles came to something of a head in the second half of 1993 with the long set of stories relating to André Holm and Jürgen Borchardt. André – who had made a previous appearance in the soap claiming to be Elisabeth Meinhart's long-lost son – reappeared as a patient in a mental hospital. He struck up a friendship with his warder Jürgen, who used his authority to get André out as required. During this period the two were at the centre of a long series of frauds and other wheezes, each more ridiculous than the other. For example, they 'invented' a new slimming pill. They produced moonshine from a still assembled in André's room, only for it to explode with duly farcical consequences. They set up a vermin extermination company which they used as a cover to get revenge on Daniel (who had refused them entry to his health club) by infesting his premises. André eventually managed to secure his own permanent release by blackmailing the head doctor and went on to feature in a number of storylines as a 'normal' member of the cast. But the mixing of styles is simply all-pervasive in *Gute Zeiten, Schlechte Zeiten*. When Tina and Yasemin were held up in the bank where Yasemin worked, Heiko arrived in heroic style and offered to exchange himself for his girlfriend. When this message was relayed by the police to the perps – who were suitably unshaven and rude of speech – they asked: 'Is anyone here Heiko Richter's girlfriend?' Yasemin and Tina both leapt to their feet and simultaneously shouted 'Me!'. This single answer combined soap, police drama, thriller and sit-com in one easy move.

A further feature of this soap is its constant 'quoting'. This can take many forms, relating to music, characters and occasionally filming techniques. Perhaps the use of music is the most bounteous source of such quotes. Thus, if a character is learning some horrendous secret, the music playing in the background may well be 'I heard it on the grapevine'. If a couple are falling out, this might be accompanied by 'Breaking up is hard to do'. Instances of this are legion. On a slightly different level, as Heiko set off to take a newly-invented toy to a trade fair, his imminent departure was announced by the theme tune to *Star Trek*. As the music reached its climax, he looked straight at the camera and said 'Energize'. This kind of thing is not entirely exclusive to *Gute Zeiten, Schlechte Zeiten*, but what is different in *Gute Zeiten, Schlechte Zeiten* is the sheer scale and unrelenting nature of the quoting, the complicity of the characters in the quotes, and their penetration into other aspects of the soap as well.

Not content with quoting other styles and techniques, however, *Gute Zeiten, Schlechte Zeiten* in fact also quotes itself. This takes a number of forms, though they are all basically variations on a theme. The cast of *Gute Zeiten, Schlechte Zeiten* have now produced a number of CDs (not to mention calendars, books – some presented as written by the characters – and more recently tattoos – 'your favourites are now up close' – and . . . a board game). When the first of these came out, a number of the characters appeared on screen during the commercial break in the middle of the programme advertising the CD. It was difficult to tell in this ad whether they were appearing as the actors or as the characters from the soap. However, the actor playing Patrick Graf – who in the soap had been elected a local councillor at the time – did clearly step into his character role when he appeared at the end of the advertisement and undercut the blandishments of the others by snatching the CD from their hands and announcing 'Not so long as I'm a local councillor'. On one occasion the launch of their Christmas CD was accompanied – quite amazingly – by the characters in mid-soap bursting into an 'impromptu' rendition of a number of the songs featuring on the CD. The actor who played Heiko, Andreas Elsholz, also developed a successful singing career on the basis of his appearance in the soap, and appeared on many occasions in the commercial breaks advertising his latest hit. But this is all part of a blurring of the fictitious and, not so much the real as the promotional – of the soap system and the star system, so to speak – which is characteristic of *Gute Zeiten, Schlechte Zeiten* as a whole. The two bands which emerged in the soap – Caught in the Act and Just Friends – have also gone on to become highly successful in 'real life'. Other boundaries are also constantly blurred. Already in 1993 voices from completely outside the soap would appear at the end of each episode asking teasing questions about the next episode: 'Will Patrick take his own life, or is there still hope? The answer, and more, tomorrow in *Gute Zeiten, Schlechte Zeiten*'. This in itself is not restricted to this production – it is quite common in other German soaps – but what *is* unusual is the overtly self-mocking nature of the complicity. Towards the end of 1994 each episode would close with one of the characters addressing the audience directly at one side of the screen as the credits rolled by on the other, likewise raising questions about what would be happening in the next episode. Further examples of this blurring of boundaries are given below.

Gute Zeiten, Schlechte Zeiten has always been a very glamorous soap: its main characters are, without exception, from the youngest to the oldest, much more glamorous than their Dutch counterparts in *Goede Tijden, Slechte Tijden*. But it is not just glamorous. *Gute Zeiten, Schlechte Zeiten* is also one of the most erotic soaps currently showing in western Europe. By this I do not mean that it is pornographic: there is nothing in *Gute Zeiten, Schlechte Zeiten* you would not be happy for your grandmother to see. There is no nudity at all, but then there is no necessary connection between nudity and eroticism whatsoever (there is a certain amount of nudity in some of the Scandinavian soaps – in *Landsbyen, Varuhuset* and *Storstad,* for example – but they are not erotic at all). The eroticism in *Gute Zeiten, Schlechte Zeiten* derives very specifically from the deliberate positioning of the viewer as *voyeur.* Sometimes the eroticizing intent is remarkably direct. For example, when Diana was knocked from a ladder by her crazed rival Anya, causing her to lose the child she was carrying, Anya then pointedly straddled a chair facing the camera and slowly applied bright red lipstick to her lips. Later Tommy and Karen kicked off their romance by squirting whipped cream over each other's faces and licking it off again. The eroticism of *Gute Zeiten, Schlechte Zeiten* was to some extent formalized in 1995 with the introduction of a new title sequence. The old and somewhat muted introduction was replaced by one in which the characters appear in close-up and coming in and out of soft focus against a pastel blue background, smiling beguilingly at camera as though on a catwalk. The old version of the theme tune was also replaced by a new, twangy and rather flaccid reggae version sung in a somewhat breathy voice redolent with sensuous overtones.

But, as with most things in this soap, sex is dealt with in ways ranging from the comical to the uncomfortable. Some of the lighter moments have been genuinely entertaining. In one storyline Matthias Zimmerman, scion of a wealthy bourgeois family and still dominated by his mother though fast approaching middle age, decides to 'hire' Nicole, a waitress, to pretend to be having an affair with him. Having introduced her to his flabbergasted parent – 'her mother may clean toilets during the day, but she'll pull out all the stops for the wedding,' he announces – they retire to his bedroom where they proceed to bounce up and down on the bed groaning and generally making as much noise as they can. Meanwhile, in the lounge next door, mother attempts to drown out the approaching climax by playing . . . Ravel's *Bolero* at full volume (an inspired choice of music by whoever came up with it). But a number of storylines provide a much darker view of sex. These tended to centre on the character of Tina Ulrich while she was still in the soap, and on occasions involved her being held up or kidnapped by men wearing balaclava masks. Thus, along with Heiko's girlfriend Yasemin, she was held up by masked gunmen in the bank where Yasemin worked. She was later kidnapped by a crazed admirer, held in a tiled basement room and handcuffed to a bed. On another occasion her accountant blackmailed her into having sadomasochist sex with him, in the course of which she tied him – as he wore full leather gear, including mask – to a bed (he in fact died during one of these sessions, a murder for which Heiko was later accused).

In turn, her own attitude towards sex was itself manipulative and exploitative.

And yet again the boundaries between the soap system and other media systems were breached when the actress playing Tina, Sandra Keller, posed for the German version of *Playboy*. During the week when she featured in this publication, she also appeared in the commercial break in the middle of the programme explaining her decision to pose for *Playboy* – if it was good enough for Iris Berben (a well-known German actress), it was good enough for her – and urging viewers to buy it. Another actress, Saskia Valencia, on leaving the soap went on to host a late-night show entitled *Peep*, which consists of a male and a female guest – usually connected somehow to the sex industry – discussing some (normally somewhat unusual) aspect of sex (at the end of the programme the female guest is presented with a cake featuring substantial male genitalia hidden beneath a marzipan posing pouch, while the male guest receives a similar cake featuring female breasts and a mound of Venus beneath frilly marzipan panties – this presentation being followed by a strip act).

With *Gute Zeiten, Schlechte Zeiten* we are, in fact, in the realm of the hyperreal. All boundaries are constantly breached; boundaries between genres, between styles, between soap and ads, between soap and pop music, between soap and other programmes. *Gute Zeiten, Schlechte Zeiten* is in fact Europe's only post-modern soap, constantly mixing, quoting, exaggerating, overplaying, undercutting. It is voracious and depthless. The storylines alluded to above are only a tiny fraction of those which have actually taken place. A striking indication of what might reasonably be called post-modern 'exhaustion' took place in *Gute Zeiten, Schlechte Zeiten* in late 1993 with the storyline of the Tights Murderer. Having started off by murdering the relatively minor character Hilde Berg, this unknown villain then killed off a number of central characters who had been in the soap for some considerable time – Yasemin, Diana and Tommy – and attempted to kill Milla before being trapped and revealed as Tobias, Daniel's muscular and mother-fixated assistant in the health club. During this storyline the voice of a different character could be heard at the end of every episode as though making a phone call in a hushed voice to avoid attention. The character asked the viewers' help in tracking down the Tights Murderer by writing in with their guess as to who it might be, the prize for the correct answer eventually drawn from a hat being a walk-on part in the soap. Apart from the now familiar blurring of boundaries, this storyline in fact signalled the narrative exhaustion from which *Gute Zeiten, Schlechte Zeiten* was suffering at the time (something similar happened in *Emmerdale* in England in 1994, but after the soap had been running for 22 years, not just one and a half). So many storylines had been devoured, so many characters exploited in so many different ways, that there was little choice but to effect at least a partial clear-out and start again. This was, in fact, a form of narrative suicide.

Gute Zeiten, Schlechte Zeiten may be depthless, but it is in no sense meaningless. Its depthlessness *is* its meaning. Its most overriding characteristic is its absolute refusal to take itself seriously, even when it is dealing with apparently serious issues. On the level of individual stories it mimics the real, but simultaneously works to subvert any two-way relationship with the real. Its references are, in fact, sideways to other products, other styles, other techniques. It is in that sense a self-perpetuating simulacrum, sustained by its own energy and its tentacular links with the media system at large. Official viewing figures show that *Gute Zeiten, Schlechte Zeiten*'s audience is overwhelmingly youthful, a very different audience from that of *Lindenstraße*. It is also by and large an affluent audience, and one which is dedicated to low-investment, high-turnover lifestyle-consumption and fashion, enthusiastically exploiting the fragmentation of German media supply and the intense competition for viewers which has developed as a result, and whose attitude towards television is very much in a pick-and-choose, mix-your-own-cocktail style.

Gute Zeiten, Schlechte Zeiten is the ultimate televisual fashion product of the 1990s: defiantly lightweight, cheerfully offering cheap and colourful throw-away storylines which never last long enough to be recognizable as last season's style, its constant winks and nudges constructing its audience as playful co-conspirators rather than as the targets for advertisers which they clearly simultaneously are. Is it really the case that, in a post-modern society, producers, advertisers and consumers have at last come together in a mutually back-slapping, create-your-own-identity spending fest? Meanwhile back in the real Germany, where real employers are downsizing real workforces, and real politicians are attacking the conditions of real workers as they strive for a different kind of convergence, recent events suggest that real life may not be quite such a wheeze after all.

In any case, *Gute Zeiten, Schlechte Zeiten* could not be shown in the UK, for example, because that kind of audience does not exist there on a large enough scale to sustain a product of this kind. It could not, for that matter, be shown successfully in the Netherlands either: the Dutch *Good Times, Bad Times* remains a modern soap addressing a modern audience through a modern treatment of its narratives. But *Gute Zeiten, Schlechte Zeiten*'s cult status shows that it has developed a very subtle understanding of its particular audience in Germany, and that, to its audience at least, it speaks a language whose syntax they fully understand.

A soap transformed: Marienhof

Marienhof (the title is the name of a square) was launched as a public service 'antidote' to the unexpected success of RTL's *Gute Zeiten, Schlechte Zeiten* (*TV World Guide to Germany*, October 1994). It is produced for the ARD network by Bavaria Film and was launched in October 1992. It is filmed in a 3000-square-metre set in Munich – one of the biggest purpose-built sets in Europe – and is set in Cologne, but there is actually very little of Cologne beyond the car licence plates and the occasional establishing shot of the Cathedral with its famous twin spires. There are only very occasional traces of the Cologne dialect, Kölsch, which is quite characteristic within German dialectology, and even Rheinish accents are something of a rarity. *Marienhof* originally went out in two 45-minute episodes per week (Tuesdays and Thursdays) at 18.25, attracting initially around 2.5 million viewers.

Marienhof revolves around the lives of people living and working in the square alluded to in the title. The main family was originally the Buschs, three generations of whom were, in the early days of the soap, involved in running the family business, a gardening shop. Although it is not a directly campaigning soap in the style of *Lindenstraße*, *Marienhof*'s public service origins were evident at the outset. It was then – and by and large continues to be now – quite slow-paced compared with *Gute Zeiten, Schlechte Zeiten*, and the Germany it portrays is at once more complex and less inviting. Graffiti adorn the walls of the local Erich Kästner secondary school, the pupils include knife-wielding neo-Nazis and drug dealers, and the atmosphere in the classrooms is often tense and confrontational.

Some time in 1994 a decision was taken to re-style *Marienhof*, no doubt as the producers became more aware of where the bulk of the audience for early-evening soaps lay: the World Wide Web site of Das Erste now describes this programme as 'young, cheeky, loud, colourful and bang up to date'. On the micronarrative level, the most obvious sign of this change was Inge Busch's decision to give up the gardening shop, leasing it to the Turkish fruit-stall owner Sülo Özgentürk, who turned it into a Turkish restaurant. She then opened a boutique, fashion being quite ubiquitous in German soaps. The entire production was simultaneously given a youth injection and a glamour implant, the arrival of a large horde of teenagers lowering the average age of the *dramatis personae* dramatically, introducing a kind of street language which many older Germans might even find confusing, and bringing increased importance to the school as the locus of an increasing number of storylines.

From January 1995 (episode 160) on, the programme moved to a five-day-a-week, 25-minute episode basis, and was kitted out with a new opening sequence and title song. The old opening sequence – which showed various shots of the main characters, some of them against the background of the gardening shop, and which finished with the title *Marienhof* having a ladybird instead of the letter 'o' ('ladybird' in German is 'Marienkäfer') – was clearly felt to be too boring, too earthy even, and was replaced by a new sequence where photos of the main characters sweep across the screen as the words 'lots of things will happen' and 'Marienhof' leap frantically from one side to another as solid red or white outline letters on a dark blue background. In the meantime the new title song (the previous opening sequence only had music, but no song) positively screams: 'Lots of things will happen / Nothing stays the same / Nothing stays the old way / It used to be before'. Following this change, audiences have increased to just under the three million mark, consisting mostly of women between the ages of 14 and 29. *Marienhof* is now sponsored by the leading German teenage girl magazine *Mädchen* and in its five hundredth episode in May 1995 featured the Irish boy group Boyzone playing a concert as part of the script of the soap.

Even so, *Marienhof*'s commitment to raising themes of topical social and political interest remained obvious even after this change. The first two episodes in 1995 contained a storyline revolving around the nineteen-year-old Simon arriving for his first day at his new school. His relatively willing attitude in class earned him general scorn from the other pupils and the unwelcome attentions in particular of a group of students with obvious neo-Nazi views. He became involved in defending Sülo from their attacks, and was clearly presented in the programme as defending the correct kind of views. He openly challenged the view that foreigners 'are taking away our jobs', and defended their right to be as 'lousy' as any German. But, just in case we failed to get the message, before both these episodes the station linkman specifically informed viewers how the story should be read. On the first occasion he pointed out: 'Today we will see the problems Simon has to grapple with, and on his first day at school too. But the young man displays civic courage.' The following day he added:

Now to the TV serial *Marienhof* in which many things from real life crop up, but which affect us all. For example Simon experiences as a school student what happens to you when you stand up for foreign fellow citizens. We experienced this close up with him yesterday. This continues today and leads to dramatic events. Will these attacks be able to influence Simon's behaviour?

Needless to say they did not (though it has to be said that prompting of this kind has now stopped). This is all on a much smaller scale than in *Lindenstraße*, of course, and is not a structural element as it is in the case of the older soap, but it clearly signals *Marienhof*'s public service genealogy, and continues to distinguish it from the commercial stations' more heavily relationship-oriented soaps.

Marienhof has in fact developed in two different directions simultaneously. On the one hand it has become more topical and more streetwise, introducing storylines relating to abortion, drugs, racism, violence, cancer and the like, but on the other it has also become in other respects more lightweight as time has gone by. The figure of Frank Töppers, owner of a plumbing and heating business and the most identifiably Rheinish of the characters, is to some extent a figure of fun with his mixture of pedantic

German and dialectical forms, his constant bungling and his insane jealousies. But *Marienhof* never laughs at other issues, however laughable they might appear on the surface. A story in March 1996 involved the school student Paula, of Brazilian origin, being terrified by a voodoo doll she has just been sent by an uncle in Brazil whom she believed to be intent on revenge against her. She was shown in a blind panic, attempting to hide the doll, and praying hysterically to a picture of Our Lady for help. 'You have no idea what *macumba* is,' she assured the others as they wrote the whole thing off as 'hocus-pocus'. There was much to laugh at here if the programme had wanted to laugh, but it kept a straight face throughout.

If *Lindenstraße* and *Gute Zeiten, Schlechte Zeiten* are the two extremes in the spectrum of current soap-opera production in Germany, *Marienhof* is (if I might put it this way) somewhat left-of-centre, tending towards its public-service stablemate *Lindenstraße*, but suffering a clear attraction in the other direction. The changes it has undergone of its own accord show more clearly than anything else the emergence of the soap opera as a predominantly youth phenomenon in the Germany of the 1990s.

An adolescent soap: Unter uns

RTL's second soap *Unter uns* (Amongst Friends) first went on the air on 28 November 1994. Like *Gute Zeiten, Schlechte Zeiten* it is a Grundy-Ufa co-production and goes out five days a week, but at the earlier time of 17.30. It is filmed in RTL's studios in the small town of Hürth near Cologne, and is also set in Cologne. It has viewing figures of around 2.5 million, which is equivalent to a market share of approximately 16 per cent. It has many technical similarities with its stablemate, including frequent exterior shots giving it an airy and expansive feel. Its actors also appear during the commercial breaks advertising all kinds of merchandising relating to the programme, and from early 1996 on, *Unter uns* also followed the older soap's lead of having characters address the audience at the end of each episode as the credits roll by. As in the case of *Gute Zeiten, Schlechte Zeiten*, all the characters speak impeccable High German. Even the two characters from Berlin speak High German without any trace of a Saxon accent, a rather unlikely occurrence in real life.

Much of the action in *Unter uns* takes place in the corner block of Schillerallee and Hölderlinstraße in a wealthy residential district of Cologne. The main characters live in the corner block, with the Weigel family occupying the ground floor and also running the bakery-cum-cafeteria which opens on to the street (the entire block in fact belongs to the grandmother, Margot Weigel, presented as something of a dragon early on). One floor up lives the Albrecht family, while the top floor is occupied by a group of young people sharing an enormous flat, the most important of whom are Corinna Bach and Jennifer Turner (a physiotherapy and a biology student respectively), who have been joined by a number of others as time has gone by.

Unter uns's opening credits signalled its target audience absolutely clearly from the very start. Anyone tuning in to the opening episode was treated to a series of MTV-style, fast-moving, grainy shots whose high-speed pans give a false slow-motion effect when played back at normal speeds. These rapidly changing shots showed, exclusively, groups of youngsters generally whooping it up against various Cologne backdrops. The accent is on youth – none of the faces appearing on screen is over twenty – fun – all the faces are smiling – fashion and general exuberance, all accompanied by frantic guitar rock music. This opening sequence has changed a little over time to accommodate new (still youthful) characters, but its basic message has remained unchanged. It was also clear from the start that the characters would be affluent. When Corinna and Jennifer arrive to inquire about the availability of the penthouse flat, Corinna informs Margot (who is concerned about their ability to pay for such a luxury apartment): 'My father is a banker', adding a little later, 'The bank has been in our family for generations. We aren't any of your awful *nouveaux riches*.'

However, a number of lines were opened up in the first episode which have not remained part of the overall set-up of the soap. These related primarily to Irene Weigel's brother Olaf Schwarz. As she roots about in a box of old bits and pieces, Irene finds a glove belonging to a pair he had once given her as a present. This eventually leads to a flashback played in slow motion and in pale blue showing Olaf as a young man running across a field towards a wall with a young woman carrying a baby. Running after them are two East German border guards carrying machine-guns. He takes the baby from the young woman and turns to face the guards as she disappears out of shot, at which point the flashback stops. We then find Olaf and the child – now the sixteen-year-old Antonia – living in a rather dingy flat in modern-day Berlin. We learn that Olaf is a paediatrician who finds himself out of work because his clinic has closed down, and that Antonia believes her mother to be dead (although she had in fact escaped to the west). Antonia persuades Olaf to go to Cologne where his sister lives.

This storyline included a number of comments of a political or even ideological nature. 'Man, the wall has been down for five years and nothing has changed,' moans Antonia to her father, pointing out, 'The claustrophobic atmosphere here in the East is getting me down.' And when Marc Albrecht later accuses her (wrongly) of stealing his bike, Margot opines 'I hope she doesn't have too socialist a view of property.' However, anyone who thought that *Unter uns* would raise serious political or ideological issues in this way was to be disappointed. These lines have not been followed up, and the possibility of any kind of political debate has disappeared from the soap, along with Olaf.

However, this storyline did introduce what was to be then, and continues to be now, one of the most important elements of *Unter uns*. When Antonia is introduced to her cousin Chris her first comment is 'Shame!' 'What's a shame?' he asks. 'That you're my cousin,' she replies. On being subsequently introduced to Chris's younger brother, Till, she informs him 'The other one was better looking.' When Chris, for his part, takes Olaf to meet his mother, he leaves them alone announcing 'There are two visitors in the house who are even more exciting than you, Uncle Olaf', heading off to help Corinna and Jennifer in their negotiations with Margot. Indeed, fancying, and being fancied by, members of the opposite sex is *the* fundamental theme of *Unter uns*, and continues no matter which individual storylines come and go.

Unter uns is by and large a fairly unexceptional (and unexceptionable) soap. It is one of an increasing number of teen soaps in western Europe which revolve around a set of fairly predictable themes. Apart from courting rituals of all kinds, these include tensions between parents and children, stories relating in a very general way to the world of business, stories with a criminal slant, problems relating to illness and disability and so on. It is not that these issues are in themselves necessarily trivial. There is nothing insignificant about kidnapping or about facing the possibility of permanent disability and life in a wheelchair. But what is characteristic of this and other similar soaps is that these themes are dealt with entirely at the level of the personal, and their broader social or political implications are never even raised, never mind explored. When asked by Olaf in the first episode why he wants to be a policeman, Chris responds 'There's so much wrong here in the city, and I want to do something, to help somehow or other.' But subsequent developments have shown that crime in *Unter uns* is not a social problem, it is down to individuals who are either crazy or simply greedy or violent or who in one way or another just refuse to play the game.

The social and political are deliberately avoided. A recent storyline involved the teenagers' friend Patricia being held on a boat against her will by her father. The group of friends attempt to involve Margot (who has mellowed considerably by this point) in a scheme to set her free. 'We should inform Social Services,' Margot protests, only to have it pointed out to her that they would take too long, that they would not be prepared to do anything until they had incontrovertible proof that some kind of crime was actually being committed, and so on. In any case, bringing in social services would have prevented the teenage characters from getting involved in the ripping adventure of saving their friend (in a 1991 *Lindenstraße* storyline dealing with child abuse both the social services and the police *were* alerted). In an earlier storyline, when they were wondering what had happened to Corinna (kidnapped by Sebastian), one of the youngsters announced 'This isn't Stephen King.' Maybe not, but it is often Enid Blyton. In very much the same way as some twenty-something characters in certain European soaps behave as if they were teenagers, the teenage characters in *Unter uns* at times behave like children in adventure stories. In the Patricia storyline there was something positively Famous Five-ish or Secret Seven-ish about them as they crouched behind railings at the docks and came up with schemes to get the father off the boat while they went to the rescue of their friend.

There is a considerable amount of humour in *Unter uns*. In the same storyline, having seen him leering at her earlier, Sandra Meier decides to use her feminine wiles to lure the deckhand off the boat to allow the rescue to take place. 'They're a bit flat,' she announces to him, sticking out her chest. 'Difficult to believe,' he muses, gawping at the thrusting bosom. 'My bicycle tyres, silly,' she retorts. 'Maybe you could help me out. I'm not very good at that.' 'Huh, women and technology,' he scoffs, shuffling off after her, failing to notice the other three conspirators standing only a couple of feet away. Conspirators in *Unter uns*, however, remain locked within the narrative world, and are not constructed by the production among its viewers.

Despite its technical and other similarities with *Gute Zeiten, Schlechte Zeiten*, *Unter uns* is a rather different kind of programme from its older stablemate. It addresses a visibly younger audience, is more self-contained and has a much more adolescent and, at times, even quite infantile feel. It mixes the comic and the dramatic but keeps the dividing line between the two in sharp focus. It is optimistic and lightweight, it is unchallenging but, by and large, enjoyable. Perhaps it performs the same function in Germany as the early-evening Australian soaps perform in the UK: keeping the young teenagers out of their parents' hair while the latter get on with the more pressing business of seeing to meals and other less adventurous subsistence tasks.

A glam soap: Verbotene Liebe

Verbotene Liebe (Forbidden Love) is based on the Australian soap of the 1980s *Sons and Daughters* which, like *The Restless Years*, was a Grundy production. The idea for a German version of this soap was originally offered by Grundy to RTL in view of their ongoing collaboration in the production of both *Gute Zeiten, Schlechte Zeiten* and *Unter uns*. In a rare miscalculation, RTL's Austrian boss, Helmut Thoma, turned the project down, claiming it was 'too Australian and too unrealistic' (*Der Spiegel*, 35/1995). Seeing this interesting product going a-begging, the WDR signed a contract with Grundy and now produces this daily soap for ARD's Erstes Programm (Grundy has also sold *Sons and Daughters* to TV4 in Sweden: see page 183). Its viewing figures have steadily increased from around two and a half million to almost three and a half million, and it has, in particular, a market share of 44 per cent for women aged 14 to 19, and 31 per cent for women aged 20 to 29, by any standards a truly impressive penetration of this particular market segment. *Verbotene Liebe* is currently sponsored by Oil of Olaz, the German version of Oil of Ulay.

Like *Lindenstraße*, *Verbotene Liebe* is filmed in WDR's Bocklemünd studios in Cologne. It is set partly in Cologne and partly in Düsseldorf. Following a pattern we have already seen, all the characters speak High German, with the difference between the middle-class Brandners and the aristocratic von Anstettens translating on the linguistic level only into differences of register (as opposed to the UK soap *Brookside*, for example, where differences of class translate automatically into differences of accent). *Verbotene Liebe* first went on air on 2 January 1995, screening at 17.55, immediately before *Marienhof*. Its opening credits were accompanied by a title song sung in English with a strong American accent. It begins as follows: 'Forbidden love goes straight to your heart / and I can't stand the pain / when I call out your name'. It was accompanied by a series of shots: sometimes a single shot filling the whole screen, sometimes two, three or even four shots on screen at the same time, constantly moving, constantly changing. As well as showing views of Cologne and various of the characters in close-up, these shots established an immediate set of contrasts: an opulent country mansion versus a man in a hard hat on a building site, a man on horseback as against a youth on a moped, teenagers in casual clothes contrasting with a beautiful young woman wearing a high-fashion strapless black dress.

The first episode was entirely dominated by the story of Julia von Anstetten, the daughter of an aristocratic German family living in the grandiose Fridenau chateau near Cologne, and Jan Brandner, the son of a more modest (but by no means working-class) family living in Düsseldorf: Jan's father Arno is in fact the owner of a construction company in that city. The episode opens with the two teenagers – on their shared twentieth birthday, though they are unaware of that at the time – quite literally bumping into each other in Cologne airport as he returns from America and she returns from London. The rest of the episode is taken up with skilfully edited shots contrasting their family backgrounds – the Brandners' well-appointed bungalow and lumberjack-style jackets versus the von Anstettens' sumptuous abode and formal evening dress – and with Jan's attempts to renew contact with Julia, by whom he has been immediately smitten. Interspersed with this is a lengthy series of flashbacks, focused mainly on Julia's mother Clarissa and Jan's father Arno, but also, to a lesser extent, on Julia's father Christoph, which make quite clear even to the most inattentive viewer that Jan and Julia are in fact twins whose parents, Clarissa and Arno, split up shortly after their birth, the mother taking the daughter and leaving the father to rear the boy (hence the forbidden love of the title).

Each parent has now subsequently remarried into their very different social strata. This is one of the most sophisticated openings to a soap I have personally ever seen – perhaps matched only by *Roseira Brava* in Portugal (see page 153) – much of its strength coming from its powerful narrative cohesion. It also revisits one of the most fruitful of romantic commonplaces – love across class boundaries.

Despite its Australian origins, *Verbotene Liebe* is very much a German product since, if the opening situation was borrowed from *Sons and Daughters*, subsequent storylines have been developed in Germany, as in the case of *Gute Zeiten, Schlechte Zeiten*. The most immediately striking difference between *Verbotene Liebe* and its Australian progenitor is the difference in social level. In the Australian original the Palmer family from Melbourne had been distinctly working–class, with the father David working as a truck–driver, while the land–owning, Sydney–based Hamiltons were middle–class. In the German version each family has been moved one step up the social ladder. 'Jan is no proletarian,' Julia would announce later to her fiancé Tim, while the von Anstettens do not simply have an aristocratic surname: Christoph is a count, and in a subsequent storyline Tanja Wittman married Benedikt von Anstetten and acquired the title of Countess. This move up the social scale is not only consistent with the narrative universe of German soaps as a whole – a universe from which the working–class appears to have been permanently banished – but also links in, at least as far as the von Anstettens are concerned, with a long German television tradition of family serials concentrating on the lives of aristocrats: programmes such as *Immenhof*, *Forellenhof*, *Schloß Hohenstein* or the immensely popular *Forsthaus Falkenau* which has already screened over 50 episodes (and in November 1996 began a new season of 23 more) and can obtain as many viewers as *Lindenstraße*.

The opening situation, with its strong contrasts of social backgrounds and lifestyles, and the overt snobbery of the von Anstettens and the von Sternecks, clearly offered ample scope for comment, direct or indirect, on many aspects of life in Germany in the 1990s. However, as in the case of *Unter uns*, anyone looking for such comment was to be disappointed. With the original situation at least formally resolved through the discovery by Jan and Julia that they are in fact twins, the contrasting backgrounds have taken a very secondary role, the social location of the characters has flattened out quite visibly, and a number of new characters have arrived to give the production a much more classic soap opera feel. It is not that stories relating to Friedenau have disappeared altogether, they are simply not foregrounded to anything like the same extent. Julia has moved in with Tim, has started to work for a newspaper and now lives in an environment which is barely distinguishable from that of any other soap character in Germany. The von Sternecks – initially part of the glamorous Friedenau set – now have a lifestyle reminiscent of that of the Richters in *Gute Zeiten, Schlechte*

Zeiten. At the other end of the spectrum, so to speak, Iris Brandner, initially a somewhat dowdy housewife wearing uninteresting denim jackets and non-eye-catching jeans, has cast aside her housewifely burden, modernized and feminized her wardrobe and her hairdo, and set about finding her real self in the public sphere (with only a few exceptions, housewives' stock is not particularly high in German soaps).

After the initial exhilaration and slightly prurient anticipation of the opening episodes, *Verbotene Liebe* has now settled down into a fairly predictable pattern. It has become a relational soap in an almost pure form, and writ large: as Julia announces to her mother in the second episode, 'If I get married, it must be to the most interesting and the most attractive man. And he must be sensitive.' Storylines raising other issues do occur from time to time – Clarissa's business plotting and industrial espionage against Arno, Sophie's fight against drugs, Tanja's marriage of convenience to Benedikt, problems between parents and their children – but it's all very small beer and never detracts from the central business of this soap. Entire episodes can pass with nothing much happening other than couples falling out, making up, snuggling up, peeling off. Shots of petticoats or duvets falling around women's feet abound: there is even one in the opening sequence. The pace is slow, the music is romantic, the mood is schmalzy. *Verbotene Liebe* is also truly a beautiful persons' soap. If the female leads in *Unter uns* are pretty, the female leads in *Verbotene Liebe* are stunning. If the male leads in *Unter uns* are handsome, the male leads in *Verbotene Liebe* are beefcakes: Jan actually eventually becomes a model in the soap. Its surface is smooth and polished, unlike the chaotic and fractal accretion of *Gute Zeiten, Schlechte Zeiten*. It's all incredibly easy on the eye and on the brain as well, but then there is no generic rule that says that soaps *have* to be socially or politically challenging.

Verbotene Liebe's glamour is rather different from that of *Gute Zeiten, Schlechte Zeiten* or *Unter uns*. In these latter soaps glamour is conjunctural, whereas in *Verbotene Liebe* it is structural. Its appeal is visual and sensual as well as emotional. It creates a narrative world where to be beautiful is to exist, but not necessarily to be happy. But to call it 'trash TV' (*Der Spiegel*, 35/1995) is much too brutal a judgement (though not entirely unexpected from this source). In its own smoochy, snuggly way it is in fact quite a gentle soap. The problems are never so dreadful as to be panic-inducing. The baddies are never so awful as to be irredeemably hateful. And there's the constant soothing and hugging and pillow talk. It's a kind of televisual security blanket: something comforting to chew on after an un-beautiful day at the office (or more likely at school). It's a kind of *Girl's Own* annual coming out every day: unchallenging and unpretentious, non-violent and non-threatening, but something for under your pillow rather than for the wastepaper bin.

A doctors' soap: Alle zusammen, jeder für sich

Alle zusammen, jeder für sich (All Together, Each for Himself) first went on air on 25 November 1996 at 17.00 on RTL2, following a fairly high-profile poster campaign in all of Germany's major cities. The head of RTL2, Harry Goering, had been looking for a soap opera for the early evening schedule for some time, describing this period as the 'main battleground' in the fight for ratings. He had even at one point considered taking over *So ist das Leben! Die Wagenfelds* following its failure on SAT1 (see below). Given that RTL2 has now very consciously styled itself as a youth-oriented channel – its new corporate image, launched on 6 April 1996, presented it as 'young, modern and good looking . . . innovative, progressive and dynamic' – it is difficult to see quite how *So ist das Leben! Die Wagenfelds* could have fitted into this new 'look' without a major overhaul of its characters and focus. In the end RTL2 followed the lead of its much larger sister channel RTL and looked to the now very considerable experience of Grundy-Ufa in this field. They are now producing *Alle zusammen, jeder für sich*. Their style is recognizable in a number of ways, including the way in which a different character addresses the viewer at the end of each episode as the credits roll.

Alle zusammen, jeder für sich is set in Berlin, though in the dozen or so episodes of this soap I have watched to date, I have not – except for the inevitable establishing shot of the corner block where all the action takes place – seen a single square inch of Berlin, since this soap appears to be filmed entirely in the studios of Fernsehzentrum Babelsberg in Potsdam. Nor is there any trace of a Berlin accent anywhere. None the less, the characters do talk from time to time about the Wall or about going shopping on the Ku'damm, so that the supposed location is in fact quite clear. *Alle zusammen, jeder für sich* adheres to a real-time convention: the approach of Christmas was accompanied by a frenzy of Christmas-tree buying, cake baking and the like by the characters, and the owner of the local café was furious that it was going to be closed over Christmas due to a food-poisoning scare, since that was when he expected to do most business.

The characters of *Alle zusammen, jeder für sich* all live and work in a corner block whose ground floor houses a café, a garage and a doctors' surgery, the entrances all being through the central patio, which becomes, as a result, a place where many encounters take place. The main family is the Baer family, consisting of Professor Hans Joachim Baer (Hajo) and his three pretty teenage daughters: the somewhat bitchy Pam, the emotional Sybille (Billy) and the rather intellectual but kind-hearted Caroline (Caro) – in fact, the actress Denise Zich, one of the members of the band Just Friends, moved from *Gute Zeiten, Schlechte Zeiten* to play the role of Billy. They have just returned to Berlin from America following the death of their mother Rebecca. The professor – a doctor of medicine – is starting up a new practice whose staff includes Bruno and Lukas. They have known each other since childhood, but there is a permanent simmering animosity between them since Bruno continues to be in love with Heike, who has married Lukas.

The early episodes of this soap dealt entirely with the problems of getting the new practice started (it is helped considerably by the outbreak of food poisoning), and on how this has affected the relationships between the various characters. Hajo has been led to believe that either Lukas or Bruno is in fact his son, and spends a considerable amount of time looking for similarities which might indicate which one it is (Lukas takes three sugars in his tea as he does, Bruno has an allergy to potatoes similar to his, and so on). Much of this is very stereotypical – there is hardly a more threadbare stereotype than the professor's beautiful daughter(s), but identifying the unknown son and the friends set against each other by their love for the same girl don't come far behind – and it already seems clear that *Alle zusammen, jeder für sich* is unlikely to break new ground in its narratives.

RTL2 is clearly not interested in competing with the four major German channels. Its stated aim is to improve its audience ratings against those of the other smaller channels such as Kabel 1 and Vox. *Alle zusammen, jeder für sich* currently has around 300,000 viewers, though it can occasionally peak at 400,000. It is too early yet to say exactly where it is heading, though it is unlikely to be anywhere terribly adventurous. It is a cut-price and rather lightweight production, but among its pluses are that it concentrates overwhelmingly on the younger characters, while the decision to focus the narratives on a group of doctors may allow it to tap into what is an extremely rich vein in current German television production, where the demand for hospital and doctor-based stories appears to be almost insatiable. All things considered, there seems no reason to believe that *Alle zusammen, jeder für sich* cannot meet the objectives which RTL2 has set for it, at least in the short term, though its longer-term success may be less certain.

The failed soaps

A middle-aged soap: Jede Menge Leben

Jede Menge Leben (Living Life to the Full) went on the air for the first time on 7 March 1995. It was produced by Colonia Media for the ZDF, being both filmed and set in Cologne (which has established something of a monopoly on contemporary German soaps), and was originally screened on Tuesdays, Wednesdays and Thursdays during the early-evening schedule at 18.30. Though a reasonably expensive soap by German standards (costing around 7000 marks per minute) it failed to attract substantial audiences, and in July of the same year it was moved to the earlier time of 17.40. A continuing poor performance saw it eventually removed from the early-evening schedule altogether, and in October 1995 it changed to a five-times-a-week format in the late afternoon schedule beginning at 16.35. Audiences at this time were around 0.8 million, two-thirds of whom were over fifty. It soldiered on for just over another year before eventually being stopped at its 313th episode on 30 September 1996.

Jede Menge Leben's initial opening sequence was very traditional when compared with the hectic and at times even frantic openings of the other early-evening soaps. It consisted almost entirely of shots of the main characters with the names of the actor or actress given at the bottom of the screen, the only other shot being a sweeping panoramic view of the Rhine showing – more or less inevitably – the Rhine bridge and Cologne Cathedral. These shots were accompanied by a title song sung in German, beginning as follows: 'Living life to the full / happiness all round / every day experiencing / a little bit more'. The early episodes included scenes shot in many well-known parts of Cologne, giving *Jede Menge Leben* a much more rooted sense of location than the bulk of other German soaps, and indeed, from time to time the characters could be seen reading the Cologne newspaper *Kölner Nachrichten*. However, following a now well-established pattern, there is nothing in the way the characters speak to indicate that we are in the Rhineland (if anything, the main character Dorothee Berger speaks with a slight Southern German accent).

The milieu is once again very comfortable. The main family is the Bergers, the husband Clemens working as a successful architect. They live in a converted millhouse outside Cologne, and are so comfortably off that his wife Dorothee has never needed to work, despite the fact that she is a fully qualified doctor. Sons Julian and Niko are still students. A second important family are the Hassenkamps: Hanna is Dorothee's best friend, and her husband Matthias is the owner of a large construction company in Cologne. As the soap proceeded a number of other characters came on board, mainly as a result of the various relationships formed by the two boys.

The first episode of *Jede Menge Leben* was extremely dramatic. It had strong similarities to the first episode of the UK soap *Castles* (see page 196), though this appears to have been purely coincidental. It begins with a large group of friends gathered at the Bergers' house for Dorothee's fortieth birthday. As the toasts are being made and the party is beginning to get into full swing, Julian arrives and announces to the astonished assembly that his father Clemens has been sleeping with his (i.e. Julian's) girlfriend Sue. Niko – returning, like Jan in *Verbotene Liebe*, from America – arrives just in time to see his parents squaring up to each other after the guests have departed. The remainder of the episode deals with the immediate aftermath of this revelation for all four members of the family. Dorothee decides to try to keep her marriage together, but the episode ends with her returning home to find Clemens and Sue kissing passionately on the couch in her living room. Subsequent episodes dealt with the immediate problems faced by Dorothee following her decision to leave Clemens. The two sons decide to stay with her, and eventually move in with her to a flat in the centre of Cologne, put at her disposal by Hanna Hassenkamp. Following a process of dispersal reminiscent of *Verbotene Liebe*, as time went by some characters would leave but many more new ones would arrive: Clemens would eventually die in a car accident, Dorothee would form a new relationship, all very standard soap opera fare.

At some point in 1996 the soap was given a new opening sequence (though the title song remained unchanged). In the new version the letters of the words in the title appeared in contrasting colours against variously coloured blocks forming a square in the centre of the screen. This was followed by photographs of the main characters sweeping across the screen. As each photograph passes, the character in it either looks straight at camera or turns to look at the camera and smiles, in a manner somewhat reminiscent of the new title sequence for *Gute Zeiten, Schlechte Zeiten*. In general the soap was given a rather younger feel at the time, but the main characters continued to be those belonging to the older generation.

Jede Menge Leben has dealt with a number of quite controversial issues as time has gone by. These include the question of whether or not to have an abortion if there is a risk that a child is handicapped, the now virtually inevitable homosexual relationship, overbearing parents who plan their children's lives without taking the children's wishes into account, the moral problem of pornographic films involving children, and so on. As in the case of *Marienhof* it is these kind of issues which reveal the public-service environment of *Jede Menge Leben*, and which demarcate it most clearly from the other (mostly Australian-inspired) soaps.

While it is true that hindsight always has twenty-twenty vision, the reasons for *Jede Menge Leben*'s failure now seem clear even from the beginning. Thus while *Gute Zeiten, Schlechte Zeiten* had begun with Heiko's eighteenth birthday, *Jede Menge Leben* began with Dorothee's fortieth birthday. While Clemens and Vera Richter or Wolfgang and Irene Weigel or Inge Busch and Peter Sommer are easily outnumbered and out-storied by the surrounding cast of younger characters, the older characters – the forty- and fifty-somethings – have remained at the centre of *Jede Menge Leben* despite the influx of more youthful faces. Experience has shown that this older age group does not constitute the dominant audience for early evening soaps in Germany. The characters in the successful early evening soaps are taking life by the horns, not trying to reorganize it following a crisis. They have to fight the beast, of course, and they are often tossed and gored, but it is the future they are fighting, not the past. Rejuvenating the cast then seemed almost pointless when *Jede Menge Leben* was moved to an earlier time-slot when *fewer* young people would be watching, not more, as shown clearly by its viewing figures. *Jede Menge Leben* was not in any sense a poor quality product – in some ways it had higher production values than many of its competitors – but it in fact attempted twice to construct an audience that was not there, and no programme can survive under such conditions. In some senses it was surprising that it survived as long as it did.

A *rural soap*: So ist das Leben! die Wagenfelds

So ist das Leben! die Wagenfelds (That's Life! The Wagenfelds) first went on air on 16 October 1995 on SAT1. It was to be this channel's triumphant entry into the field of soaps (prior to that it had no German soaps in its portfolio of programmes at all) and was part of a larger overall programming strategy officially launched in early December of that year, aimed at improving the channels' ratings and making it more attractive to advertisers. *So ist das Leben! die Wagenfelds* was produced in Munich by Bavaria Film in co-operation with Iduna Film. The first episode was a special two-hour-long event broadcast at 20.00, with subsequent episodes being one hour in length (later reduced to 30 minutes) and going out at the earlier time of 18.00, the period during which most soaps are screened in Germany.

So ist das Leben! die Wagenfelds was preceded by a great deal of advance publicity and hype. Its name was originally to have been simply *Die Wagenfelds*, but this was abandoned for fear that it would be too reminiscent of *Die Goldenburgs*, a German family drama of the 1980s (whose full title was in fact *Erbe der Goldenburgs*) dealing with the clash between two brewery-owning families, and seen at least to some extent as a German riposte to *Dallas* and *Dynasty* (Jurga, 1995: 59). SAT1 did not present *So ist das Leben! die Wagenfelds* as a soap either, preferring to style it a 'family drama'. Its audience was to be aimed not at the youth market targeted by other soaps, nor the female market targeted by the medical dramas, but the entire family: as the advance publicity put it, everyone 'from the techno-teenie to the knitting granny'. It was in fact announced as 'the most expensive daily family drama anywhere in the world'. Though a little over the top, these claims were not entirely without foundation. The producers built from scratch the sprawling Bavarian country house which was to feature as the guest house 'Zum Schwarzen Hahn' in the serial, at a cost which is given variously as two million marks (*Der Spiegel*, 35/1995) and over three million marks (*TV Movie*, 23/95) – in either case a very large sum of money. The production costs of 6000 marks per minute are also very much at the top end of the German soap opera scale.

The complex nature of *So ist das Leben! die Wagenfelds*'s projected appeal was obvious from the start. The opening sequence featured the title in large blue letters moving over a sepia background which first shows a family with three teenage children (two older boys and a younger girl) followed by each individual member of the family, then by a number of other people of varying ages who would also appear in the soap. It is accompanied by the title song entitled 'Stay together', sung in English by the band Bed and Breakfast, which has in fact outlived the serial. The family featured are, of course, the Wagenfelds: the parents, Stefan and Katharina, and the children, Johannes, who is preparing for an examination to be able to study biology at university, the seventeen-year-old Danny, who appears to have 'dropped out' and is at constant loggerheads with his father and, to a lesser extent, with his mother, and Lena, all of whose energies are invested in improving her times for the 100 metres freestyle in her attempt to become a champion swimmer.

A number of very important contrasts were then developed as this first episode unfolded. The first was a generational conflict, and a second that of town and country. Katharina receives an unexpected phone call from Anton Reitmeyer informing her that her aunt, Käthe Huber, the owner of a guest house in Bavaria, is seriously ill. She sets off for Rosenburg by train, only to discover that Käthe has merely fallen from a ladder while pruning a tree. Anton has, however, brought her to Rosenburg in this way to make her aware of the financial problems her aunt is suffering, and to warn her that Käthe is in danger of losing the guest house, where Katharina grew up. The contrast between city and country life is played up in many ways. The music which accompanies scenes shot in Hamburg is either harsh guitar music or moody ballads, whereas as Katharina travels to Rosenburg, the music is more relaxed, even jaunty. And the pace of the editing slows down considerably. Our view of Katharina walking slowly through the guest house and out into the garden where she sits on a swing takes the form of a single, uninterrupted shot 2 minutes 47 seconds in length – quite extraordinary, even by the rather ponderous standards of soap operas. In the meantime, Stefan is unable to make it to the swimming-pool in time to see Lena win her race because he is caught in a traffic jam.

On returning to Hamburg, Katharina is unable to persuade Stefan to leave his job and come to Bavaria with her, but she decides to go anyway when the sultry Nadia Enge appears at her door at one o'clock in the morning and tells her of her affair with her husband. Subsequent episodes develop the many problems she and her children have adjusting to their new environment, Stefan's unsuccessful attempts to persuade them to come back to Hamburg, and their slowly developing relationships – both personal and business – with their new neighbours.

So ist das Leben! die Wagenfelds shares – in fact to some extent borrows – a number of features of other German soaps, and adds a few of its own. The linguistic uniformity noted already is also the norm here. No one in Hamburg has a recognizable Hamburg accent (which has very easily identifiable characteristics) and, in the parts of the production set in Bavaria, only the elderly Anton has a Bavarian accent. The title song in

English repeats the appeal of *Verbotene Liebe*, linking in to the youth pop market, much of which is sung in English even by German groups. The family are affluent, the characters may not be of the pin-up variety to be found in *Verbotene Liebe*, but they are all good-looking. Again, following the lead of the Grundy soaps, the actors – very much out of character, however, as opposed to *Unter uns*, for example – addressed the viewer directly at the end of each episode.

What *So ist das Leben! die Wagenfelds* offers that is different is partly shared by *Jede Menge Leben* and is partly unique to it alone. What it shares with ZDF's unsuccessful soap is a focus on what might loosely be called the middle-aged characters, in particular Katharina. What it adds is a number of even older characters still. These not only outnumber the elderly characters in other German daily soaps, but are also more important than them in narrative terms: there are even a specific set of conflicts between them and the middle-aged characters. This was clearly part of SAT1's attempt to achieve a broad appeal throughout the age groups. A further difference is the emphasis on country life. While this links in with a long tradition of *Heimat* films and productions in Germany – Katharina actually describes Rosenburg in an early episode as her 'Heimat' – and had also been a feature of the 1980s series *Schwarzwaldklinik* (Frey-Vor: 1995: 139), it represents a decisive break with the other contemporary German soaps all of which are, without exception, city-based.

So ist das Leben! die Wagenfelds's target was three million viewers (*Der Spiegel*, 35/1995). In fact, it was never to reach this figure. It bumped along at two million and falling, before finally being taken off the air only six months after it had started. In part, its failure was linked to the overall failure of SAT1's new programming strategy. The hour-long format was difficult to sustain in terms of narrative interest in a time-slot when the audience has been accustomed to shorter programmes, and the two-hour-long opening episode in particular had dragged, not because it was uninteresting, but because the dynamics of soaps are not, by and large, suited to episodes of that length. RTL2, which at the time had no soap of its own, offered to take it over. Negotiations were entered into, but no agreement could be found, and as a result *So ist das Leben! die Wagenfelds* disappeared from German television screens for ever: a rather sad end to a programme in which not just so many hopes, but indeed so much time, money and effort had also been invested.

The discounted soaps

Despite their considerable number, the programmes covered in the preceding sections do not entirely exhaust the category of soap opera in the Germany of the 1990s. There are a further two productions which are sometimes included in this category, but which I have decided not to go into in detail for a number of reasons. However, I summarize them below in the interests of completeness.

A production sometimes included among the list of German soaps is *Macht der Leidenschaft* (literally Power of Passion, but officially translated as Family Passions). Its first episode was shown on 5 December 1994 by ZDF in the late-afternoon slot at 16.00. Having seen a number of episodes of this (actually rather awful) production, I am unable to convince myself that it is in any meaningful way German. Though some parts of it were in fact shot in Hamburg and Heidelberg, it was produced mainly in Canada by the Canadian production company Baton Rouge and used overwhelmingly Canadian sets and Canadian actors whose English dialogue was dubbed into German. As *Die Zeit* of 2 December 1994 put it in a preview of the programme: 'ZDF has got together with a commercial Canadian company and produced in Toronto – which gives the series an unintentionally comic side when a Canadian actor tries to portray a businessman from Hamburg the way that scriptwriters from America imagine the life of bigwigs from the Hanseatic city.' *Macht der Leidenschaft* ran for one season before disappearing without trace.

On 29 January 1995, only three weeks after the start of *Verbotene Liebe* on ARD, RTL launched a new hour-long once-a-week soap starting immediately after the end of *Lindenstraße* on Sundays. It was entitled *Westerdeich*, and was a specifically-acknowledged German rewrite of the Australian soap *E-Street*, with the original Australian scripts reset in the small (fictional) community of Westerdeich on the northern Frisian coast. However, like *Wittekerke* in Flanders (see page 36), *Westerdeich* cannot be viewed as a truly domestic product (like *Wittekerke*, *Westerdeich* was also produced in Leuven in Flanders, though the location shooting was done in the northern German coastal town of Cuxhaven). Despite attracting over four million viewers on its first showing, making it the third most popular RTL programme that day, it ran for only one season, and has not been renewed.

Analysis

In terms of the sheer number of productions available (see also the Postscript below), there can be little doubt that Germany is currently the European capital of soap. It is not, however, the heartland of European soaps: that distinction still belongs to the United Kingdom, and in particular to England. Germany's most popular soap, the once-a-week *Lindenstraße*, gets on average about half the viewers of the three-times-a-week UK soap *EastEnders* despite the considerably greater size of the German television market (37.4 million television homes as against 23.4 million in the UK). The greater number of channels in Germany is only a partial explanation: the real difference lies in the varying social reach of the respective programmes. Only *Gute Zeiten, Schlechte Zeiten* even creeps into prime time in Germany, while all the major UK-national soaps are prime-time soaps. Nonetheless, the growth of domestic soap opera in the 1990s in Germany has been by any standards quite stunning. And it is not finished yet. In October 1996 ARD announced the launch of yet another soap opera in Autumn 1997, to run on Mondays at 20.15 (*Express*, 1 November 1996). Entitled *Die Anrheiner*, it will be set in Cologne, will deal with the everyday life of a family of five members, and will have storylines relating to shipping. The characters will not speak Kölsch (the Cologne dialect), but a light Rheinland dialect. The yearly budget will be of the order of ten million marks.

It is by no means a coincidence that this unprecedented growth has accompanied the break-up of the former public service monopoly with its restrictive advertising regulations. As Eva Schabedoth correctly puts it (1995: 153), 'The extent to which the serial narrative form shapes television today can be seen absolutely correctly as a true child of the advertising situation which has accompanied the introduction of the dual [public-service/commercial] broadcasting system on German channels.' Or, to quote *Der Spiegel* (35/1995): 'A daily soap is not just any television programme, the daily soap is *the* television programme, it is the most reliable money-making machine a television channel can have – in Germany they cost 5000 marks per broadcast minute and bring in 115,000 marks per advertising minute.' And the private channels are clear in their mind as to where the most lucrative section of the audience from the point of view of advertising revenue lies. *Der Spiegel* (34/1993) quoted RTL's head of programming as follows:

'The ideal audience,' says Conrad, 'are young married couples who have two children, who are building a house and want to buy a second car.' In view of this RTL makes a considerable effort to frighten off older viewers: their favourite programmes (such as *The Price Is Right*) are relegated to the early morning schedule or dropped altogether.

This is clearly not just a young(er) audience. It is a younger audience with substantial disposable income. Those whose spending power is weak or non-existent are rendered invisible by such a targeting strategy: this includes the bulk of Germany's non-Germanic population which, with the very notable exception of *Lindenstraße*, is scarcely represented at all in the German soaps (a similar observation was once famously made of the Australian soap *Neighbours* by leading Australian feminist Germaine Greer (see Crofts, 1995: 101)).

Lindenstraße is in almost all senses a soap apart in Germany. The demographic make-up of its audience is different from that of the other soaps, its style and its narratives are different, and as a result its relationship with its audience is different. If we remove *Lindenstraße* from the equation, the most striking feature of the current German five-day-a-week soaps is their extreme ghettoizing both in terms of their timing and in terms of their audience: they are without exception crammed into the three-hour-long, early-evening schedule and are aimed clearly and undisguisedly at a younger audience, the audience most eagerly targeted by advertisers. As *Die Zeit* (2 December 1994) put it in a lengthy article on German soaps, 'Successful daily soaps guarantee the advertisers an encounter at the same time every day with their most sought-after target group, the fifteen to thirty-year-olds. This guarantees the channels stable advertising revenue.' Station bosses – even the public service station bosses – in Germany are quite open about the function of the early-evening soap in their overall schedule. For example, shortly after *Verbotene Liebe* was first launched on ARD *Der Spiegel* reported (35/1995):

Two million viewers watch it every day at 18.00 on Das Erste, and the media people are also eagerly snapping up advertising spots at a cost of 17,850 marks, with the result that ARD's director of programmes was able to point out recently that with this quality serial the ARD had once more proved its 'ability to entertain ... we have won young viewers back'.

The relentless and all-pervasive targeting of a youth (or at least relatively youthful) advertising audience is the single most important factor in explaining the nature of current five-day-a-week German soaps. For example, it determines the kind of characters that can populate them. Middle-aged or even elderly characters are OK, so long as their numbers are small and they are not a major focus of attention: in fact, they are at their most successful when they provide continuity in the soap as waves of youngsters succeed each other. As Georg Feil of Colonia Media (the producers of the unsuccessful *Jede Menge Leben*) put it rather sourly in *Der Spiegel* (22/1996), speaking of programme commissioners:

They usually ask how old the protagonist is, and if he's over 50 and already a 'crumbly' it's turned down right away. It's probably the twerps from the advertising agencies who've put them up to this terrible equating of protagonists and target group.

Terrible or not, there appears at the moment to be no escape from this rule: the two productions which tried to defy this equation – *Jede Menge Leben* and *Die Wagenfelds* – perished in the attempt. German soaps are overwhelmingly about young people's relationships with each other, to a lesser extent about young people's relationships with their parents, only to a relatively minor extent about their parents' relationships with other members of their generation, and only exceptionally about their parents' relationships with *their* parents' generation. The gradual loss of both narrative and moral authority by Inge Busch in *Marienhof* is symptomatic of this trend (and something not entirely dissimilar has even happened to Helga Beimer in *Lindenstraße*).

The pressure to model the narrative world on the idealized world of the target group also defines the broad social milieu of the German soap. To some extent this can be seen as the intensification of a pre-existing trend, since the narrowing of the narrative universe to the social horizons of the petite bourgeoisie was already visible in the early days of *Lindenstraße*. As Jurga points out in relation to this programme (1995: 59):

The working class is otherwise completely excluded. We are dealing here with what is perhaps a specifically German narrowing of social reality to the representation of the middle class. This is no doubt mostly due to the poorly developed tradition of representing German working class culture.

As far as the 1990s are concerned, this trend is not specifically German: it is perfectly visible throughout Europe, including the UK, where the working-class nature of soaps such as *EastEnders* and *Coronation Street* has, in my opinion at least, frequently been overstated, and is in any case changing (see page 207). However, two things can be said. One is that the 'symbolic annihilation' of the working class has, with some notable exceptions, been a feature of televisual output in Germany for rather longer than it has in countries such as the UK or Sweden. And the other is that the teenage soaps have taken this trend to new heights. The unspectacular, vaguely sleeves-rolled-up petty bourgeois world of *Lindenstraße* pales into insignificance compared with affluent new-middle-class society constructed by these soaps. The current German soaps are the realm of the young, the beautiful and the wealthy: they implicitly practise ageism, 'lookism' and taken-for-granted consumerism. The small number of misfits which *Gute Zeiten, Schlechte Zeiten* brought with it from its early Australian scripts have since disappeared, no doubt never to return. These soaps advertise the bounties of German consumer society not just by being surrounded and penetrated by adverts, but by themselves acting as an inexhaustible display of why-not purchasing power. They are a world of cosmopolitan fashions, international rock music and American-speak: it is, in fact, instructive to note how many of the younger characters in these soaps have spent time in the United States: Jan in *Verbotene Liebe*, Simon in *Marienhof*, Nico in *Jede Menge Leben*, the three daughters in *Alle zusammen, jeder für sich* and others. But they have not come from the real USA. They have come from the USA of imported television series and films – the ultimate electronic icon of nonchalant consumer indulgence. The youngsters mope and brood their way through the usual soap opera tribulations, of course, but who cares when all around them is such a cornucopia of abundance?

Linked in with this idealizing of consumer-oriented space is the flight from the geographical which is obvious (if in differing degrees) in all the

German weekday soaps. Where there is a specific setting it is entirely token in nature. *Unter uns* and *Verbotene Liebe* may be set in Cologne, but they might just as well be set in any other city, since Cologne does not impinge in any meaningful way on the narrative world. The same could be said of Berlin in *Alle zusammen, jeder für sich*. The complete dominance of High German is the outward physical sign of this homogenization – as *Der Spiegel* (22/1996) puts it:

If a German TV production is set in a specific city . . . it seldom gets beyond the level of the postcard view. The protagonists in our domestic productions speak polished High German, even when death approaches or sex knocks on the door.

These soaps are not about Germany's regional variety: they are not in a potentially variegated geographical space, they are in a homogenizing lifestyle where variety is having the means to choose freely from a uniformly available, if large, set of goods. From this point of view, *Gute Zeiten, Schlechte Zeiten*'s flight from the geographical is perhaps a more honest statement of what these soaps are actually about. Where they cannot be, however, is in the countryside: *So ist das Leben* tried this and paid the price. The countryside in contemporary German culture – as in Europe in general – is linked to discourses of nature and traditional values: renewal through renunciation – an impossible conjunction for the dominant discourses of these consumer-celebrating soaps.

The more issue-oriented storylines are also overwhelmingly about themes of primary interest to a younger rather than an older audience: drug abuse, contraception, abortion and so on. The soaps with a more highly developed public service pedigree are much more likely to raise such issues as a matter of course: before its demise *Jede Menge Leben* had planned storylines dealing with alcoholism and marriages of convenience as a means of being granted political asylum. They are also more likely to raise what might broadly be called more overtly political issues such as neo-Nazism, racial intolerance and the like, but again will deal with these as they affect the younger members of the cast. The soaps on the commercial channels also make a point of raising issues of topical interest, of course, and the pairing of *Marienhof* and *Verbotene Liebe* on Das Erste shows that the distinction between public-service and commercial soaps is not entirely clear-cut. However, even when quite overtly political issues are raised, their political dimensions are seldom explored. Everything is kept at the level of the personal, of the small-scale, of the debating club: such issues are a matter of individual conscience. As *Der Spiegel* again puts it, referring to Rainer Werner Fassbinder's classic series of the 1970s (22/1996):

A cheerfully instructive course in anti-capitalism like Rainer Werner Fassbinder's *Acht Stunden sind kein Tag*, stories portraying the class struggles of the industrial workers in the Ruhr ... pleading for losers and underachievers, all that has now been shelved.

The debate as to whether these soaps are actually just 'giving people what they want' (a view often professed by Helmut Thoma) or whether they contribute to an ongoing process of depoliticization is essentially a false and in the final analysis unresolvable debate, as the endless arguments on screen violence amply illustrate. Presenting the issue in such oppositional terms rather than attempting to synthesize them is itself part of a much larger and vigorously disseminated macro-discourse of methodological comminution which works to obstruct rather than to facilitate understanding. What can be said is that narrative formations which bestow moral protagonism on youthful characters eager to invest their time, their money (and presumably also their parents' money) in identity-conferring consumption is clearly more to some people's benefit than others, that it contributes little or nothing to raising awareness of social problems such as homelessness or unemployment (taboo subjects in these soaps), and that these soaps are doing nothing to encourage viewers to break out of that kind of cycle.

There can be no doubt that the current German teenage soaps *are* meeting some kind of demand from their viewers, otherwise they would not be watched, and in the analyses above I have tried to suggest what these various appeals might be: the floundering of *Jede Menge Leben* and *So ist das Leben* shows that there is no automatic relationship between soaps and success. But they have somehow been appropriated by a discourse of anti-authoritarianism which itself emanates from the currently dominant neo-liberal ideology. Watching soaps has become the visible sign of opposition to the old public-service, paternalistic moralizing. They have been subsumed into a widely touted strategy of post-modern liberation theory where collage is the guarantor of coolness. As the German student magazine *Audimax* put it in an article entitled 'Are we all serial criminals?' (September 1996):

Today the television magazine lies on top of Adorno, the medical dictionary or the Civil Code ... It's quite simply cool among students to write an essay on Wittgenstein and at the same time be a *Dallas* fan.

And no doubt the community-building potential of these and other soaps is quite real (see Vogelgesang, 1995). But what kind of communities are being built? With the partial exception of *Marienhof*, these soaps waltz endlessly round each other within extremely narrow self-imposed horizons. A kind of division of labour has emerged, almost spontaneously: *Gute Zeiten, Schlechte Zeiten* appeals to a slightly older and more sophisticated audience than *Verbotene Liebe*, which in turn appeals to a slightly older and more sophisticated audience than *Unter uns. Marienhof*, with its rather more developed social-issue agenda, appeals to a different section of the audience again, but is still very much a youth product. How much longer they can continue to crowd together in this highly restricted, largely narcissistic discursive space remains to be seen. In the meantime *Lindenstraße* continues its solitary path, simultaneously progressive in its tactics and conservative in its strategy, but at the very least moving forward.

Postscript

On 2 June 1997 SAT1 returned to the soap front with *Geliebte Schwestern* (Dear Sisters), a doctors-and-nurses soap, filmed in Cologne and set in Berlin. It goes out every weekday at 19.10. Like *Alle zusammen, jeder für sich, Geliebte Schwestern* taps into a powerful German tradition of doctors' series or *Artzserien*. It is a world of beautiful nurses and handsome doctors and distinguished older surgeons with younger wives and even younger mistresses, all spiced up by a good whodunnit to get the action going. It attracted around 1.3 million viewers for its first episode, but has now settled down at just over one million. This is not a particularly encouraging performance, and *Geliebte Schwestern* appears to have arrived too late. The *Süddeutsche Zeitung*'s review on 3 June, entitled 'Between a quickie and a Maserati', says it all.

On Monday 22 September 1997 RTL launched a new once-a-week soap entitled *Hinter Gittern: der Frauenknast* (Behind Bars: the Women's Prison). The first episode attracted an audience of 3.26 million, a share of just over 11 per cent. Though no mention was made of the Australian soap *Prisoner* in the credits, the similarities between the two productions are fairly obvious.

There are also persistent rumblings in the German press that Pro 7 is also due to start its own soap soon. As *Der Spiegel* (38/1997) put it: 'soaps are part of the staple television diet'.

Greece

Television in Greece

Greece was the last country in western Europe to introduce a national television system, with EIRT (later renamed ERT) coming on stream in 1966, and not being fully operational until a year later. The arrival of television also coincided with the coming to power of the Colonels, whose junta lasted until 1974. The former military channel YENED was later converted into the state-owned company ERT2, becoming part of ERT's operations in 1987, the two stations at that point being named ET1 and ET2. ERT's third channel, ET3, was launched in 1989 and is based in Thessaloniki in northern Greece, and its transmissions are restricted mostly to Thessaloniki and Athens. Its audience share can on occasions be less than 2 per cent.

The early association of television with dictatorship, and its subsequent rather cynical manipulation by a series of parties in power, helped to develop a mistrust of the national broadcasting system, an unease which contributed to the rapid changes in Greek television at the end of the 1980s and the beginning of the 1990s. This period was characterized by the mushrooming of private local channels, and the growth of a few of these channels to become in effect national channels completely dominating the Greek television market (Tsaliki, 1995b). The most important of these was Mega, which started broadcasting in November 1989 and quickly became (and remains) the market leader, followed by Antenna, launched in January 1990, and now in second position. Since then, Star and Skai have also emerged to take third and fourth positions respectively. Since the arrival of the commercial stations, the three ERT channels have seen their combined share of the audience sink at times to less than 10 per cent of the total, the most catastrophic collapse of any public service broadcasting corporation in western Europe.

Domestic Greek soaps

One of the first signs of the changing nature of the television landscape in Greece was the phenomenon of the American daytime serial *The Bold and the Beautiful* in the late 1980s and early 1990s. Having been originally bought in by the first state channel ET1, it proved enormously popular, with the streets of Greek towns and cities reportedly emptying when it was on air. In a scenario which would be repeated in Italy shortly later, it then gave rise to Greece's biggest-ever television bidding war (Allen, 1995: 15) before eventually being taken over by the private channel Antenna.

Greece's first and now longest-running domestic soap was *H λαμψη* (*I lampsi*, or Splendour), launched in September 1991 and broadcast on a daily basis by the commercial station Antenna. It is written and directed by Nikos Foskolos, and originally screened from 19.45 to 20.30. The second domestic soap, entitled *Καλημερα ζωη* (*Kalimera zoi*, or Good Morning Life), first went on air in November 1993. It too is broadcast on a daily basis by Antenna, showing originally from 18.40 to 19.10, and, rather astonishingly, it too is written and directed by Nikos Foskolos. In 1996 *I lampsi* had average audience ratings of 45.7 per cent, making it the most popular serial in Greece, while *Kalimera zoi* had average ratings of 40.5 per cent (*Διπλο Τηλεοραμα*, 4 October 1996), though this situation has now been reversed. *I lampsi* reached 1200 episodes (and thereby entered the Greek *Guinness Book of Records*) on 30 May of the same year. Antenna's own research shows that the bulk of the audience for both programmes lies in the 45+ age group.

Given the quite astonishing success of *The Bold and the Beautiful* in the years preceding the launching of *I lampsi*, it is tempting to see the Greek soaps as a response to, and in some sense a Greek version of, that production. And indeed, similarities between *The Bold and the Beautiful* and *I lampsi* and *Kalimera zoi* are not difficult to find. The Greek soaps really *are* different within the European context. They are much more glamorous than anything available elsewhere. The characters are indefatigably good-looking. The women are beautiful, the men are handsome, the fashions are expensive and classy, everyone is well-off, the characters are lawyers, district attorneys, chiefs of police, doctors, film directors, high-flying businessmen; they live in plush surroundings and eat in exclusive restaurants. All of these elements can be found in *The Bold and the Beautiful*, and indeed, *I lampsi* nodded strongly in the direction of the American soap in 1996 when one of its actors – Dan McVicar, who played the role of Clarke Garrison, the chief fashion designer in *The Bold and the Beautiful* – turned up in the Greek soap as the American preacher Jesus MacLester (with a corresponding increase in viewing figures).

I do not wish to rule out the possibility (far less the likelihood) of some kind of influence of *The Bold and the Beautiful* on the Greek soaps, but I do want to suggest that such links might not be as straightforward as they might at first seem. The complicating factor is the writer/director Nikos Foskolos, now in his late sixties or perhaps even early seventies, who, before becoming involved in these productions, was one of the best-known film-makers in Greece in his own right, his very considerable fame resting mostly on two productions: the film Υπολοχαγος Νατασσα (*Ipolohagos Natassa*, Lieutenant Natasha), released in 1970, and the television series *O αγνωστος πολεμος* (*O agnostos polemos*, The Unknown War), shown in 1971.

Ipolohagos Natassa is a melodrama dealing with the experiences of the young Natasha Arseni under the occupation of Greece by the Germans during the Second World War. I want to stress that I am not using the term 'melodrama' in any kind of negative sense here: well-crafted melodrama can be just as powerful as any other dramatic convention, and *Ipolohagos Natassa* is one of the best-made and most stirring melodramas I have ever seen. It was the most successful Greek film of all time, selling three-quarters of a million tickets in Athens alone.

In the opening scenes we see Natasha in the concentration camp at Dachau in 1965. As she boards a train to return to Greece, she remembers the events of her youth. We see the beautiful heroine – physically reminiscent of Angélique, protagonist of an entire series of French *romans rose* – dash around the Greek countryside in her brightly-coloured clothes and plunging décolleté, her lustrous blond hair blowing in the wind, while all the other women around her wear the drabbest of peasant garb. She marries Orestis, a soldier, and later becomes involved with him in covert military operations against the occupying forces in the Peloponnese, but she is captured and tortured, denying not only her mother but also her young son whom the Germans bring to her in an attempt to make her reveal her true identity. Having been saved from the firing squad in a daring rescue by Orestis dressed as a German commander, both are then shot by mistake by Greek partisans taking him for one of the enemy. She survives and is taken by the Germans to Dachau where the Americans find her at the end of the war. She is in a state of mental collapse, and spends twenty years in a hospital with no idea of who she is, and without speaking a single word. In 1965 her memory returns (this is the point at which the film begins), and she returns to Greece to be honoured for her courage. Here she meets up again with her son, who rides towards her out of the sunlight in his military uniform in just the same way as Orestis had ridden towards her on their first meeting. He addresses her very formally, without giving any indication of who he is, and explaining how he had been told she was dead. She responds

'I feel you, my child', her first words in twenty years. He throws himself into her arms crying 'Mother!' The End.

O agnostos polemos was Foskolos's first involvement in Greek television, being shown on the YENED channel in 1971. It repeated the success of *Ipolohagos Natassa* by achieving audience figures of over 90 per cent. I have seen only the first episode of this series in a version reissued for the video market, but this was sufficient to show that it shares a number of elements already present in *Ipolohagos Natassa*.

O agnostos polemos is set in the period immediately predating the invasion of Greece by Mussolini's forces. Like *Ipolohagos Natassa* it has a beautiful heroine, Hristina Psahou – again very blond, despite the fact that (naturally) blond hair is rather less common in Greece than dark hair – with a small son. And there is a strong military presence, with all the leading male characters being soldiers. The Greek army is presented very much in a heroic mould in this series – Greece did in fact repel the Italian invasion in 1940 – which no doubt explains how it was possible to broadcast it on what was an essentially military channel. However, *O agnostos polemos* is no apology for dictatorship, since fascism is unequivocally presented as barbaric and inhuman. In one scene there is a confrontation between the Greek commander and a black-shirted Italian envoy in which the commander leaves his visitor in no doubt as to his views on fascism. While it is clear that neither *Ipolohagos Natassa* nor *O agnostos polemos* are simply 'about' the Second World War in any uncomplicated way, the enormous success of these productions suggests that their dominant meaning for their viewers may well have been different for the meaning they had for the military.

I want to suggest that the new Greek soaps are in fact best seen as a continuation and updating of Foskolos's earlier work within the broad tradition of American daytime soaps (in fact, two of the leading actors in *O agnostos polemos*, Hristos Konstantopoulos and Nikos Apergis, both appear in *I lampsi*, the latter as one of the major characters, Sevos Drakos). It is Foskolos's influence which above all helps to explain the occasionally filmic quality of these soaps. More than any other soaps anywhere in Europe *I lampsi* and *Kalimera zoi* make use of techniques such as slow motion and superimpositions, particularly in the many scenes involving shootings of one kind or another. Everyone who was shot in *Ipolohagos Natassa* – most dramatically Natasha and Orestis – was shot in slow motion, as was the Italian spy who broke into Hristina's house in *O agnostos polemos*. Other continuities can also be found: the use of clangorous music, the melodramatic style, the presence of authoritarian men in uniforms (in both *I lampsi* and *Kalimera zoi*) and an alarming propensity by men when angry to strike the women they are involved with. I actually do not believe there is a single other western European country where scenes of this kind would be currently possible in a soap. It is not that violence against women does not occur in other soaps, indeed it does, but it is seldom made explicit in this way.

The most powerful influences at play in *I lampsi* and *Kalimera zoi* are, therefore, Greek, not American. The enduring popularity of Foskolos's works – he is often the object of highbrow criticism for the hyperbolic nature of his productions, but there is simply no disputing the breadth of their appeal – points to complex continuities in Greek society and culture, despite the many changes which have occurred on numerous levels in the intervening twenty years.

A glittering soap: I lampsi

The image with which *I lampsi* opens, accompanied by the soap's dark but truly compulsive theme tune, is one of a spinning Van de Graaff sphere sending arcing electrical discharges out in all directions. This image is suitably symbolic of both the high level of glamour and the underlying darkness of this soap. *I lampsi* is set in Athens and revolves around the lives of various groups of extremely wealthy and, by and large, very beautiful people. The most important of these are the two brothers Sevos and Yanko Drakos. Yanko is a successful and very wealthy businessman with a stake in the family company Giant, and for some years now he has also been involved in politics. He is married to Virna, who works as the Procurator Fiscal in Athens, and he has three grown-up children from an earlier marriage. He lives in an elegant villa which, together with its swimming pool and the enormous skyscraper where Giant has its offices, is seen in the opening sequence – the skyscraper strongly reminiscent of a very similar scene in the opening sequence for *The Bold and the Beautiful*.

Yanko's older brother, Sevos, also involved in Giant and in politics – he was at one time President of the Popular Revival Party – was married for a long time to the considerably younger Sandra with whom he had a particularly stormy relationship. During one of their many separations she had also been Yanko's mistress, a period during which she tried to ruin her own husband's political ambitions. Later, having returned to Sevos, she would then attempt, with Sevos's agreement, to destroy Yanko's political career by involving him in a sex scandal. Later still, having divorced Sevos, she would eventually marry Yanko's son Timos.

Following the tradition of Foskolos's earlier work, *I lampsi* is a highly melodramatic soap, about as far removed from the notion of 'kitchen-sink drama' as it is possible to imagine. Antenna's trailer for the one thousandth episode in September 1996 featured brief clips from key storylines from the first five years with the following words superimposed on them: 'love, intrigue, beauty, tenderness, passion, tension, mystery, glamour, agony, scheming'. Perhaps I can best give some impression of the experience of watching this soap by reproducing the summaries for a week's episodes screened in January 1994, taken from the popular television magazine

Τηλεθεατης (15 January 1994):

MONDAY: Elvira, a prisoner of her addiction to drugs, ends up on the street. Having sold off everything she owned and some things she didn't, she decided to sell her body as well in order to get her next fix. In the meantime the traffickers in white death are attempting to buy her house for a pittance. Vanda is worried that the men who raped her may have infected her with some disease and she visits various doctors for tests.

TUESDAY: Vanda is still having medical examinations when she learns that the police have arrested someone suspected of her rape. She goes to the police station and identifies him. In the meantime, Virna announces that Hasna is to be extradited to Italy to face charges for the murder of the Italian harbour guards. Hasna rages against the injustice she feels is being done to her.

WEDNESDAY: Commissioner Vourvahis cannot control his fury when he is taken to interrogate his daughter-in-law's rapist. A little later Vanda comes to her attacker's cell to see him and speak to him. Sandra is worried that Yanko will betray her plans to have Sevos deposed as president of the party. In the meantime Tatiana begins specialist drug treatment and physical exercises in order to be able to keep the baby the next time she is pregnant.

THURSDAY: Alexis continues his attempts to save his marriage. However, nothing he tries is successful since he himself causes every new beginning to fail. His passion for Virna has not waned after his marriage to Lili. On the contrary it is growing all the time. In the meantime Vanda gets the results of the medical examinations: she is in excellent health. She, however, believes herself to be ill.

FRIDAY: Sandra is carefully preparing her final 'blow' against Sevos. The day of the opening of the national conference of the 'Popular Revival' party is approaching, and she wants to be ready for his fall from the presidency. Vermiso, who is still in love with her, comes across her by chance in her husband's office and does not hesitate to declare his love for her yet again. In order not to ruin her ambitious plans, she gives in to his advances.

This is a normal week's business for *I lampsi* (Hasna, incidentally, had been involved in smuggling arms to Bosnia when the Italian harbour guards had been killed). Suddenly *Brookside* seems rather sedate.

A *pseudo-medical soap*: Kalimera zoi

Like *I lampsi*, *Kalimera zoi* is set in Athens and deals with the lives of a group of very wealthy people living in that city. The opening sequence starts with a view of an electronically generated sea over which the words *Kalimera zoi* appear in large gold letters, the capital omega (Ω) of *zoi* taking up virtually the entire screen. Once the faces of the various characters have all appeared inside the omega, the background scene changes to an aerial view of the real sea as we sweep in over an exclusive residential area of Athens, complete with swimming pools in extensive back gardens.

Kalimera zoi is based on two main families, the Arhos and the Theoharis. Leonidas Arhos is an enormously wealthy and powerful businessman (following a technique likewise used in the American soaps, he has also appeared in *I lampsi*) and, when I joined this soap, he was living with his wife Antigone, his son Hristophoros and his daughter Xenia. The Theohari family consists of Stathis, a police commissioner, his step-brother Nakos and his three sisters Agapi, Ilektra and Savina, together with their various partners.

The opening sequence of *Kalimera zoi* ends with the camera closing in on a private clinic in Athens, and a certain amount of the action does take place there. Ilektra works there as the administrator, and at various times a number of different characters have been treated there. This gives the soap something of a medical feel, but *Kalimera zoi* is not in any sense a medical soap. The clinic is merely yet another setting for storylines based firmly on relationships between the characters. *Kalimera zoi*'s title song suggests the same mixture of darkness and light as can be found in *I lampsi*. Its final verse is as follows: 'Be mine / My paradise and my hell / In the north wind's blast / Good morning life'. Whether we are in the clinic or the police station or any of the characters' houses, this is a better indication of what *Kalimera zoi*'s storylines are actually about, at least on the surface.

With its less ponderous theme tune and its sunnier opening, *Kalimera zoi* did seem in its earlier episodes to be somewhat lighter in touch than its stablemate. However, any initial lightness it might have had has long since gone and in some ways it is now even more troubled than *I lampsi* with its tales of madness and betrayal, its attempted suicides, its ghastly revelations, its writhing drug addictions, its shootings, its compulsive gambling, its graphically depicted illnesses and death.

What has been, for me at least, the most shocking scene in *Kalimera zoi* occurred in August 1995. It featured in the episode in which Markos Palaiologos is about to leave his wife Ilektra and their young daughter. As he picks up his things, he suddenly crashes against a small glass table before collapsing on to the sofa in the grip of an epileptic fit. As Ilektra places a wooden wedge in his mouth to stop him from biting his tongue and his sister-in-law Savina rushes to help, the camera closes in on his face, completely covered in foam, before coming to rest on his quivering hand. This entire scene was shot from an angle high above the participants, as a number of scenes in *Ipolohagos Natassa* were, again in slow motion, again to the accompaniment of deafening music (not only have I never seen anything like this in any other European soap, I do not believe that it would currently be *possible* to see anything like this in any other European soap). There seems little to say 'Good morning' to in life as presented now in *Kalimera zoi*.

Analysis

As the preceding descriptions will have made clear, *I lampsi* and *Kalimera zoi* have a great deal in common, both in terms of their production and in terms of the narrative world they create. Both are shot almost entirely in the studio. In the numerous episodes of these soaps I have been able to watch, I have seen only two outside shots, both of which appeared in the same episode of *Kalimera zoi*. They were very short, and occurred during a flashback in which Xenia recalled some moments of her earlier relationship with Nakos, and showed them splashing in the sea and frolicking in a field. Apart from this, everything has been indoors, with Athens itself limited to the occasional establishing shots, often showing the city at night. The sets are often absolutely minimalist: a few files in a bookshelf and a desk to show we are in the police station, a white screen or a bed to show we are in the clinic. There is an all-pervasive lack of visual depth, with everything happening in the foreground, and a heavy concentration on medium-to-very-close-up shots, with virtually every scene ending with a sustained close-up of one of the characters' faces.

Both share the same ineluctable glamour. There is of course something mildly but unmiscallably erotic in the endless procession of beautiful people, tumbling hair and sexy, low-cut, elegantly-tailored clothes. This erotic intent is quite deliberate. For a period in mid-1995 in *I lampsi* a very curvaceous blond maid called Ariel was employed in Yanko Drakos's villa. With her dark-blue, one-piece, cross-over, figure-hugging 'uniform' she dressed as surely no actual maid has ever dressed in real life. However, her outfit was not at all dissimilar to that worn by 'maids' in, for example, Bavarian soft-porn, roll-in-the-hay movies.

In a lengthy interview published in the Greek magazine *Dolce Vita* (it is Greek, despite its Italian title) on 9 September 1996 Nikos Foskolos was asked the question 'What has played a decisive role in your work? What has influenced you?' His response was as follows: 'Life, the everyday tragedy of the anonymous little man, the arrogance of the few and the powerful, the unhealthy passion for wealth, the corruption and degradation of Greek society.' Given the glamour and wealth of the inhabitants of *I lampsi* and *Kalimera zoi* this seems like a rather remarkable statement. There is, of course, and never can be any simple connection between what those involved in the production of any cultural product claim it is about and the range of potential meanings, or actually dominant meaning which that product opens up in any given society. But I want to argue in the remainder of this analysis that Foskolos's remarks are less incongruous than they may at first appear.

It goes without saying that the bulk of *I lampsi*'s and *Kalimera zoi*'s viewers do not inhabit worlds characterized by anything like this level of glamour. But this mixture of glamour, eroticism and soft pornography is not, in fact, restricted to these two soaps. It suffuses Greek commercial television as a whole, its chat shows, its comedies, its variety shows, and above all its advertisements, as well as the halo of related publications which surrounds it. With the exception of ERT's *Ραδιοτηλεοραση*, current Greek television magazines such as *Διπλο Τηλεοραμα*, *Τηλεθεατης*, *7 Μερες TV* or Thessaloniki's *Τηλε Θ* are a journey into a world dominated by double-page adverts for slimming courses featuring topless models with, of course, perfect figures, full-page adverts for facial hair removal, adverts for beauty products, features providing beauty tips, fashion features, all combined with a relentless fascination with the lives of the rich and famous, both Greek and international. There are feature articles entitled 'Sharon Stone, synonym of sex', or *faits divers* columns headed 'Zooming in on the personalities' or 'People and happenings' or (in English) 'Who is who', all showing an insatiable curiosity for who is dating who among the glitterati of city society (Athens or Thessaloniki), who was seen out with whom in which night club. Central to this entire industry are, above all, images of glamourous women, always young, often blond, usually in revealing clothes, sometimes wearing none at all or next to none. Taking all this into account, what I want to suggest is that glamour, at times tending towards mild eroticism and even forms of soft pornography, is the currently dominant *mode* of commercial television in Greece. This is the preferred language through which everything else is conveyed. This is no doubt due, at least in part, to what was seen as the austerity of the former state television monopoly, since something rather similar happened, to take only two examples, in Italy in the 1980s and in Portugal in the early 1990s, but it also relates, as argued in the Introduction, to the appropriation of glamour as part of the emancipatory rhetoric of neo-liberalism.

Within the morphology of this language, the tales told by *I lampsi* and *Kalimera zoi* are among the most stressful and, in the final analysis, the most distressing of any European soaps. These are the most violent soaps I have ever seen. The bulk of the violence is verbal, it is true, but it is nonetheless inescapable. The opening sequences of both soaps show all the characters in turn, either in a large rectangle taking up most of the screen in *I lampsi* or in the capital omega of the title in *Kalimera zoi*. But they are not looking beguilingly or smilingly at the audience as they do, say, in *Gute Zeiten, Schlechte Zeiten* in Germany or *De syv søstre* in Norway. They are talking. What they are saying can't be heard, since only the title music is audible, but there is no doubt that what they are doing is talking. Endlessly. The characters in *I lampsi* and *Kalimera zoi* talk as they talk nowhere else.

European soaps are, like soaps everywhere, in general dominated by dialogue rather than deeds. But the standard convention is for dialogue to proceed in small chunks shared out between or among those involved, in a more or less 'naturalistic' style. It is very unusual for anyone to hold the stage for any length of time. In *I lampsi* and *Kalimera zoi* it is not at all unusual for a character to talk for thirty seconds, one minute or, on occasions, two minutes, sometimes even longer without interruption. They do not converse, they perorate (many of the actors also work in theatre). And they shout. These two soaps are without any shadow of a doubt the loudest soap operas in Europe. Everyone shouts at everyone else. Conversations which start off on an amicable footing frequently end up in slanging matches. Fathers shout at children, brothers and sisters shout at each other, parents shout at each other, superiors shout at their subordinates, all frequently accompanied by strident music (the same musical sequences being shared by both soaps). Everyone intimidates everyone else. The rich and the powerful use their money and their authority to browbeat those around them. Stathis throws the files on the floor in his rage at his second-in-command Olga, only to find himself later bawled out by his superiors brigadier Leventagas and the police chief of staff. And there is no escape, no outlet. Everything is closed in. Nakos actually spent a long period in the soap in a cell in the psychiatric ward of the clinic with bars on its only window. We go from one resoundingly claustrophobic set to another. Even the relationships permutate to the point of quasi-incestuousness. Despite the beautiful people and exhilarating fashions, there is something truly nightmarish about these soaps.

The characters in *I lampsi* and *Kalimera zoi* are in fact searching for the Truth. 'Tell me the truth', 'I want to know the truth', 'Don't tell me lies', 'Why are you lying to me?' – these are the *leitmotivs* which run through these serials like Ariadne's thread. Scarcely an episode passes without one of the characters saying something along these lines to one of the others. They are even searching for themselves. 'Who am I?', 'I don't know who I am' are also phrases which surface in many storylines. Sometimes these questions *are* the storyline, as when Markos suffers an attack of amnesia after his epileptic fit and wakes up to find that he does not know who he is or who any of those around him (including his wife and daughter) are. 'Who are you?', shouts Ilektra at her brother Stathis in a tense storyline in September 1996 during which she actually points a gun at him. Vourvahis fails to recognize his son Alkis, also pointing a gun at him. Heraclitus is being revisited; τα παντα ρει (everything is in flux).

The most striking difference between *Lampsi* and *Kalimera zoi* and Foskolos's earlier work is that while his melodramas of twenty-odd years ago almost always ended in the re-establishment of their own internal values following the original disruption – the classic narrative schema – nothing is ever resolved in these soaps. The values which their narratives embody and enact are entirely inadequate to the themes and issues which those very narratives themselves raise. *Lampsi* and *Kalimera zoi* construct a society where consensus is fragile at the level of the everyday – precisely the level at which both hegemony and soap opera function (or dysfunction) most effectively – where frustrations are many and where channels of redress are few: precisely the kind of society mentioned by Foskolos in his interview. It is a world whose traditional (melodramatic) narrative cycles retain their appeal to, but have simultaneously lost their explanatory power for, their ageing audience since the society they first arose in has now changed beyond recognition, while the newly emerging proto-hegemonic narratives of Greek society address a different and much younger audience altogether. Their undeniable popularity suggests strongly that this is a world which their viewers recognize and are able to identify. And there *are* undeniable tensions within Greek society. Greek politics, notoriously dysfunctional with political parties relying on charismatic leadership, *caciquismo* and widespread clientelism (Tsaliki, 1995a: 368) rather than programmes in the modern sense of the word, appears – like the Greek middle classes of which it is ultimately an expression – unequal to the task of modernizing and democratizing the country properly. In fact, it is at least arguable that Greece never went through a genuinely 'modernizing' period. It did not produce a developed welfare state at the time when this was being instituted elsewhere, and neo-liberal rhetoric is now in full swing when there is relatively little welfare state to dismantle. What is happening is that a to some extent pre-modern society where the bulk of people could achieve an acceptable standard of living by combining work in the relatively low-paid public sector with small-scale 'individual enterprise' outside it is under attack from a late-modern ideology where 'individual enterprise' is being appropriated more and more by the powerful.

As Greece's economic crisis has deepened in the 1990s – the recent strikes by teachers, farmers and longshoremen are a sign of the growing tensions within the country – social discipline has frequently been maintained by channelling the internal frustrations of Greek society outwards. Greece is without any doubt the country in western Europe where the notion of the Enemy has outlived the Cold War most successfully. The press in particular constantly reproduces an image of Greece as a last frontier against eastern barbarism, with cartoons featuring the kind of barbed-wire bulwarks once associated with East Germany, or newspaper headlines like 'The Far West on Our Frontiers' (*Ελευθεροτυπια*, 29 August 1994). The accompanying highly aggressive nationalist discourse both quells internal dissent and diverts attention elsewhere. The astonishing popular mobilization in Greece around the issue of the name 'Macedonia' in late 1992, when over two million people attended rallies in Athens and Thessaloniki, provided, as Tsagarousianou and Sofos put it (1993: 54), 'a unique opportunity for most of the Greek political élites and personalities to get out of the impasse which had been reached as a result of their inability to formulate convincing solutions for the country's pressing economic and social problems'. And other Enemies constantly lurk on the horizon, most notably Turkey, but even at times Albania, the object of bitter hostility in the Greek media in 1994 during the trial of the so-called

Omonia Five in Tirana, hostility deriving from Albania's persecution of the Greek-speaking minority living in the south.

I want to suggest that the violence and the shouting in the Greek soaps can be seen to narrativize in the private sphere the frustrations and tensions which, in different areas of public life, are mobilized in other directions. But there is as little advance there as there is in the soaps: in an unwittingly symbolic move, the actor who plays Yanko Drakos, Hristos Politis, stood as a candidate for the unsuccessful Political Spring party in the 1996 general elections (it won no seats at all). The tensions, in politics as in the soaps, are constantly being recycled and the pieces of the jigsaw moved around, with occasionally a new one added or an old one discarded. This is more appealing if it is at least visually pleasurable, but beneath the gloss and the glamour, the pieces never fit.

The Republic of Ireland

Television in Ireland

The first television channel to go on air in the Republic of Ireland was launched by the state broadcasting company Telefís Éireann – now Radio Telefís Éireann (RTÉ) – on New Year's Eve 1961, with the second channel RTÉ2 – now known as Network 2 – beginning broadcasting in 1978. Ireland is currently one of only three western European countries to have no domestic commercial television channels (the other two being Austria and Switzerland). The franchise for a commercial channel to be known as TV3 was in fact awarded in 1989, with the commencement of operations announced for 1991 (Kelly and Truetzschler, 1992: 111–2). However, the project did not prove to be economically viable, mainly due to the small size of the Irish market (a population of around three and a half million) and the already existing competition of the British channels, and the projected station never got off the ground, despite encouragement and assistance from the government at the time, keen to promote internal competition.

As this episode shows, the television market situation in Ireland is considerably complicated by the fact that virtually all areas of the country receive British television stations, and many British programmes continue to be very popular in Ireland. Indeed, the influence of, and competition from the UK channels has been a powerful factor in Irish broadcasting practice from the beginning.

On 31 October 1996 the Irish-language television channel Teilifís na Gaeilge came on air. However, its audiences have always been extremely small, averaging 0.5 per cent, scarcely ever exceeding 1 per cent, and occasionally being as low as 0.2 per cent (Watson, 1997: 224).

Domestic Irish soaps

The Republic of Ireland has one of the longest traditions of television serial production of any western European country, with the earliest productions dating back to the 1960s. The most important of these were *Tolka Row*, an urban soap which ran from 1964 to 1968, *The Riordans*, a rural soap which ran from 1965 to 1979, and Ireland's currently longest-running soap, the village-based *Glenroe*, which began in 1983. Further information on these productions can be found in McLoone and MacMahon (1984), Sheehan (1987), Silj (1988), O'Connor (1990) and Devereux (1997). Teilifís na Gaeilge also produced a four-times-a-week Irish-language soap entitled *Ros na Rún* (Watson, 1997: 226), though I currently have no further details of this production.

Some brief mention should be made of the British soap *Coronation Street* which is relayed by Network 2 at the same time as it is being broadcast in the UK, thereby adding around three-quarters of a million to its viewing figures, and which usually features in the ten most popular programmes in Ireland. This is an entirely unique case of one European country broadcasting another country's soap opera in prime time, and testifies to the continuing close relationship between the Republic of Ireland and the UK, a relationship which has, for example, also resulted in a number of television co-productions between the countries.

Given the increased pace of urbanization in Ireland in the second half of the twentieth century – by the end of the 1980s only 15 per cent of the population still worked in agriculture (Kelly and Truetzschler, 1992: 108) – it was no surprise that, as the 1990s drew near, demand for a convincing urban soap was clearly growing. Barbara O'Connor's audience research in the second half of the decade revealed a preference for 'the more socially-conscious British serials', particularly among younger viewers (1990: 12). In her committed and energetic analysis of Irish television drama, Helena Sheehan also pointed out that questions were being asked, both inside and outside RTÉ, such as 'Why, with all the interesting storylines inherent in earning a living, raising a family, understanding the world and coming to terms with the complexities of urban life, can RTÉ generate no Irish equivalent to *EastEnders* or *Brookside*?' (1987: 367). The urban serial which would eventually emerge would be placed in Dublin. It was called *Fair City*, taking its title from the first line of one of Ireland's most famous songs, 'Molly Malone' ('In Dublin's fair city, where the girls are so pretty, I first set my eyes on sweet Molly Malone'). Although *Fair City* first went on air in October 1989, it seemed churlish to exclude it from this study for the sake of a few months.

Fair City goes out on RTÉ1 on Tuesday and Thursday evenings at 20.00. My first acquaintance with this soap dates from early 1994, by which time it had been running for just over four years. I was immediately struck by how little of what was suggested by the opening sequence of this soap was actually delivered by its narrative. The opening sequence consisted of a series of aerial views of Dublin, eventually homing in on a large housing estate, almost certainly a corporation housing estate going by the general design and arrangement of the houses. Over these views were superimposed a series of snapshots of daily life in the form of a photograph whose content was constantly changing. These scenes included, for example, several of children playing in the yard of what looked like a rather rundown school, complete with graffiti on the walls, two men reading a newspaper outside a bookmaker's shop with part of the name of the shop missing, presumably as a result of vandalism, and a closing shot of a man cutting a hedge in a garden while two women with teacups in their hand, one of them smoking a cigarette and wearing a full-length pinny, chatted to each other over the hedge. Having viewed all this, I confidently expected a very proletarian soap.

I was quickly disillusioned. From the outset *Fair City* has been set in the fictitious Dublin district of Carrigstown, where the characters variously run pubs, pizzerias, lingerie businesses, garages, beauty salons and the like. Nothing very proletarian here, needless to say. In fact, the large housing scheme of the opening shots simply never came into view. All the scenes were either indoors – *Fair City* appears to be subject to rather severe budget constraints (Sheehan, 1993: 5) – or in the road in front of McCoys bar which looks as though it has been specially built for the programme. But this is not a road of corporation houses: it is a street of much older and more up-market housing stock, with most of the ground-floor units transformed into shops of one kind or another. And not only does the scheme itself not come into view, neither do any of the wide range of problems which in one way or another beset Dublin's *real* housing schemes such as Finglas, Tallaght or Ballymun, and which are of course widely known in Ireland and have been the subject of many current affairs programmes over the years (Kelly, 1984: 101–2). Unemployment is nowhere to be found, drugs were not mentioned (at least not in the episodes I was able to view), there were no signs of obvious deprivation. No one was conspicuously wealthy, but no one was poor either and the problems raised by the narratives were overwhelmingly personal in nature.

After a quite lengthy break (dedicated mainly to viewing soaps from other European countries), I renewed my acquaintance with *Fair City* early in 1997 to find a programme which had changed in a number of significant ways. The nature of these changes was instantly announced by the new-style opening sequence. Gone were the overhead views of the corporation housing scheme and the snapshots of downtrodden, working-class life. They had been replaced by a new title sequence which quite deliberately develops the theme of a modern and affluent post-industrial Dublin rising from the dereliction of a grimy and sooty past, with scenes of smoke stacks and abandoned factories giving way to street markets overflowing with fruit and vegetables and shots of the sandbanks in Dublin Bay or of downtown Dublin straddling the resplendent river Liffey. As far as the narrative is concerned, that flattening out into an undifferentiated middle-class which is now characteristic of so many European soap operas is well underway. Eamonn Clancy, the only businessman to operate on any kind of scale in the earlier years, has disappeared, and virtually everyone else is on the way upwards.

Gary, former employee of the pizzeria, is now joint-owner, with Hazel Hendricks, of a restaurant rather pompously known as the Bistro. As well as her stake in the Bistro, Hazel is planning to open a new leisure centre. Charlie Kelly, quondam hotdog stall-owner, now jointly owns an antiques business with Bella Doyle. Pauline Fitzpatrick, who runs her own upholstery business in the same lock-up as Charlie and Bella, is being romanced into a joint venture by Ivor O'Neill who is refurbishing a hotel in Kaven, meaning that she would have to move out of Dublin if she accepts (which she does). Hughie Phelan and Natalie Carr, £9000 richer thanks to compensation paid to Natalie following a car accident (sudden enrichment via windfalls has become an almost structural feature of *Glenroe*: Sheehan, 1993: 4) have just secured a mortgage and are looking for their own house in a different part of Dublin: 'I'd be the first in my family off the corpo books,' exclaims Natalie. Noaleen McCoy, Kay ('sure money's the least of my worries') McCoy's stepdaughter, even sends her son away at her stepmother's expense to a very exclusive boarding-school in Dun Laoghaire ('Just think of the people he'd be mixing with, Kay, I mean, it could set him up for life') in order to be able to spend more time with Gary (so much for the rundown neighbourhood school of the original opening sequence). Even the accents have changed. Hazel Hendricks and her estranged husband Alistair as well as Ivor O'Neill have brought with them refined accents which had not been heard before in *Fair City*.

In a combative analysis of current Irish television drama in 1993, Helena Sheehan suggested that in the 1990s 'the situation has not only not improved, but it has substantially disimproved. There is less drama than ever and what there is is tamer than ever' (1993: 4). On the basis of my admittedly somewhat piecemeal viewing of *Fair City* so far I find it very difficult to disagree with this judgement. *Fair City* is in many respects a disappointing production because it fails to live up to the tradition in which it appears to place itself. It is not the case that it would be impossible to find soaps which are less socially committed than *Fair City* elsewhere in Europe. On the contrary, such soaps abound, but they place themselves fairly and squarely within other traditions – the Australian teen soap tradition or the American daytime glamour soap tradition – which do not create any expectations of such an approach. *Fair City*, on the other hand, places itself quite clearly, even in its restyled version, within the tradition of British 'social realist' soaps, to which it was explicitly linked in its origins. This is quite clear in a number of ways: in the humdrum surroundings, in the unglamorous characters (the only glamorous woman, Sandie Dowling, is also depicted as slightly tartish, which is surely no coincidence), in the down-market fashions, in the use of items from 'real life' (real newspapers, references to real places), even in quite specific narrative techniques such as the lack of extradiegetic music – indeed, the Irish and British soaps are unique in Europe in the total absence of non-literal music. But *Fair City* fails to deliver anything like the level of social comment which current British soaps provide. It seems obsessed with the personal and private. And even then it has great difficulty getting to the point.

The dialogue is often among the most tortuous that I ever recall encountering. For example, in an episode screened in early 1994, a conversation between Mary O'Halloran and Lilly Corcoran went as follows (Mags Kelly was present at the time, and was just being offered a cup of tea by Mary):

Mary:	Here you are.
Mags:	Thanks Mary.
Mary:	Oh!
Mags:	What?
Lilly:	What?
Mary:	What's that?
Mags:	What?
Lilly:	What?
Mary:	What's that mark?
Lilly:	Where?
Mary:	There.
Lilly:	It looks like lipstick.
Mags:	Cherry Desire . . . the colour.
Mary:	How did it get there?
Lilly:	It's not mine. Is it yours?
Mary:	Don't be ridiculous! Cherry Desire?
Mags:	Must be Clona's.
Mary:	Mm. Well, whoever washed that cup didn't do a very good job with it.
Lilly:	Don't look at me. You washed up last time.
Mary:	I did not.
Lilly:	Yes you did. I remember distinctly.
Mary:	Well, even if I did, I didn't wash that cup.
Lilly:	We can see that.
Mary:	No, no, no. That cup was not among the dishes I washed.
Lilly:	So you're saying I washed it?
Mary:	I'm saying that whoever washed it didn't do it properly.
Lilly:	Well, it wasn't me.
Mags:	Look, it doesn't matter. I don't mind, it's only lipstick.

Mary: No, no, no. Lilly, would you get another cup please?
Lilly: Me?
Mary: If you don't mind.
Lilly: [Long pause] Right.

[*Lilly gets up to leave. As she does so Mary hands her the offending cup.*]

Mary: Oh Lilly.
Lilly: What?
Mary: Would you take that please. If you put it in to soak all that lipstick will
          come right off.

This is a truly agonizing pace, this conversation taking no less than 1 minute
20 seconds out of a 27-minute episode. And in the same episode, a
conversation between Paddy Clarke and Charlie Kelly over the latter's hot-
dog stand took the following circuitous route (Charlie has just been
explaining to Paddy that he could not face just sitting around at home with
nothing to do):

Paddy: So here you are instead, your own boss, out in the world.
Charlie: In the hub of things, meeting people, having a chat, bit of craic, seeing
          what's going on around you.
Paddy: I know what you mean.
Charlie: I'm not sure you do, Paddy.
Paddy: Sure it's the same as serving behind the bar.
Charlie: Ah not quite. I mean, take this morning, for example.
Paddy: What about it?
Charlie: I saw your man Clancy.
Paddy: What was he up to?
Charlie: I don't know. He was coming out of your Anne's flat.
Paddy: Probably calling for the rent.
Charlie: Aye, maybe you're right . . . it was a bit early, though.
Paddy: Well, he might have been looking at the flood damage.
Charlie: Aye, that's probably it. He's, em, he's a married man, isn't he?
Paddy: Why?
Charlie: Oh, nothing. I've just never seen him with his wife, that's all.
Paddy: But sure they live in Howth.
Charlie: Ah, there'd be no need for her to come around here then.
Paddy: What are you talking about Charlie?
Charlie: Oh, nothing, just talking, passing the time.
Paddy: Oh, it'll pass anyway.

Though a certain lack of directness may traditionally be held to characterize
a kind of conversational strategy not uncommon in Irish society, there
would simply not be time for this kind of beating about the bush in a more
energetic and forceful production. It seems to me that the level of circumlocution pervading *Fair City* at the level of dialogue is merely the
emergence at that level of a much more vast scale of circumlocution which
characterizes the production as a whole.

And beyond the circumlocution, there are constant mismatches between what characters say in *Fair City* and what their comments relate to. When the Gardai (the Irish police force) move Charlie Kelly along because he does not have a permit for his hot-dog stall, Clancy muses to Gerry Gaffney: 'I wonder if this has anything to do with Europe – Jacques Delors and all that.' It goes without saying that membership of the European Union has had fundamental consequences for Irish society, but to link them to a hot-dog stall is simply ridiculous. But these mismatches are not limited to the political. As Eamonn Clancy and Anne Clarke discuss the future of their relationship (she is concerned because she believes her father has found out about it), the following exchange occurs:

Clancy: Oh come on, Anne, we're not teenagers. This is better than romance. This is danger. This is excitement.
Anne: I don't know if I want this much excitement.

It is difficult to convey the sheer incongruence between a conversation like this and what is actually happening on screen and in the narrative. Dramatic tension has been entirely supplanted by simply talking about it.

A further rather remarkable aspect of *Fair City* is the level of sexual innuendo. Again, I am not suggesting that references to sex cannot be found elsewhere – all soaps are in one sense or another about sex. What is specific to *Fair City* is the *innuendo*. A few examples should suffice to illustrate this point:

1.   When Paddy Clarke warns his daughter not to let Clancy take advantage of her as her landlord, he points out 'He's a hard man', not realizing they have just spent the night together. She arches her eyebrows in response.

2.   As Hannah Finnegan and her lodger, retired soldier Pascale Mulvey, argue about the jumble sale she is about to hold in the house, he picks up his African spear and announces, 'I'll have you know this is a sacred symbol of warrior manhood . . . I don't want anyone to interfere with my spear', to which she responds laconically, 'At your age there's not much chance of that.'

3.   When Liam Casey tries to persuade Hazel Hendricks to come for a meal with him, she finally agrees, saying, 'Well, OK, just dinner', to which he responds 'Don't worry, Hazel, I won't bite . . . not unless you ask me to.'

4.   As Anne Clarke and Liam Casey (they are also business partners) argue about his relationship with the somewhat older Hazel, he points out 'Some things improve with age: wine, women.' She responds 'And don't some things turn sour . . . like wine, I mean', to which his rejoinder is 'Only if they're not laid down properly.'

Talking about sex on television has a long and complicated history in Ireland (of which the famous Bishop and the Nightie episode in 1966 was a well-known landmark: see Earls, 1984: 109–11), but enormous strides have been made in recent times in the direction of more liberal attitudes, particularly among the younger generations. It is difficult to imagine this kind of innuendo still appealing to anyone other than those still enmeshed in some way in the webs of institutionalized prurience. Whatever the age breakdown of *Fair City*'s actual viewers, this would seem to be the age range of the viewers the programme is attempting to construct (RTÉ's own figures show that *Fair City*'s largest source of viewers is the 35-plus range, its percentage take-up among this group often being twice as large as its take-up among 15- to 24-year-olds, and ranging between one-third and two-thirds larger than the 15–34 age group).

Analysis

To sum up, *Fair City* looks in many respects like a British soap, but fails to deliver anything like the corresponding bite, at least partly because its dentures are soaking in a glass somewhere else. Not only are there very few teenagers – teenagers provide a lot of the spice in *EastEnders*, for example – but 'not being teenagers' or 'not being young any more' is something other members of the cast talk about with remarkable frequency. It is not that *Fair City* does not occasionally touch on some of the tensions and transformations of contemporary Irish life – Gary Maguire freely admits that he no longer goes to church, and Hughie and Natalie have no intentions of getting married; there are a number of people living on their own after failed marriages – Bella Doyle, Pauline Fitzpatrick, Hazel Hendricks; there is the single mother, Noaleen McCoy; the local priest, Father Costello, who dresses in civvies and seems to spend as much time in the pub as everyone else, is clearly not all his parishioners' cup of tea – but virtually nothing is made of any of this beyond the occasional difficulties in finding (or keeping) a new mate. Even *High Road*, that leafy idyll of urbanite Scots (see page 193), appears radical by comparison, with its storylines relating to bullying at school and violence between rival taxi firms.

And beyond that, *Fair City* never really engages convincingly with the realities of specifically *urban* life. Helena Sheehan suggests that 'The opening sequence evokes Dublin, but Carrigstown does not feel to me like Dublin. It is more like a 1950s rural village than a 1990s city. Everybody lives in each other's pockets and knows each other's business.' This again strikes me as being a very perceptive remark. In an episode of *Glenroe* screened in February 1994 Fidelma Kelly fumed 'The worst about a place like Glenroe is that everyone knows your business' – a not unreasonable statement, perhaps, given that Glenroe is actually a village. In an episode of

Fair City screened the same week Anne Clarke complained about the impossibility of keeping her relationship with Eamonn Clancy secret in a place like Carrigstown: the fact that real estates such as Ballymun or Finglas can have as many as 50,000 inhabitants gives some idea of the distance between Carrigstown and the realities of contemporary Dublin.

Both Sheehan (1987, 367–8) and Kelly (1984, 101–2) point to a long-standing difficulty both in Irish television drama and in current affairs programmes of representing the working-class in a way which shows any grasp of the complex realities of working-class life. They point to an irresistible tendency to equate the working-class with the lumpenproletariat, and to concentrate on violence and petty crime. *Fair City* clearly does not fall into that trap (though Leo Dowling, Sandie's husband, is less than squeaky clean), but nor does it come to terms with the working-class proper.

This has also proved a very difficult area for Irish television, the most resounding setback for fiction dealing with working-class experience being the axing of the drama series *The Spike* in January 1978, only eleven years before the commencement of *Fair City*. Set in a run-down further education college in a working-class district of Dublin, *The Spike* was outspokenly critical of many vested interests in Irish society, including the church, the government and an education system which produced youngsters with absolutely no prospects in life. It was taken off the air amid storms of protest after its fifth episode which featured shots of a model posing nude in one of the college's evening art classes. Since then, there has been a great reluctance in RTÉ to be involved in drama dealing convincingly with the realities of Irish working-class life. Sheehan (1987: 374) suggests that 'Noel O'Briain, producer and director both of *The Spike* and *Inside*, has often made the point that RTÉ drama has never recovered from *The Spike*. It has erected barriers of self-censorship that have yet to be breached in the years since.' The legacy of this fear is clear in *Fair City*'s circumlocutory lack of nerve. If the British soaps walk a constant tightrope between being conservative and being progressive (see page 210), *Fair City* is currently bouncing up and down on a loosely-sprung trampoline with no risk either of falling off or of executing an unexpected loop-the-loop. The legacy of *The Spike* is also clear in the almost total absence not only of working-class characters from *Fair City*, but also of anything very much which is recognizable as working-class experience. Whereas in the British soaps working-class experience is *dis*placed into petit bourgeois class positions (see page 210), in *Fair City* working-class experience is *re*placed by petit bourgeois aspirations. In this sense at least the new opening sequence is rather more honest than the previous one.

It is generally agreed that the earlier Irish nationalist consensus, based on a vision of a rural Ireland where to be Irish was much more important than belonging to any particular class, entered a period of irreversible decline in the 1960s, when Irish television was in its infancy. As McLoone puts it (1984: 59): 'Irish television came into this cultural climate at a time when this nationalist consensus began to break down and for the last two decades has mediated the ideological ruptures that have ensued.' As the power of the Old Right, and of the church in particular, slowly declined, the 1960s and 1970s saw many confrontations between this old order and those championing a more modern form of society based on social-democratic liberal welfarism. McLoone argues powerfully that the mini-series *Strumpet City* was part of an 'ideological project' within RTÉ championing such a view of society. That the old order was not yet prepared to concede such a change despite their own declining influence can be clearly seen in their ability to generate large-scale protests against programmes such as *The Spike* or certain episodes of *The Late Late Show* (Earls, 1984). The 1980s increasingly saw the rise of the New Right, whose emergence was also chronicled in productions such as *Bracken* and *Glenroe*. Sheehan (1987: 344) says of the former, 'The most important difference perhaps was in the undercurrent of values, deriving more from the entrepreneurial spirit of early capitalism, bourgeois individualism and the Protestant ethic, than from traditional Catholicism', while adding of the latter:

Glenroe has drifted more and more into a preoccupation with the problems of people of property and a soft-centred indulgence of the minor joys and sorrows of their lives. In a period of recession, when more and more sections of the population have been threatened with marginalisation and impoverishment, it has not really been telling the truth of the times to construct a scenario where sudden unearned wealth and/or entrepreneurial skill has allowed virtually every character to be upwardly mobile and prosperous. It has given a very easy ride to the spirit of the entrepreneurial 1980s. (p. 360)

Fair City continues and consolidates the dominance of that view. I am not really able to agree with Sheehan that it lacks, following her quotation of Lukács, a 'Weltanschauung'. It constructs, even if only by default (which is, after all, at least partly what hegemony is about), the new neo-liberal consensus of classless individuals moving up the ladder of personal wealth (though never very far) thanks to their own individual endeavours. The real (and very obvious) imbalances of Ireland's 'tiger economy' in the 1990s are nowhere to be seen. Economic power is everywhere in microscopic amounts in *Fair City*, but nowhere in substance: it is a placeless utopia, neither rural nor urban, but combining elements of the mythologies of both.

If it is true that Irish society and culture are in general conservative, then there is, of course, nothing inherent in that conservativeness. It remains in place because a great deal of time, effort and, in the final analysis, money is put into keeping it in place (the sheer expense of continuing to teach Irish Gaelic in all Irish schools is indicative of the broader endeavour) and because oppositional forces are unable to challenge that hegemony convincingly. Like all cultural products *Fair City*'s relationship with the dominant ideological environment is essentially dialectal, in this case simultaneously constrained by it and reinforcing it. There is little point in complaining about this, since producers have a quite different set of priorities from academics, and with around 740,000 viewers per episode *Fair City* may be a little way behind *Glenroe*'s 830,000 and even fractionally lower than *Coronation Street*'s 750,000 (RTÉ figures for week ending 16 March 1997), but it is still among Ireland's ten most popular programmes. Soap operas have their own inertia, of course, and it can be great, but there is nothing inevitable about their continued success. As I demonstrate in a number of other chapters in this book, numerous soap operas in a variety of European countries have disappeared because viewers – in their own inimitable way – refused to put up with them any longer. Recent figures actually show that viewers for both *Glenroe* and *Fair City* are dropping (by around 500,000 and 100,000 respectively since 1994). Ireland will only get a more energetic urban serial when and if its viewers demand something different from what is currently on offer.

Italy

Television in Italy

Italy's first television channel, the public service station RAI (Radio Audizione Italiana), started broadcasting in 1954. The second PSB channel, RaiDue, came on stream in 1961 and the third, RaiTre, a channel with strong regional inputs, in December 1979. In the early 1980s four commercial channels were set up, taking advantage of the almost complete lack of effective regulations governing the establishment of television stations at the time, a situation so chaotic that it has, on occasions, been described as the 'Wild West' (Mazzoleni, 1992: 176). One of these quickly disappeared, while the others – Canale 5, Retequattro and Italia 1 – eventually came under the control of Silvio Berlusconi and his Fininvest trust. The resulting competition between commercial and public channels – coming at least five years before similar developments in most other continental European countries – had far-reaching consequences for all areas of Italian television. For example, between 1976 and 1986 the number of hours of television available to Italians rose from 6000 a year to 34,000, while between 1983 and 1987 the number of adverts on Italian television went from 40,000 per year to 300,000 (Wolf, 1994: 587).

The three RAI channels began to develop more distinctive identities, with RaiUno and RaiDue aiming for the broad family market, and RaiTre introducing a range of innovative programming formats. The three Fininvest channels also diversified, with Canale 5 taking on RaiUno in the battle for the mainstream audience. Though it originally produced virtually nothing, as the 1980s wore on it realized – as many other European commercial stations were to do later – that if it wanted to challenge seriously for the family audience it would have to start producing at least some of its own programmes too, some of which proved to be extremely popular. Italia 1 was restyled as a youth-oriented channel, while Retequattro specialized in imported soaps and *telenovelas* during the day, often showing seven or eight in a row, while broadcasting repeat programmes from the other two channels in its evening schedule.

Though competition continues to be acute in the 1990s, things have, to some extent, settled down, and RAI and Fininvest (now renamed Mediaset) now constitute an effective Italian duopoly, dominating Italian television viewing to a very large extent. Viewing figures for January 1997 were RAI: 49.5% (RaiUno: 23.74%, RaiDue: 15.24%, RaiTre: 10.52%), Mediaset: 40.5% (Canale 5: 22.42%, Italia 1: 9.68%, Retequattro: 8.46%).

Domestic Italian *telenovelas* and soaps

Like many other European countries, Italy had no experience of long-running domestic television serials until relatively recently: as Fenati and Rizza put it (1992: 162) 'State television had never welcomed the concept of serials at the programming level and even less at the production level', and commercial television was also slow to see the potential of this kind of output. The 1980s were dominated not by domestic serials but by, on the one hand, American soaps – and not just supersoaps such as *Dallas* and *Dynasty*, but also, rather uniquely, daytime soaps such as *Loving* and *The Bold and the Beautiful* – and on the other by short-run Italian series. The most successful of these was undoubtedly *La Piovra* (The Octopus), dealing with a lone policeman's fight against the Mafia, and, with average audiences of around fourteen million and occasionally peaking at over seventeen million, outperforming the American soaps by some distance (Buonanno, 1994: 44). *La Piovra* has so far clocked up seven seasons, and has continued to be one of Italy's most popular domestic productions in the 1990s.

Telenovelas

Italy's first domestically produced (relatively) long-running serial was the 1991 *telenovela* entitled *Edera* (the name of its heroine), followed a year later by a second *telenovela* initially entitled – somewhat inappropriately – *Senza fine* (Without End). This latter production was beset by problems of all kinds. It was first shown on Canale 5 in July 1992, but was halted due to plummeting ratings after only three episodes were screened. It then moved to Retequattro with the new title *Camilla* (also the name of the heroine), but was again halted after only three episodes. It finally settled down over a year later on Retequattro once more, at 16.00–17.00, where it ran in the early part of 1994. It was described by the Italian (former Communist) daily

L'Unità (17 January 1994) as follows: 'Here, as well as emotions, we can find a lot of mystery and a lot of sex. A very Italian mixture which wanted to renew the genre, but has merely betrayed it.' The reviewer complained that the director 'had tried in vain to imitate the slowness of the South American *telenovelas*'. A different reviewer described it two days later in the same newspaper as 'a real flop', a judgement to some extent reflected by its very unattractive timing.

A melancholy telenovela: Passioni

The third attempt at a long-running domestic serial was yet another *telenovela*, entitled *Passioni* (Passions), shown in 33 one-hour episodes starting on 19 January 1994. This was the first such production I was able to view myself, at least in part. *Passioni*, which was described by one of its producers as being 'experimental' (*L'Unità*, 11 January 1994), was jointly produced by Reteitalia productions and Titanus, the company which had earlier produced *Edera*. It was a fairly lavish production. *L'Unità* – a newspaper which is not noted for its sympathy with the serial format – described it as 'a kind of Italian-style *Dynasty* ... with a cast of 123 actors' (19 January 1994). Some of its actors were extremely well-known: Virna Lisi, for example, had starred in – among other productions – the highly popular serial ... *E la vita continua* of the 1980s. *Passioni* was part of a publicly stated strategy by Fininvest to fight off foreign competition. As *L'Unità* (19 January 1994) put it: 'because it is precisely over this genre that Fininvest is doing "battle" – producing a serial which is totally Italian in order to compete with those from across the Atlantic which have constantly invaded our television market'.

Passioni represents the confluence of a number of different influences. From previous Italian fiction series it draws its concentration on the rich and the powerful. The bulk of the story is set in Rome, and the main family, the Boldanos, live in an incredibly lavish mansion with lush interiors and large, beautifully manicured gardens. Antonio Boldano is the head of a powerful business empire with international interests, including interests in Brazil, where a certain part of the story actually takes place. This kind of milieu was noted by Silj as a dominant feature of the most popular Italian television series of the 1980s (1988: 184), and is in fact presented by Milly Buonanno as one of her 'substantive criteria' of Italian television fiction (1994: 179): 'the world of Italian fiction is predominantly the world of the *haute bourgeoisie*, or at the very least a world of the well-to-do classes, populated by established professionals, leading financiers, industrialists, managers, top civil servants, intellectuals, designers'. The strong crime element in *Passioni* also has a long and well-established Italian genealogy, and taps into the incredible popularity of Italian detective series of the 1980s and 1990s. Many of the most dramatic moments of the production belong to this narrative line.

However, the mark of the South American *telenovela* is also visible, even though it has been to some extent transformed. This influence is present in the melancholy mood announced by the wistful title song *Per lei* (For Her), sung as large raindrops cause slow ripples to spread out over the gently undulating surface of a pond where dead leaves float slowly by. And, when action is not on the agenda, *Passioni* is characterized by hushed, almost whispering conversations, spoken slowly with long pauses between exchanges, often to the accompaniment of bittersweet, nostalgic music. The dialogue is intimate in a highly stylized, at times almost poetic, way. In the much more hard-nosed atmosphere of British soaps, for example, where the conventions of 'social realism' have achieved an astonishing degree of hegemony, it would be genuinely difficult to imagine a format in which anyone could convincingly deliver similar dialogues to any kind of prime-time audience.

La Repubblica (9 September 1994) described the final episode of *Passioni* as a 'happy ending'. Despite this, my own overwhelming impression of this production is the melancholy mood, the slow, whispered, at times anguished dialogues, perhaps above all Virna Lisi's sorrowful, brimming-eyed, suffering Eleonora, a woman on whom fate – in fact, the narrative – appears to heap one calamity after another. *Passioni* is, in short, predominantly a melodrama, but it is a very good melodrama (I do not consider this to be a contradiction in terms), well-made and well-acted by experienced and skilful actors. Its production values are also high, much higher than those sometimes found in certain South American *telenovelas*. But in the end it was only a limited success. It achieved average audiences of just under 2,500,000. These figures are roughly similar to those achieved by the leading South American *telenovelas* in Italy such as *Milagros* and *Perla negra* shown on Retequattro, and are only roughly half those achieved by the American daytime soap *The Bold and the Beautiful* shown on Canale 5 in the early afternoon. This suggests strongly that an exploitable prime-time market for domestic *telenovelas* on a mainstream channel does not yet exist in Italy. This part of the market appears to be being served to its own satisfaction by the imported products (occasionally Italian co-productions) on a channel specializing precisely in that kind of supply.

Soaps

Italy's first soap: Un posto al sole

A short article appeared in Italy's best-selling daily newspaper *La Repubblica* on 5 July 1995 entitled 'Stories of respectable people: here is the Italian "soap"'. It went on to give details of a soap entitled *Un posto al sole* (A Place in the Sun), a forthcoming co-production between RAI, the production company Format, and Grundy Productions (Italy). According to this article the soap was to go on the air in February 1996 on RaiDue at 20.30. In fact *Un posto al sole* would not be launched until 21 October 1996, eight months later than scheduled, not on RaiDue – a channel which in the late 1980s restyled itself as primarily a provider of fiction (Buonanno, 1994: 13) – but on the minority-viewing channel RaiTre, and not in prime time but at 18.30, two hours earlier than the originally planned slot. Its current viewing figures are around 1.6 million, a not unreasonable score for RaiTre, whose most successful programme *Milleunadonna* has around 2.3 million viewers. This figure is, however, only a third of the viewers of *The Bold and the Beautiful* shown on Canale 5 (4.8 million) and is around 800,000 lower than that of prime-time *telenovelas* on Retequattro, and it pales into insignificance when compared with the figures for Italy's most successful programmes such as the satirical news programme *Striscia la notizia* or the only occasional blockbusting film such as *Basic Instinct* which can still attract over ten million viewers.

La Repubblica's summary of the opening situation of this new soap, based on information given to it by Giovanni Miloni of Format, was as follows:

A group of young people ... unexpectedly inherits a top floor and attic flat in an aristocratic mansion in the centre of Naples. The group moves, lock, stock and barrel, into the various floors of the noble building, bringing along with their stereos and their t-shirts the inevitable chaos of their generation.

Which will, willy-nilly, involve the aristocrat downstairs who's come down in the world, the rich middle-class family on the second floor, the bachelor living on the ground floor, the surveyor, the caretaker and his daughters.

Some small changes to this outline had taken place by the time the first episode went on air. The mansion is now at the water's edge, overlooking the Bay of Naples, the flat was inherited by only one of the young people – Anna Boschi – rather than by a group, there has (so far at least) been no sign of a surveyor, though there is a doctor, and the caretaker has a son, but no daughters.

The article in *La Repubblica* which first announced *Un posto al sole* described the story as being 'completely Italian'. This is not, however, strictly speaking correct, at least not as far as the opening situation is concerned, since *Un posto al sole* has very obvious and very striking connections with the German soap opera *Unter uns* (see page 67), which is likewise a Grundy co-production. *Unter uns* is also set in a town house with a group of youngsters (initially all girls) moving into the top floor and attic in the first episodes. The character Michele is clearly modelled on Achim in the German soap: both manage to wangle their way into the all-girl apartment by pretending to be gay (and both are eventually discovered in their deception). The character of Luca De Santis is also based to some extent on that of Olaf Schwarz in *Unter uns*: both are doctors, and both have lost their wives in dramatic circumstances in the past (though in rather different circumstances, since the East Berlin story of *Unter uns* is not easily transportable to Italy). There is, in fact, quite a strong physical resemblance between the two characters with their gaunt, long-haired, six-o'clock-shadow, slightly bohemian look.

However, *Un posto al sole* combines these characters and situations from the Grundy library of off-the-shelf storylines and situations with recognizable Italian precedents. Thus the basic set-up in *Un posto al sole* to some extent reproduces that of the popular series of the 1980s *Quei 36 gradini* (Those 36 steps). The mansion house in *Quei 36 gradini* was set in a middle-class district in Rome, and the main characters included the caretaker Pietro, the middle-aged Matilde who is separated from her husband, and Countess Dora, their counterparts in *Un posto al sole* being the caretaker Raffaele Giordano, the middle-aged and separated Giulia Poggi and Countess Federica Palladini. Indeed Countess Federica tries to get rid of Raffaele in *Un posto al sole* in much the same way as Countess Dora tried to get rid of Pietro in *Quei 36 gradini* (Silj, 1988: 171).

In fact, this mixture of standardized Grundy techniques and Italian settings and traditions is evident already in the opening sequence for *Un posto al sole*. The title song, which accompanies various views of Naples, is positive and up-beat in tone: 'A new day is here / for us also / a truer world / will awake'. The Grundy influence is instantly visible in the almost universal good looks of the characters, from oldest to youngest. As the song comes to an end, the sun rises from a stylized sea in the form of a yellow spiral. It moves to form the letter 'o' of the word 'sole' in the title, all of whose other 'o's are also yellow spirals, the other letters being in green.

If the opening sequence of *Un posto al sole* is fairly predictable, the closing one is rather unexpected. At the end of (almost) every episode, as the credits roll by, two pairs of eyes – one blue and one brown – appear on the screen. Two voices – a female voice (Fiamma) accompanying the blue eyes and a male one (Fabbio) accompanying the brown ones – then proceed to comment on what has happened during the episode. For example, at the end of the episode in which Maria Boschi announced that she knew how the old count had died (an episode which was broadcast on a Friday), their conversation went as follows:

Fi: Fabbio, now we're going to have to wait till Monday to find out from Maria who's responsible for Count Giacomo's death.
Fa: [*Unintelligible noises*]
Fi: Oh, stop chewing. You've done nothing else during the entire episode.
Fa: Fiamma, watching television makes me hungry, you know that.
Fi: But all that noise of chewing gets on my nerves. It distracts me.
Fa: Huh, *I* distract *you*, when all you've done is make comments out loud throughout the entire episode. Fiamma, you know what you are.

Fi: Yes, yes, I know, but why don't you tell me on Monday morning on RadioDue
    at 8.05?
Fa: In *Fabbio e Fiamma e 'la trave nell'occhio'*.

The voices, in fact, belong to the presenters of a daily radio programme
broadcast every weekday on RadioDue (its title appears in the last line
above), and every morning they comment on the episode of *Un posto al sole*
of the evening before: a case of what Milly Buonanno calls 'intermedial
dialogism' (1994: 196) which I have not encountered – at least not in this
particular form – anywhere else in Europe.

Un posto al sole is set in Naples, which figures considerably as a location
in the soap. However, the Naples constructed by *Un posto al sole* is a very
selective one, and is rather different from the Naples which is traditionally
found in Italian television fiction. Traditionally, Naples has figured in
Italian televised fiction as a site of crime and underworld activities of all
kinds, often related with the Neapolitan version of the mafia, the *camorra*.
This is, as Milly Buonanno points out in her fascinating study of Italian
television fiction, part of a much larger and long-established tradition of
constructing the South as the 'territory of evil', a tradition whose most
emblematic expression is undoubtedly *La Piovra*, set in Sicily. Referring to
the 'criminal trinity' of the mafia in Sicily, the *camorra* in Naples and the
'ndrangheta in Calabria, she writes: 'In televised fiction the south means
predominantly crime, illegality, the cult of silence and of violence, dark and
lugubrious settings, bloodshed, ambushes and armed encounters ... '
(1994: 159). Buonanno herself suggests that a certain 'slippage in the view
of the South' may have been in evidence in season 1992–93 (161). Whatever
the reason, the Naples which emerges from *Un posto al sole* simply does not
correspond to this stereotype at all. It is a modern and dynamic city where
no one would feel at all ill-at-ease walking around at night. Even the tramps,
whom Anna once helps to feed as part of a charitable action organized by
Alberto Palladini, are courteous and gentlemanly.

This somewhat unorthodox view of the city actually surfaced in the
narrative itself when Michele's girlfriend Monica arrived from Milan and
tried to entice him back to Milan with the offer of a job in her father's
newspaper. As they sat on the veranda overlooking the moonlit Bay of
Naples he challenged what he called her 'prejudices' about Naples, their
conversation continuing as follows:

Mi: Leaving Naples just now would mean missing out on the most interesting
    time in this city, on its renaissance.
Mo: Yes, unemployment, criminality and robberies, they are also part of its
    renaissance.
Mi: Unemployment would undoubtedly go down if they developed tourism, and
    I know that people are working to bring crime under control.

He goes on to assure her that Naples is a city where 'reality is not just greater than fiction, it towers above it'.

The second most striking gap between the Naples of *Un posto al sole* and the real Naples is the total absence of any trace of the Naples dialect in the production. Everyone, from the oldest to the youngest and from the highest to the lowest, including the motley band of workers who work in the Palladinis' boat-building company, speaks standard Italian. This differentiates *Un posto al sole* from *Quei 36 gradini*, for example, where the characters spoke in Roman dialect, and is rather surprising given that Neapolitan – or rather a certain, almost standardized version of the Neapolitan dialect – is well understood by Italian viewers in general. As Ortoleva points out of the new television landscape which emerged in Italy in the 1980s (1992: 261):

In this mass culture on a national scale, the very function of the vernacular, in particular of Neapolitan and Roman, was to a certain extent delocalized. These dialects were transformed, so to speak, into 'national' dialects, and became in the national media more static and rigid than those current in the local language. Thus they were transformed into a generally understood language. More than dialects of specific regions, they were the 'vernacular Italian' of popular culture, of song, cinema, light theatre and entertainment broadcasting.

Part of the 'problem' may be, as Milly Buonanno points out, that 'Naples is, in spite of everything, too strongly codified in the Italian imaginary in a register of comedy' (1994: 163), a register which the producers of *Un posto al sole* would certainly want to avoid. Nonetheless, the lack of 'linguistic realism' remains striking. It may be an attempt by the producers to relocate Naples discursively in the north (see O'Donnell, 1994), or it may be part of the general Grundy strategy of departicularizing the local (see the sections on Germany and the Netherlands), or it may have to do with the kind of audience being constructed by this soap.

Un posto al sole's appeal is complex and fractured, an amalgam of, to some extent, discrete elements rather than a homogeneous whole. It is difficult to avoid concluding that the delay in its launch was due to a number of changes being effected in the production as a whole (though it is also the case that 1996 was a period of some turmoil for the RAI following the centre-left's electoral victory in the early part of that year and the removal of the governors appointed initially by Berlusconi in 1994), and perhaps the lack of coherence and sense of dispersal are symptomatic of the fact that this production has not yet quite figured out who it is. The teenage element is, of course, important, but in its current form different parts of the soap are designed to appeal across a range of ages and to as wide an audience as possible. It is too early to say if it will succeed in establishing itself as staple viewing even for a niche section of the Italian viewership, or whether it will ever challenge *The Bold and the Beautiful*. However, for the time being at least, there seems no reason why the 230 episodes originally planned should not be shown and perhaps even be extended in the future.

Analysis

The path towards a long-running domestic serial in Italy has not been an easy one, and indeed, successful arrival at the point of destination is not yet assured, even if *Un posto al sole*'s ability to hold and even slightly increase its audience seems at least promising. Milly Buonanno, who describes Italian culture as having a 'strong intellectualising and elitist orientation' (1994: 10) offers the following partial explanation:

The reasons why seriality in the strong sense has not yet been produced in Italy . . . are linked to the history of Italian public service broadcasting, which from the outset has sought inspiration, as far as the production of fiction is concerned, in the narrative models found in the theatre and in cinema, within the more general framework of a privileged reference to high culture and high-brow literature . . . Nor could the widespread climate of (intellectual) opinion which is still fiercely opposed to seriality encourage the birth of, if not a commitment to, then at least of an openness towards serials. (1994: 191)

None of this is unique to Italy, of course, but there are some specific characteristics which make the Italian case at least to some extent different to what is encountered elsewhere.

In the first place, commercial television came considerably earlier to Italy than to any other continental European country, and, as a number of commentators have pointed out, despite a series of highly visible presentational differences, the new commercial channels did not in the end radically break the mould of Italian television. As Ortoleva (1992: 283) puts it:

Once commercial television had affirmed its presence, however, questions began to be asked about how 'new' it was. While the reorganized RAI, even if with great uncertainty and reluctance, tried out some new forms of expression, the private television stations explicitly became the direct extension of the 'old' television, from which they borrowed planning patterns, personalities and programming models.

By the time the 'new wave' of soaps arrived in Europe the Italian duopoly had, in fact, already by and large sorted out the various identities of its constituent parts, so that there was little room for soaps to play the kind of pioneering, identity-creating role they have undoubtedly played elsewhere.

Secondly, the traditional cultural élites maintained their position of dominance and control much longer in Italy because the structures which allowed them to do so were a material part of the almost 45 years of uninterrupted Christian Democratic ascendancy – referred to by some as a 'blocked democracy' (Di Tota, 1997: 225) – a phenomenon which has no real parallel elsewhere in western Europe: indeed, a central element of these structures was the transformation of the three RAI channels – or, more particularly, of their news programmes – into spheres of influence of the main political parties and their associated intellectuals (Mazzoleni, 1992: 124). *Un posto al sole*'s emergence has broadly coincided with the at least partial dismantling of that structure.

In fact, early attempts at Italian serial fiction aimed at two different kinds of audiences, both of which were inherited from the past: on the one hand a predominantly female niche audience, as in the case of *Edera* and *Senza fine/Camilla*, whose desire for melodrama seems to be amply met by Retequattro; on the other, as in the case of *Passioni*, an audience still locked to some extent into the dominant narrative patterns – luxurious settings, crime stories – of the 1980s. But as Italy struggles to find a new *political* identity following the end of the Christian Democratic ascendancy and the subsequent collapse of the Berlusconi-led coalition Polo delle Libertà, these cultural patterns no longer seem able to bring together the truly national audiences of the great successes of the 1980s, while simultaneously pre-supposing an audience from which many young people in particular no doubt feel excluded. *Un posto al sole*, for its part, appears to be attempting to construct a national audience along rather different lines: not around great national problems such as the mafia or the north-south divide – a fiercely debated polemic in Italy (see Bocca (1990)) – but around problems of day-to-day social co-existence narrativized through the low-impact personal dramas which are so characteristic of Grundy-style soaps.

La Repubblica's preview of *Un posto al sole* announced confidently that the soap would be aimed firmly at a youth audience. It is not at all clear from the form in which the production eventually appeared that this is actually now the case. Of course, the appeal to a youth audience is there, and is unmistakable. The large number of young characters and the importance they are given sees to that, and they bring the inevitable youth-oriented themes with them. But the focus is not exclusively a youth-centred one. Some of these storylines are approached from other angles, with issues of class, social problems and at times even industrial relations also cropping up. Thus Maria Boschi's physical abuse by her husband Pietro causes a discussion between Michele and Anna about the question of domestic violence (complete with statistics). And how will Alessandro solve the dispute with the workers in his boatyard? Will they accept his offer of shares and directorial control instead of a wage rise? These themes take the soap beyond the strict purview of an exclusively younger audience.

The family itself is also a theme in *Un posto al sole* in a way in which it never emerges in the youth-oriented German daily soaps, for instance. By and large, it is presented as a much more complex amalgam of feelings, mutual responsibilities, rights and obligations than it is in the German case: as a social structure with its potential strengths and weaknesses, it is to some extent – however stereotypically – problematized from the point of view of characters spread over the entire age range of the soap. This view of the family may not be idyllic, but it does to some extent depart from the dominant 'tragic' view of Italian family life in RAI productions dating back at least to the 1980s (Silj, 1988: 179), as well as from that of Fininvest's more entertainment-oriented productions where 'the family loses many of its problem features and crisis-ridden characteristics to become a place where, barring temporary upsets, serenity reigns' (Buonanno, 1994: 189). And *Un posto al sole* breaks with other trends of Italian television fiction in other ways. Certainly, no one is poor, not even the Giordanos, but its mix of characters is more variegated than would appear to be the norm in Italian fiction, and there is nothing to match the lavishness of *Passioni*. Renato Poggi is not by any stretch of the imagination a 'leading financier', and the Palladinis, despite their Ferrari and their expensive furniture, do not seem to be fabulously rich: the Cantieri Navali Palladini definitely make yachts rather than ships. For all their titles, the Palladinis appear to be very much minor aristocrats and middling capitalists.

Silj (1988) also suggests that the Italy of the leading series of the 1980s was 'a country without housewives' (p. 184), where 'women are portrayed as strong, emancipated and independent ... these women work, have professions ... and are sure of themselves' (p. 181). While this sense of independence and self-confidence is present among the younger women in *Un posto al sole*, the older women simply do not conform to this pattern. None of the three main older women – Federica, Giulia and Rita – works, and the latter two are seen from time to time doing the ironing, making the meals and so on: very much housewives, indeed.

In fact, *Un posto al sole* appears to be attempting to create a quite different Italy from the one (or ones) which have dominated Italian fiction so far. Traditionally, the local has been celebrated and class divisions have been emphasized as a source of tension and narrative energy. In *Un posto al sole* the local is delocalized, almost nationalized (perhaps Naples, discursively, if not geographically, the turning-point between north and south, was an inspired choice), and class warfare, if not class divisions, is presented as inefficient and a thing of the past. The various social strata involved in the soap are not disguised, in fact their existence is signalled in many different if rather stereotypical ways, but there is (relatively) little social friction, what little there is being mostly provided by the machiavellian Countess Federica, and being generally presented as out of touch with the modern world.

Politics in the party-political sense never raises its head in *Un posto al sole*, but politics is not absent as it appears to have been in the series of the 1980s (Silj, 1988: 184). This became quite clear during the dispute between the aristocratic Alessandro and the workers in his boatyard. He stands out against the old-fashioned views of his father who simply wants to sack his workforce and take on others ('We can't take on the trade unions,' he protests, 'and we need skilled workers'), and criticizes his fiancée, Tiziana, for seeing the dispute in terms of 'them' and 'us' when it is, according to him, a question of 'everyone contributing'. His offer of shares to his workers, thereby giving them a controlling interest in the company, is presented very much in the 'let's-all-pull-together' spirit:

I believe in fact that a climate of co-operation is the only effective way to save the company ... This represents a radical revolution in the management of the company, and it means that the structure of command itself will be changed ... All my decisions will require your approval.

Despite their initial opposition, the workers – an uninspiring bunch, easily influenced by shop steward Lippi – eventually agree. This episode represents, needless to say, a rather optimistic view of Italian industrial relations, but it is symptomatic of the kind of convergent audience *Un posto al sole* is attempting to construct: one built around notions of consensus and agreement, similar to those constructed by – albeit from different vantage points – *Familie* in Flanders (see page 37) or *El súper* in Spain (see page 175). And this is not restricted to the soap: Alessandro's offer to his workers coincided with the then relatively recent election victory of the centre-left alliance symbolically named 'Ulivo', or 'Olive Branch'.

From this point of view, *Un posto al sole* is much more 'experimental' than *Passioni* ever was, something also signalled by its presence on RaiTre. It disperses the southerness of Naples, otherwise the resultant discursive precipitation would skew its audience's expectations, and hence the audience itself. It plays the youth card fairly consistently, but is careful to appeal to older audiences as well. No one is either fabulously rich or grindingly poor, but everyone is good-looking and well-dressed. It avoids party politics, but suggests a society where all, from aristocrats to caretakers, pull together. *Un posto al sole* is in fact attempting to create a nationwide audience more interested in what it has in common now and in the future than in what may have divided it for geographical or other reasons in the past. As Italy struggles to throw off the (largely corrupt) political structures of both the more distant and the more recent past and create new ones for the future, it may well be the case that such an audience is emerging, but *Un posto al sole*'s scheduling and ratings suggest that the desired encounter between consumer and product is a developing rather than an established one.

Postscript

According to *La Repubblica* of 30 June 1997 RaiUno is currently producing its longest-running serial of all time. It will take 60 weeks to complete, will go on air in Spring 1998 while production is still in progress, and will have the extremely unusual format of 26 episodes of 100 minutes each. Entitled *Incantesimo* (Magic Spell) it will be based on a young surgeon called Barbara and the adventures of her professional and private life.

The Netherlands

Television in the Netherlands

The Netherlands has the most complex public service television system in Europe, perhaps even the world. During the period of the PSB monopoly, which lasted from the 1950s until the late 1980s, programming was provided by a group of independent broadcasting organizations representing specific social groups and recruiting membership from the public at large (Ang: 1991: 121–2). This system, known as the 'pillar system', and designed at least partly to reduce the likelihood of any one social group monopolizing media output, was imported into television from radio where it had been introduced in the 1930s (Brants and McQuail, 1992: 153). With the gradual decline of the pillar system in Dutch society at large from the 1960s onwards came new non-confessional broadcasters such as the Dutch Broadcasting Foundation NOS (mainly responsible for news, current affairs and sport), the more overtly entertainment-oriented VOO (originally the pirate station Veronica, and now operating a television channel in its own right) and TROS (the move towards more entertainment-based television is also sometimes referred to as 'trossification'). Between them, these organizations account for the bulk of programming on the three PSB channels, Nederland 1, 2 and 3.

The death-knell of the PSB monopoly in the Netherlands was definitively sounded by the launch of the satellite-borne commercial station RTL-Véronique in 1989 (Nieuwenhuis, 1992: 210). The irresistible rise of RTL-Véronique (now known as RTL4) led to the legalization of commercial television in 1990. Since then new stations have included RTL5 and Veronica, which together with RTL4 form the Holland Media Groep (HMG), as well as SBS6 (partly owned by ABC Sports and Paramount) and the dedicated sports channel Sport 7.

Domestic Dutch soaps

A *lachrymose soap:* Goede Tijden, Slechte Tijden

Prior to 1990, the Netherlands had no experience of domestic soap opera whatsoever, despite the astonishing popularity enjoyed there by the American supersoaps of the 1980s (Ang, 1985: 55). The first Dutch soap, *Goede Tijden, Slechte Tijden* (Good Times, Bad Times), produced by Joop van den Ende Productions, was launched by the newly-established satellite channel RTL4 in October 1990, and was the first new European soap of the decade. It was part of an aggressive strategy which quickly made RTL4 the most watched station in the Netherlands, a strategy graphically described by RTL4's then deputy director Ruud Hendriks as 'war' (*De Telegraaf,* 5 December 1992). *Goede Tijden, Slechte Tijden* immediately became extremely popular, with very stable audience ratings of around two million viewers, and it is often the top programme on weekdays (Infomart figures via teletext on RTL4).

However, at least to begin with, *Goede Tijden, Slechte Tijden* was something of a hybrid product: though produced in the Netherlands, it was, in fact, in its early stages – like its German counterpart *Gute Zeiten, Schlechte Zeiten*, with which it shares a number of characters (see page 56) – a rewrite of the now long-defunct Australian soap *The Restless Years* (1976–80). *The Restless Years* was written by Reg Watson, who is acknowledged at the end of each episode of the Dutch soap, and produced by the Australian company Grundy. *Goede Tijden, Slechte Tijden* is in fact a co-production between Joop van den Ende (JE) Productions and Grundy's export arm, Grundy International. As Cunningham and Jacka (1996: 163) point out:

There was . . . no tradition of making soap opera in Holland – no factory production of stripped serial drama. Expertise was needed very quickly, so the Grundy scripts and know-how were important elements in Dutch television. Reg Watson adapted the scripts and they were separately translated. Together with Michael Murphy, at Grundy International, he set up the production process at JE Productions; this whole process took eight to nine months. *Good Times, Bad Times* was the first stripped soap opera to be shown on Dutch television.

Following a pattern which has since been followed in Germany, the Australian scripts were simply translated during the first two seasons, with the original settings and characters being replaced with Dutch ones. It was only from 1992 on that genuinely original Dutch scripting took over from the earlier Australian scripts.

Despite its now fairly thoroughgoing 'Dutchification' *Goede Tijden, Slechte Tijden*'s Australian origins were visible in a number of ways. One was the importance given to young people in the early storylines. From this point of view it is not difficult to agree with Cunningham and Jacka's suggestion that this was an important factor in the early success of this soap, since the youth market – in particular the teenage market – had long been neglected by the Dutch public service providers (1996: 163). Another is the fact that virtually all the actors chosen to play the parts are good-looking. However, it is important to stress that the characters are not themselves glamourized in any way (something which becomes immediately clear if *Goede Tijden, Slechte Tijden* is compared with its 'sister' German production *Gute Zeiten, Schlechte Zeiten*). Within the narrative world of *Goede Tijden, Slechte Tijden* glamorous dress, for example, is associated only with glamorous occasions (weddings, birthday parties and the like), or is used to identify a female character as a seductress: in this respect, Linda Dekker's change from potential villainess to acceptable character was accompanied by a notable increase in the everydayness of her clothes. The characters are often seen carrying out quite mundane tasks such as doing the dishes, polishing their shoes or oiling their gardening tools. For the first four years of the soap – until the opening sequence was changed in 1994 – the photograph of Laura Alberts with which this sequence ended showed her hanging out the washing.

The *dramatis personae* of *Goede Tijden, Slechte Tijden* is a multifarious one. At the centre are the two brothers, Jeff and Robert Alberts, and their respective families. As well as being brothers, Jeff and Robert are, at different times in the soap, both business partners and business rivals, having first run a company together, then having gone their separate ways during a lengthy period of estrangement, and then coming back together again. The business element of *Goede Tijden, Slechte Tijden* is in fact fairly low-key – small beer when compared with Van Den Bossche Systems in the Flemish soap *Familie* or the Dahlén shipping line in the Swedish soap *Rederiet* – but it provides an opening for numerous business/personal intersections in the narrative.

Given their economic positions, the social milieu of the characters is, by and large, comfortable, but it is not in any sense splendid. While Robert and Laura Alberts live in a large and well-appointed detached house in a leafy suburban area, where not only they, but also their son Arnie and his girlfriend Roos appear to live mainly off Robert's income, the younger characters, for their part, live mostly in flats, while Helen Helmink, the youngsters' former teacher, lives in a high-rise block. The only characters who appear to be in any way working-class are immigrants. The Surinamese Frenk Peters, while he was still in the soap, appeared to be a manual worker of some kind, though it was never altogether clear what kind of work he actually did. A short storyline concerning Fatima Yalmiz's clothing workshop showed it peopled exclusively by Asians working at the sewing machines.

Despite its Australian origins, *Goede Tijden, Slechte Tijden* is now very much a Dutch product, particularly since the scriptwriting was taken over by Dutch writers, and indeed many of its current viewers are unaware of the fact that it was ever hybrid in nature. Nonetheless, it lacks anything like the kind of clear physical location associated with many other European soaps. The particular kind of Standard Educated Dutch spoken by the characters is almost certainly enough for most Dutch viewers to locate this soap fairly clearly in the north-west of the Netherlands. The (very occasional) outside shots showing extensive wharfs and quays also help to locate it in a large harbour city. Amsterdam seems an obvious candidate, but in fact the actual location (in narrative terms, that is) of the soap is not at all derivable from anything which actually takes place within it. While the opening credits of many European soaps feature shots of their (at least supposed) location, *Goede Tijden, Slechte Tijden* begins with photographs of each of the main characters coming briefly to life. Outside shots are extremely infrequent, and when they occur they often last no more than a few seconds. No mention of the city is ever made, and the characters read the entirely fictitious newspaper *Het Spectrum* (in fact it appears to be the Amsterdam paper *Het Parool* with a specially made-up front page).

Elements of the characters' lives which lie outside the work/emotions interface are, by and large, avoided. None of this is, of course, coincidental. Anything that might help to identify the actual location of the soap is being deliberately avoided. *Goede Tijden, Slechte Tijden* is not in the Netherlands but *of* the Netherlands. While *Landsbyen* creates a nostalgic Denmark of the past and *Familie* creates an elegant Flanders of an idealized present, *Goede Tijden, Slechte Tijden* creates a rarified Netherlands of the emotions: it is a world where feelings come first, and where only enough of the real Netherlands appears as is required to locate these within the viewer's national frame of reference.

With its lack of physical location and absence of geographical extension *Goede Tijden, Slechte Tijden* is one of the most claustrophobic of European soaps. All soaps are potentially claustrophobic – both physically and emotionally – with their constantly recurring locations and their unending two-steps-forward-one-step-back narrative shuffle, but, in Europe at least, only the Greek soaps are as claustrophobic as the Dutch ones. *Goede Tijden, Slechte Tijden* is a world of rooms without windows or of windows which look out on to nothing: no sky, no buildings, no trees, no passers-by, nothing but a uniform grey.

(A striking exception to all this did take place, however, at the end of 1995, when Dian Alberts and Frits van Houten got married on the Caribbean island of Bonaire. Here the viewers were treated to ample shots of the island as Frits and Dian lounged on the beach or sped around dirt tracks in their open-top 4x4. This particular episode was made with help from the Bonaire Tourism Corporation and the Harbour Village Beach Resort, and it may be that such scenes will become more common as advertisers realize the potential of such a relationship with the producers of soaps. However, it remains the case that the Dutch setting of the soap has never been, and probably never will be, the object of such expansive filming.)

But the claustrophobia extends to the relationships between the characters as well. The only stable relationship so far appears to have been that between Arnie and Roos. All the other relationships rotate in endless permutations which border on a combinatorial explosion, the kind of endless grouping and regrouping that characterizes current Australian soaps such as *Home and Away*, for example. In short, with its numerous characters constantly crowding each other out of doomed relationships, *Goede Tijden, Slechte Tijden* is the dark star of European soaps: a densely compressed world, a world where characters constantly search for warmth and light. If the Greek soaps are the noisiest of European soaps, and the Danish soap *Landsbyen* is the most lyrical of European soaps, *Goede Tijden, Slechte Tijden* is by far the most lachrymose of European soaps. Characters, both male and female, cry frequently and copiously (even the villainous Frits van Houten cries when spurned by Martine Hafkampf). In fact, the title of this soap is largely misleading, since the 'good times' are few and far between. Its title song makes the emphasis much clearer, something which stands out even more forcefully if it is compared with the title song of *Gute Zeiten, Schlechte Zeiten* (see page 58): 'The time of carefreeness is over / Today begins the long road towards tomorrow ... Good times, bad times / A day that appears to be a night'.

It would be easy to mock *Goede Tijden, Slechte Tijden* for its cut-price production values. It is undoubtedly a low-budget production. The dominance of studio shots has already been mentioned. Sound quality can be indifferent, with characters sometimes drowned out by the background music. The actors regularly spill all kinds of liquids – coffee, wine, champagne, coke, soup, anything spillable in fact – but the shots go on air with the spillages rather than being retaken. Characters slam telephone receivers on to their bases only to see them fall off again. The end of the Instituut Karma storyline, in which Laura and the other members of her family were held at knife-point by members of a sect, and were then rescued by Arnie wielding a hockey stick and Jeff wielding a suitcase (an entire summer passed between the beginning and the end of this sequence), served, above all, to illustrate the fact that there is a complex expertise involved in choreographing fight scenes which was simply not available to those working in this soap.

However, although it might be low-budget, *Goede Tijden, Slechte Tijden* is not, in any sense other than the strictly financial, 'cheap'. It can be silly – the dénouement of the Instituut Karma storyline, for instance. It can be over the top – as in the case of Helen Helmick's constantly frustrated attempts to tell Peter that she is his mother. But it always takes its storylines seriously. It lacks the grimness of the UK soaps and those European soaps most directly influenced by them, but it is an unremittingly serious soap. No one is ever invited to laugh at or even with any of the characters. Storylines often run for months on end, giving rise to other storylines directly related to them and providing a close-knit narrative cohesion which is often lacking in soaps. The long storyline of the death of Laura's daughter Lotje was a case in point, but the many storylines and the topics it set loose were treated seriously throughout. The funeral scene in particular – one of the longest outside sequences ever to be shown on *Goede Tijden, Slechte Tijden* – was, however clichéd it might sound, genuinely moving, as Arnie placed Lotje's teddy bear on her coffin before it was lowered into the ground.

On recently re-viewing an episode I had taped from 1992, I was immediately struck by how much the younger characters, in particular, had changed. The inevitable fact is that the teenagers of 1990 have now become twenty-somethings (though, in a now very frequent displacement, they still continue, by and large, to behave like teenagers). The classic solution to this problem is to renew the teenage group – either on a 'naturalistic' basis as in *Home and Away* through the mechanism of fostering, or in more desperate fashion as in *Gute Zeiten, Schlechte Zeiten* where characters get murdered (about half a dozen were murdered in 1994 by the Tights Murderer), die of brain tumours, go on the run and the like – but so far the rate of renewal in *Goede Tijden, Slechte Tijden* has been relatively slow, and the bulk of the new younger characters who have appeared are also in their twenties. The truth is that, despite its origins, and in striking contrast to its German counterpart, *Goede Tijden, Slechte Tijden* is no longer a teenager's soap. Perhaps it never really was.

A brooding soap: Onderweg naar Morgen

Following a pattern which is now well-established in a number of European countries, the success of a soap opera on a commercial channel often leads to the appearance of a rival on public service television, or vice versa. In the case of the Netherlands, this rival was *Onderweg naar Morgen* (Heading Towards Tomorrow), launched in January 1994 on the PSB channel Nederland 2. The term 'rival', however, requires some qualification here since, quite apart from the unique nature of the Dutch PSB channels, *Onderweg naar Morgen* is, like *Goede Tijden, Slechte Tijden*, also produced by Joop van den Ende Productions (which, therefore, shares with Ufa in Germany the distinction of producing soaps for rival public and commercial channels simultaneously). It was originally screened jointly by TROS and Veronica and was a reasonably successful production, with average audiences of between one million and one-and-a-half million per day (figures supplied by Joop van den Ende Productions). When Veronica established its own independent channel in 1996, *Onderweg naar Morgen* moved over to that channel, abandoning Nederland 2.

As against *Goede Tijden, Slechte Tijden*'s Australian original, for this second soap JE Productions turned to an American model, the soap opera *Ryan's Hope* launched in 1975 by the US channel ABC and dealing, according to Halliwell (1982: 541), with 'the young hopefuls of New York': the authors of *Ryan's Hope*, Claire Labine and Paul Avila Mayer, are acknowledged at the end of each episode of *Onderweg naar Morgen*. However, only the basic set-up was taken from the American model, and the scripts for *Onderweg naar Morgen* have always been Dutch. Using a technique which is common in American daytime soaps and in other productions influenced by them – most notably the Greek soaps – *Onderweg naar Morgen* runs a number of storylines simultaneously (usually not less than half a dozen) but actually only features about half of them in any one episode.

The similarities between *Onderweg naar Morgen* and *Goede Tijden, Slechte Tijden* are immediately striking, as is perhaps only to be expected given that they are produced by the same company and indeed in the same building. Like its rival, *Onderweg naar Morgen* is fully 'Dutchified'. It is likewise just as anonymous in terms of its location as *Goede Tijden, Slechte Tijden*. It features the same enclosed world as its competitor, with the same featureless windows and even fewer outside scenes. And its title song reproduces the brooding, apprehensive mood of *Goede Tijden, Slechte Tijden*, part of it going as follows: 'Heading towards tomorrow / An unpredictable step / A path that is sown with joy and sorrow / You know so little of / The future has hidden so many things from you'.

The action in *Onderweg naar Morgen* also revolves essentially around two families, the Reitsemas and the Cowenbergs, connected mainly by the fact that the two fathers – Jan and Ed respectively – work as doctors in the Beatrix Hospital, as have various of their children at different points. Perhaps the most notable difference between *Onderweg naar Morgen* and *Goede Tijden, Slechte Tijden*, apart from the medical interest, is that the thriller elements are much more to the fore in the former, adding to its generally sinister tone. Physical violence is not uncommon, and is quite graphically portrayed. When Reina de Zeeuw, daughter of Cor de Zeeuw, a businessman with sinister underworld connections, was raped by the criminal Olaf Kleemans, she was shown huddling under a desk with her clothes torn and her face covered in blood. When Olaf was then murdered in his hotel room – was it Reina who did it? – the camera returned insistently to his dead body lying on the floor with a knife sticking out of his stomach and blood coagulating on his shirt. More recently Alexandra Di Maxis, who had tried to blackmail Cor de Zeeuw during a diamond-smuggling storyline, was roughed up by the latter's men in some detail.

Onderweg naar Morgen is, in fact, if anything even more claustrophobic than its rival. The sets seem smaller, they often appear cluttered (books piled high in corners, shelves laden with ornaments or videotapes), and the characters almost always appear in medium shots or close-ups. The colours are stronger and more sombre and the lighting is often shadowy, contributing to the sense of being hemmed in. The *mise-en-scène* is the gloomiest of any serial production I have seen. The tone is frequently strident and angry. While *Goede Tijden, Slechte Tijden* is melancholy and even languid at times, *Onderweg naar Morgen* is brooding and sinister.

A teen soap: Goudkust

The Netherlands' third daily soap, entitled *Goudkust* (Golden Coast), first went on air on the new commercial channel SBS6 on 11 May 1996. Like the others it is also produced by Joop van den Ende Produkties, and the scripts are partly written by the Dr Proctor Scripts group, which is also involved in scriptwriting for *Goede Tijden, Slechte Tijden* and *Onderweg naar Morgen*.

Goudkust in fact begins at very much the same point that *Goede Tijden, Slechte Tijden* had begun six years earlier: with a group of youngsters, all around nineteen years old, in their last year at secondary school preparing for their final exams. They live in an elegant and leafy seaside town (the waves rolling in form the background to the opening sequence), and attend the Duindaals Lyceum together. Unlike its predecessors, *Goudkust* is an entirely Dutch product since it is not based on any foreign model, and it differs from the other Dutch soaps in being much more glamorous, with looks and fashions playing a major part in its general appeal, and who's-going-out-with-who being a major source of drama. It has, in fact, filled the space which the evolution of *Goede Tijden, Slechte Tijden* – whether 'natural' or otherwise – had left empty, though it does so with a rather different set of values.

My acquaintance with this soap is very limited, and certainly insufficient to offer any sustained analysis. Its own publicity specifically contrasted it with the Netherlands' other 'more serious' soaps, though my own impression on the basis of the small number of episodes I have seen is that what it has in common with the other two Joop van den Ende productions is rather more obvious than what separates it from them. Apart from a somewhat greater percentage of outside shots, its production techniques and values are broadly similar, it contains (again according to its own publicity) all the 'well-known soap elements such as evil, romance, deceit, heroism, sacrifice, love, illness, death and fraud', and its general mood is downbeat and difficult. Even so, with its array of youthful characters and its sexy fashions it is probably closer to the German soap *Gute Zeiten, Schlechte Zeiten* now than *Goede Tijden, Slechte Tijden* was at any point since the domestic scriptwriters took over in both countries. But while *Gute Zeiten, Schlechte Zeiten* goes out on Germany's most viewed channel, *Goudkust* is shown on what is still a minority channel within the Dutch media system. It went out in a first packet of 200 episodes, and is not currently (May 1997) on air, though screening is expected to resume in August 1997.

Analysis

The most striking element of the two major soaps analysed above is their general down-in-the-mouth quality and unrelentingly sombre tones. Humour is extremely rare, the tension is all-pervasively palpable; they are a Vale of Tears. There is even something mildly Calvinistic about them: salvation through (at least symbolic) self-mortification and pain. They are constantly heading towards the unknown.

The title which Cunningham and Jacka give to their analysis of the success of the Australian serial *The Flying Doctors* in the Netherlands is 'Social values in a serious culture' (1996: 160). Dutch culture has been, traditionally, a predominantly serious one. It would be wrong to overstate the point, of course. There are many comic programmes on Dutch tele-vision, from sit-coms such as *Zeg'ns en Aaa* or *In de Vlaamsche Pot* to satirical reviews such as Kees van Koten and Wim De Bie's *Keek op de Week*, which are often extremely funny. And RTL4 screens a whole range of game shows and chat shows which are every bit as down-market as anything else available in Europe. Indeed, the company which produces many of these programmes, Endemol – Europe's largest independent production company, made up of Joop van den Ende Productions and John de Mol Productions – exports a number to many other countries, in particular Germany. But even in the case of these transnational games the Dutch versions appear more reserved and understated than their foreign manifestations. In an interview published in the *Guardian* on 5 May 1993, Linda de Mol contrasted the Dutch and German versions of the *Dream Wedding* show – both of which she hosts – as follows: 'The Dutch candidates are far less emotional than the German ones'. Asked if she would like to live in Germany she replied: 'No. I'd get swamped by fans. In the Netherlands, stardom doesn't exist. Maybe we're too sober, or the country's just too small.' Linda de Mol is reproducing here a discourse which is well-established in Dutch society. For example, Albert van de Heuvel, for eight years vice-chairman of NOS, suggested in an interview in the newspaper *Trouw*, on 15 October 1993, that Dutch culture was 'poor in emotion . . . our culture is uncomfortable with emotion', by which he clearly meant any *display* of emotion.

This lack of display permeates all levels of these two soaps. The Netherlands is one of the wealthiest countries in Europe and has an industrial infrastructure and powerful multinational companies which a number of other countries with larger populations could not match, and a considerable level of affluence is available to a substantial sector of the population. But none of this is on show in these soaps, again in contrast to their German counterparts. Everyone in the Dutch soaps is financially comfortable, but conspicuous consumption is entirely absent. In a country with a (at least officially) strongly egalitarian and tolerant culture (itself partly the driving force behind the unusual set-up of the PSB channels), display signifies an absence of solidarity.

The Italian experience suggests that the arrival of commercial stations in a particular country leads initially to a tremendous split in terms of programme supply as the new stations attempt to establish a personality which is clearly different from that of the existing stations, but that after a while a mutual regrouping will slowly emerge around the currently dominant cultural values of the country in question. I am not suggesting that this regrouping either constitutes a simple return to the old *status quo*, or that it leads to a stage where public and private stations are virtually indistinguishable – this is clearly not the case – but television stations which want to be mainstream have to find ways of addressing the population at large, and this invariably means a slow but inevitable process of at least partial convergence – involving movement on both sides, of course – in at least some respects. It is arguable that such a process is now underway in Germany, at least as far as ARD and RTL are concerned, and the ease with which *Onderweg naar Morgen* moved from Nederland 2 to Veronica suggests that something similar may now be happening in the Netherlands. These two Dutch soaps – which do not see themselves as niche products in the way many of the German soaps do – have found themselves irresistibly drawn into that orbit.

What I want to argue is that the seriousness of *Goede Tijden, Slechte Tijden* and *Onderweg naar Morgen* belong to a broader discourse of continuity as opposed to a discourse of change expressed by *Goudkust*. This continuity is both cultural and social. It is probably fair to say that Dutch culture – or at least Dutch television culture – continues to maintain a division between 'drama' and other forms of fiction according to which drama is seen as an essentially serious business. Drama can have comic elements, of course, or it can be tragi-comic, but it is expected to deal with serious topics seriously: fiction which does not conform to this would be classified not as drama, but as 'entertainment'. A similar division has also characterized dramatic output in the Scandinavian countries: in the Swedish tabloid *Aftonbladet* of 27 August 1988 Gunder Andersson, on the basis of an analysis of *Dallas, Varuhuset, Cinderella* and *Hamlet*, argued that 'Perhaps what distinguishes serious drama from entertainment-drama is precisely the fact that serious drama dares to recognize the fact that life can be hell most of the time.' And *Goede Tijden, Slechte Tijden* and *Onderweg naar morgen* are classified, not primarily as soap opera, but as drama. Indeed, at the end of 1992 *Goede Tijden, Slechte Tijden* was voted second-best *drama* production in the Netherlands after the (likewise rather serious) medical series *Medisch Centrum West*.

On a broader level, the continuity – again as in the case of the Scandinavian countries – is with social values of restraint, tolerance and solidarity. The growth of *Goede Tijden, Slechte Tijden* into an adult soap while *Gute Zeiten, Schlechte Zeiten* has remained resolutely adolescent is in that sense not surprising, nor is the Dutch soap's modern mode of address, as opposed to the German soap's post-modern one; nor, for that matter, is the fact that the one truly teenage 'rich kid' soap goes out on a minority channel. Whatever else is happening in the Netherlands – its highly-developed social security system has indeed been under attack for some time now (Brants and McQuail: 1992: 152), and the demonstrations and subsequent police response at the recent Amsterdam summit show that unemployment and its threat to the general social order is an issue of growing importance – there is as yet no 'serious' mass cultural outlet for the discourses of triumphant individualism and its accompanying personal display. The worlds of *Goede Tijden, Slechte Tijden* and *Onderweg naar Morgen* may be dark ones, but their audiences seem to prefer their darkness to the lure of the consumerist spotlight.

Norway

Television in Norway

A national television service was not introduced in Norway until 1960 (Lundby and Futsæter, 1993: 95). This single-channel service, run by the Norsk Rikskringkasting and known by its initials NRK, remained the only Norwegian channel of any kind until the mid-1980s, though the situation was attenuated to some extent by the fact that many people in the east of the country could pick up Swedish television by overspill, Norwegian and Swedish being, to a fairly large extent, mutually intelligible languages (for a fascinating analysis of how this situation affected the purchase of American soaps by NRK in the 1980s – and for a very interesting overview of television in Norway in general – see Gripsrud, 1995: 71–85).

NRK's *de facto* single-channel monopoly of Norwegian-language television – a single channel from which, incidentally, advertising was banned – lasted until 1987 when the satellite channel TV3 began beaming Norwegian-language programmes (mostly dubbed) from London. However, its uptake was then and continues to be now, small: in 1996 its most successful programmes seldom attracted more than 400,000 viewers. In 1988 two further satellite channels were launched, TVNorge and TV1, these eventually merging under the joint title TVNorge (Petersen, 1992: 621), now known more commonly as TVN. Penetration of this new channel was also slow. By 1993 it accounted for only 9 per cent of Norwegians' viewing time, and today its programmes rarely get more than 200,000 viewers.

Norway's second terrestrial channel, TV2, was launched on 9 September 1992. It is a private channel, though it has public service obligations and is subject to a range of restrictions both as regards the form and content of its programmes and the amount of advertising it can broadcast (Østbye, 1992: 179). It is, by a long distance, Norway's second most popular channel, with programmes occasionally attracting as many as a million viewers. On 31 August 1996 NRK launched a second terrestrial channel, NRK2 (at which point the old NRK became NRK1). NRK2 deliberately targets a more youthful audience, and, as well as films, includes lengthy news programmes and documentaries. Its audiences currently peak at around 150,000.

Domestic Norwegian soaps

On 26 November 1996, Norway's best-selling daily newspaper, *VG*, carried as its front-page headline: 'Soap Fever devastates Norway'. The cause of this headline was the arrival in Norway, for the first time ever, of two domestic soaps running every week: *Offshore* (this is the actual title, not a translation) and *De syv søstre* (The Seven Sisters). Since each of these goes out only once a week – *Offshore* on NRK1 and *De syv søstre* on TV2 – this hardly amounts to 'soap fever' by the standards of most other European countries. But these programmes are extremely popular, and their joint success does mark an important landmark in the history of Norwegian television and in Norwegian society in general.

In its inside pages, the same issue of *VG* offered a brief résumé of what it saw as the history of soap opera in Norway. It listed Norway's first soap as *Hjemme hos oss* (At Our House), broadcast in 1980, followed fourteen years later by *Vestavind* (West Wind) and *I de beste familier* (In the Best of Families), both beginning in 1994. It also mentioned TV2's 'youth soap' *Sommerfugl* (Summer Bird) which began in January 1996. While *Vestavind* and *I de beste familier* were both very successful, with audiences of over one million each, *Sommerfugl* was something of a disaster, with viewing figures peaking at 400,000.

However close *Hjemme hos oss* may have been to the soap genre in other respects (I am not personally familiar with this production), it was certainly not a soap as far as its production methods was concerned. In a conversation I had with Anne Birte Brunvold Tørstad of NRK in early 1995 – she was the project leader for *I de beste familier* and occupies the same position now for *Offshore* – she explained in detail that the production methods used in *I de beste familier* had never been tried in Norway before, and that both writers and directors had to be 'educated' in order to cope with the particular pressures and restrictions which such a production method inevitably brings with it. *Vestavind* (which I have seen) is quite definitely not a soap following the criteria outlined earlier in this book. Its subtitle is, in fact, 'The chronicle of a family in post-war Norway 1945–1972', and, as this subtitle suggests, it is essentially historical in nature. In fact it has certain broad similarities with the Swedish production *Det var då*, broadcast in 1989 and 1990 (see page 180) or the Finnish serial *Puhtaat valkeat lakanat* of the early 1990s (see page 49).

A fairytale soap: I de beste familier

The first Norwegian production which might reasonably be termed a soap – and which was certainly seen this way by the Norwegian press: the *Arbeiderbladet* of 3 October 1994, for example, described it as 'NRK's first plunge into the unknown waters of what can be called Norwegian soap opera' – first went on the air on Sunday 23 October 1994 at 20.00. The first episode lasted 45 minutes, with subsequent episodes lasting half an hour. It was entitled *I de beste familier* (In the Best of Families), was screened by NRK and went out in a first season of 21 episodes. The possibility of extending this serial beyond this was built in from the start: as the accompanying information provided by NRK's Drama Department put it, talking of the fictitious village where the serial is set: 'provided that the series becomes a hit with the public, it isn't inconceivable that we might spend additional seasons in Sanden'. In its early weeks *I de beste familier* had average audiences of 900,000 and was one of the most popular programmes showing in Norway at the time. As the 'last' episode approached, viewing figures climbed even higher: the twentieth episode was watched by 1,023,000 viewers (out of a total population of some four-and-a-half-million), and was the fourth most viewed programme of the week (*VG*, 7 March 1995).

I de beste familier is centred on the Wahring family which owns and runs the local hotel, the Sanden Strandhotell, itself in real life the quite well-known Hurum Hotell in the village of Filtvet on the western side of the Oslo fjord. Elin, 40 years old, both owns and runs the hotel and lives in it with her two children, the seventeen-year-old Petter and the twelve-year-old and incredibly precocious Lillema (a truly virtuoso performance by young actress Vera Karena Øian). Elin had previously been married to Willy Wahring, who had been lost in an accident at sea some four years before the narrative started (in true soap style, his body had never been found, leaving open the possibility of an unexpected return), and at the beginning of the serial she has recently begun a new relationship with Magne Asbjørnson, a teacher from Oslo who has just got a permanent job in the local school. Her mother-in-law, the wealthy and, at least initially, interfering and rather snobbish Marie Wahring (also a quite excellent performance by established Norwegian actress Ingerid Vardund, who had also appeared in *Hjemme hos oss*), lives in a large house not far from the hotel. Vemund Wahring, Marie's other son and Elin's brother-in-law, is the local policeman. Elin's older brother Geir Lervik runs a mechanical workshop also close to the village, and lives with his wife Sissel and his teenage daughter Kristin, who is the same age as Petter.

The opening sequence to *I de beste familier* began with a helicopter shot of shimmering sunlit water with the hotel eventually coming into view. Views of the main characters, either singly or in pairs, were then alternated with further helicopter views of the hotel grounds and other houses where the characters variously live. This was accompanied by a soft and relaxed theme tune with the melody first picked out on an acoustic guitar and then on an oboe. The mood created by the music and the shots of the characters is one of harmony and good-naturedness: all very appropriate, since *I de beste familier* is without any doubt the most idyllic soap opera to have appeared anywhere in Europe in the course of the 1990s.

The opening scene of the first episode involved a conflict between Petter and his mother over the fact that she has started a new relationship, with Marie Wahring initially taking Petter's side. This leads to a number of anxious moments later when Elin and Magne organize a formal dinner to announce that he is moving in with her. But, with one exception to which I shall return below, this is about as tense as *I de beste familier* gets. And the conflict doesn't last. Lillema eventually convinces Petter that he is being selfish, and he and Magne become good friends. Even Marie eventually changes her spots and pays for Elin and Magne to take a week's holiday in London and basically works herself to a standstill running the hotel for them in their absence. By the end of episode 21 we are sorry to see her go.

No long-running narrative – and, however short by soap standards, 21 episodes is fairly lengthy for a television narrative – can survive without complications and conflicts of one kind or another. And, of course, these do crop up regularly in *I de beste familier*. Bendik absconds from the army and ends up in trouble with the military police. He begins a relationship with Kristin, who becomes pregnant. Vemund finds it difficult, initially, to adjust to the fact that his new assistant is a woman. There are occasional tiffs between Elin and Magne. But it's all extremely understated. The only conflict in this soap which produces real heat as opposed to sparks relates to Geir and Sissel. His business runs into trouble, she takes on a job as a cleaner at a local school, opens her own bank account, and this disruption of their accustomed roles leads to frustration and resentment all round. They bawl and shout at each other while the alienated Kristin is on the phone, and indeed he eventually moves out to live on his own, but theirs are the only voices to be raised in anger in all 21 episodes.

In fact, despite the upsets and occasional spats, *I de beste familier* is a world which radiates warmth. There is no room here for either glamour or passion. Elin and Magne are not passionate about each other, they are fond of each other, the occasional fall-outs notwithstanding (in one scene in the first episode he actually tears off his shirt in mock passion, much to her amusement). Kristin is bewildered and vulnerable in her unexpected pregnancy, but after his initial shock, Bendik accepts his responsibilities, and appears to feel real affection for her. In fact, the only character who speaks about sex at all – at times unstoppably – is the irrepressible Lillema. *I de beste familier* is not really about sex in the way that many European soaps are. It's about a mini-society whose members offer each other unstinting mutual support.

All of this reached its fitting climax in the twenty-first episode when Geir and Sissel came back together, Bendik asked Kristin to marry him, Vemund and Silje finally left hand-in-hand after having tiptoed nervously around each other for a good number of episodes. The last scene showed Elin and Magne standing on the jetty: 'Magne, I think maybe we should have a little baby together,' she says, before they head back to the warmth of the hotel glowing against the dark winter sky. There was a bit of a punch-up at Petter's eighteenth birthday party, but none of it seemed to matter very much as the rowdy elements were bundled off in a taxi by Bendik, Trine kissed Petter better on the stairs, and Kristin finally said 'yes' to Bendik's question – an ending entirely in keeping with the narrative as a whole; a seamless finish to a warm and cosy duvet.

A suburban soap: De syv søstre

The first episode of *Familiesagaen: De syv søstre* (Family Saga: the Seven Sisters) went out on TV2 on Saturday 21 September 1996 at 20.00. It is produced for TV2 by the independent production company Rubicon, and the storylines are, in fact, written by two Swedes, Peter Emmanuel Falck and Christian Wikander, whose wide experience of the soap-opera format includes the Swedish soaps *Varuhuset*, *Storstad*, *Rederiet* and *Tre Kronor* (see pp. 180–3). In order to keep their storylines in tune with current events in Norway, they read several Norwegian newspapers every day for six months prior to the beginning of production. *De syv søstre* is a once-a-week soap, each episode lasting 30 minutes. It was planned to show a minimum of 52 episodes, with the option of continuing 'endlessly' (*VG*, 26 November 1996). In fact screening was suspended around February 1997, though it is due to resume in Autumn 1997.

De syv søstre is set in Solbekk, a suburb of a fictitious Norwegian town which is not in fact identified. However, the first shot of the opening sequence – a view of a somewhat craggy fjord – together with the accents in particular of the younger characters suggest somewhere on the west coast. Its action centres mainly around four families: the Frydenlunds, the Birkelands, the Sivertsens and the immigrant Shah family; and indeed, after the initial establishing shot of the fjord and of one of the houses which feature in the soap, the opening sequence consists of the various family groups posing for photographs. The title of the soap is taken from the name of a circle of women friends which includes all the important female characters (as well as the homosexual Roy Bakke as a kind of 'half-sister'). In the first episode the women involved celebrated the fortieth anniversary of the circle, Nelly Frydenlund having been a member of it throughout that entire period.

De syv søstre raises tough issues: adolescent sex (Gry Birkeland is fourteen, and the fifteen-year-old Steinar Frydenlund believes he is the father of her baby), alcoholism, gang violence and petty crime. It tackles prejudices, such as racial prejudice or anti-gay prejudice, openly. Frode Birkelund's homophobia in relation to Roy is explicitly raised by the soap. Frode is unequivocally constructed as the villain in this particular respect, and in the end agrees to visit Roy's club with him – the Club Garbo – where he eventually dances with him and even agrees to kiss him. But the prejudices raised by *De syv søstre* are not just personal. The Shah family suffer from institutional discrimination both from private companies and from the public authorities. On the one hand a health inspector threatens not to give them a health certificate without good reason to deny it, on the other they find it extremely difficult to get insurance for the Café Bristol, this problem only being solved when Nelly convinces her husband Haakon – despite his initial reservations – to use his influence within the local business community to rectify the situation ('There's always been injustice in the world,' he says, 'And should we just accept it?' she answers sharply).

After a slowish start – it had around 350,000 viewers in the first weeks – *De syv søstre* eventually established itself as one of the most popular programmes in Norway, and certainly one of the most popular programmes on TV2, with over 600,000 viewers in November 1996, simultaneously topping the viewing charts for 12- to 24-year-olds (*VG*, 26 November 1996).

An industrial soap: Offshore

NRK's second soap opera, *Offshore*, began in November 1996. It goes out on Sunday evenings at 20.00, in half-hour episodes. There was to be a minimum of 60 episodes, but in fact the serial is still running in late 1998. As NRK's Head of Drama Oddvar Bull Tuhus put it – presumably referring to *I de beste familier* – 'NRK will never again stop a successful soap opera the way we did before' (*VG*, 26 November 1996). As the title suggests, some of the action takes place on an offshore oil platform (though the bulk actually takes place on land).

Offshore has a very dramatic opening sequence. It begins with a shot of an oil rig taken, presumably, from a boat as it sweeps past at a distance of perhaps a couple of hundred yards. This section is accompanied by a rather melancholy air played on what sounds like a panpipe. The words 'Offshore' then appear at the bottom of the screen in large, overlapping, orange letters, the music switches to fast-paced electric guitar music with a heavy drum backing, and the scene changes to views of oil workers abseiling down hawsers, tightening drilling pipes with enormous wrenches, even dancing in their oilskins and hard hats on the deck. With the rig still in the background, the centre of the screen then shows various scenes featuring the main characters. The sequence then ends with the camera appearing to go into the giant flame caused by the gases being burned off at the rig.

The extent to which this opening actually adumbrates the serial itself varies a great deal from one section to the other. The part that the production most signally fails to live up to is the muscularly industrial roughneck images of the second section. Although there are a number of establishing shots of the rig used at regular intervals in the soap – shots of helicopters landing on helipads and the like – the bulk of the action there takes place, for very obvious reasons, in those parts of the rig which could be more or less convincingly mocked up in the studio: the cabins, the canteen and the kitchens. In the episodes of *Offshore* I have seen so far, I have yet to see anyone doing what might reasonably be termed industrial work (in this respect *Offshore* differs radically from the 1996 British production *Roughnecks*, for example, where entire episodes could be set – and at least partly filmed – on a rig and oily-faced characters were often seen doing the kind of work oil workers might actually be expected to do).

Offshore is based on three main family groups, the Torgersens, the Hartlovsens and the Bergs. Hroar Torgersen is the managing director of North West Oil, the company which owns the Huldra oilrig on which a certain amount of the action takes place (the various establishing shots were actually filmed on the Statfjord C-platform in the North Sea). Both he and his wife Barbara are involved in much business intrigue, for example when they scheme to have the drilling contract awarded to Atlantic Drillers, in which Barbara has shares, as opposed to Norsk Drilling with whom they have always worked in the past. These business intrigues include attempts to outmanoeuvre the oilworkers' trade union, promoting awkward people into jobs where they can control them more easily, and so on.

The Hartlovsens live close to the Torgersens, with the mother Hanne living with Steinar Lindbek, who at the beginning of the serial was the deputy platform chief on the Huldra. While the Torgersens and the Hartlovsens appear to be well-off and live in large and well-appointed town houses, the Berg family, who live in the more northerly part of Norway between Trondheim and Tromsø known as Nordland, is much more proletarian. The son, Gunnar, works on the rig and lives in the rather cramped family home with his parents Aslaug and Ola, his wife Charlotte and their very young baby Ola William.

The age range of the characters in *Offshore* is more compressed than that of *De syv søstre*, with young teenagers and OAPs having only a token presence. On the other hand its social range is much greater, from the *haute bourgeoisie* to the platform workers and the catering staff. Its geographical extension is much greater, and it is more linguistically varied: as well as differences of lifestyle, there are also notable differences of accent between the various groups, the Torgersens' more or less standard *bokmål* contrasting perceptibly with the strong west-coast accents of much of the platform staff and the more *nynorsk*-leaning speech of the Bergs and, at times, even of the Hartlovsens.[1] Class differences are openly acknowledged. During a meeting between management, trade unions and outside consultants regarding safety on the rig following a fire, Hroar complains that it's difficult for him to 'play ball' as shop steward Thorbjørn Lindbek asks if no one will pass it to him. 'But we're not playing in the same team,' responds Thorbjørn.

Unlike *De syv søstre*, *Offshore* is definitely not a young person's soap. In the week in which *De syv søstre* topped the young viewers' chart, *Offshore* did not even make the top ten, with only 75,000 viewers in this category (*VG*, 26 November 1996). Despite this, it is, by some distance, the most popular fiction programme in Norway today and is one of the most popular television programmes in general, having worked its way up from 600,000 viewers to almost a million, and it looks set to run for some considerable time to come.

Analysis

I de beste familier was presented by NRK as being based more on a British model and as being deliberately opposed to what it saw as an American style of programme-making. As NRK's own documentation puts it:

this series is meant as a counterbalance to the often unrealistic American TV series which many people associate with this genre ... In Britain classic series such as *Coronation Street* (with 40 years on the box) and *EastEnders* still command a wide and loyal viewing audience. And it is in fact this British tradition, with its realistic view of people's daily lives, which is the ideal for *In the Best of Families*, rather than American series such as *Dynasty* and *Dallas*, which depict jet-set lifestyles that very few viewers can identify with.

The overall aim of this approach – helped by visits to the producers of *EastEnders* and *Emmerdale* in England as well as to the producers of *Rederiet* in Sweden – was to 'create an entertaining family serial with roots in our recognisable environment'. However, if the commitment to recognizable, unspectacular and by-and-large convincing narrative settings is, in a broad sense, 'British' rather than American – at least as far as soap operas are concerned – that is really about as far as any similarity between *I de beste familier* and the British soaps goes. Life was never this harmonious in the Crossroads Motel – *Crossroads* being the only British soap to feature an establishment similar to the Strandhotell – and it is certainly not this harmonious in any of the UK's more-or-less rural soaps: *Emmerdale* in England, *Pobol y Cwm* in Wales or *High Road* in Scotland. And the contrast between the kind of world constructed by *I de beste familier* and *EastEnders* or *Brookside* is positively striking.

Although the social extremes are much less far apart in Norway than in Great Britain, for example, and Norway's very considerable wealth – it is one of the richest countries in the world in terms of GNP per capita – together with its long period of social democratic government and highly developed welfare state have combined to produce a society with a high level of general affluence, this does not mean that Norway is not a class society, nor that social tensions do not exist there. However, the idea of being part of a *structurally* differentiated society is almost completely lacking in *I de beste familier*. This is perhaps the most striking difference between *I de beste familier* and Swedish soaps such as *Varuhuset* or *Rederiet*. The employing class – or however we wish to classify them – are not simply ex-nominated in the Barthesian sense (Barthes, 1973: 138); they just aren't there (or, to be more precise, they are reduced to Geir Lervik's extremely small-scale mechanical workshop). To the extent that *I de beste familier* is about Norway rather than just about the Wahring family, it is also Norway that is being presented as 'In the Best of Families'.

I de beste familier featured the rather bohemian character Sverre Avløs, whose eleven-year-old son turned up unexpectedly about halfway through the episodes. Terje strikes me as being particularly important in this respect. The fact that he is black is in no sense coincidental. On his first appearance in *I de beste familier* I was immediately and involuntarily reminded of a key moment in the closing ceremony of the Lillehammer Winter Olympics in February 1994 (the whole question of a 'non-American' approach had been very much a key issue in the preparations for these Games as well (see Bryn 1993)). One of the main parts of the opening ceremony was a lengthy snow ballet featuring mythical creatures known as the *vetter* who lived underground in Norway and emerged to bring a message of harmony and peace to the world. The *vetter* reappeared in the closing ceremony, dressed in white, just as the Declaration of Human Rights was being read out. At this point the camera very deliberately focused on one child in particular who was black. The television producer took the view that this was one of the most important moments of the televised version of the event:[2] it presented Norway as a country where to be Norwegian was not just to be Nordic or Sámi (the Lapp minority in the far north of the country, who also featured heavily in the opening ceremony), but to be black, brown or indeed of any other colour/ethnic origin. I find myself drawn more and more to the conclusion that, if the story of the *vetter* was a Norwegian fairytale for international consumption, *I de beste familier* is, on at least one level, a Norwegian fairytale for internal consumption. Even the bad fairy Marie Wahring becomes a fairy godmother at the end, looking forward to the arrival of new grandchildren via Vemund.

I de beste familier attracted a certain amount of criticism in the Norwegian press for being a soap opera in which 'nothing very much happened'. While, at least from an action-oriented perspective, this is to some extent true, the popularity of the programme was beyond dispute: viewing figures of over one million are very healthy by Norwegian standards. And yet the production was not, in fact, continued, the twenty-first episode broadcast in March 1995 proving to be the last (and there seems no possibility that it will ever be resuscitated now, not least since two of the actors, Christoffer Staib and Kalle Øby, who played Petter and Geir respectively, are currently appearing in NRK's new soap *Offshore*). There are technical reasons which might go some way towards explaining this. The woman whose brainchild *I de beste familier* was – Karin Bamborough, NRK's Head of Drama – left the NRK even before the serial was completed. But the real reasons may lie in the narrative itself. A number of lines were left open at the end of the twenty-first episode: Would Geir and Sissel stay together? What would become of Kristin and Bendik? Would Magne and Elin begin a family? What would Petter's future life look like? Not much to go on, in fact, and it would almost certainly have been impossible to maintain interest in these developments and, at the same time, maintain the idyllic nature of the narrative as a whole. Something would have had to give, and the bubble would have burst. In the end, soap opera and fairytale are almost certainly incompatible in the longer term.

The Norway constructed by *De syv søstre* is a very different and much more complicated Norway than that constructed by *I de beste familier*. As regards the social standing of its characters, *De syv søstre* is shot with a wide-angle lens (with some blind spots) as opposed to *I de beste familier*'s narrowly-focused aperture. It combines the slightly old-fashioned, upper-class family business environment of Frydenland & søn with the lower-middle-class Birkelands and Shahs and the downwardly-mobile Sivertsens. Beneath this – jumping over the working-class almost entirely – is the rather intimidating criminal world previously occupied by Espen Hjeltevik and, at the beginning of the serial, still occupied by Jannicke Haugland, who, at that time, was working as a prostitute in Oslo. Bjarte Sivertsen also lives on the edge of this world, throwing a bomb into the Café Bristol after losing it to the Shahs. Even the Birkelands are drawn into this violent world by him when it turns out – to everyone's astonishment and horror – that he is the father of Gry's baby, and that she had become pregnant after having been raped by him.

Offshore is in turn a very different kind of soap opera from *De syv søstre*. Issues are dealt with at what might almost be called a philosophical level.

When Robert Torgersen is discovered lying about crashing the car he finds himself on the receiving end of a stern lecture from Hroar about the importance of self-respect in a person's life. When Charlotte Berg informs her parents that she has no intention of fulfilling their wish for her to become a concert pianist, she informs them that she does not know who she is and that they have no idea who they are themselves either. The unusual nature of this approach can be highlighted by comparing the treatment of this last storyline with a somewhat similar one in the German soap *Jede Menge Leben* (see page 77) dealing with Frau Padun and her musically-gifted daughter. Granted the daughter was much younger in the German soap, but the conflict was essentially the same. However, in *Jede Menge Leben* the conflict was reasoned out by the adults involved using what might be called popular psychology ('you are simply using your daughter to gain vicarious glory for yourself'), while in *Offshore* the questions raised are of an entirely different order ('try to find out who you are, it's never too late').

Linked with this more philosophical approach is the whole style of the production. *Offshore* is slow and moody, sombre even. While there is a kind of general rule in European soap operas that at least one of the concurrent storylines should be lighter than the others (see, for example, Geißendörfer (1996) for the 'rules' followed in *Lindenstraße*) it can happen that all the storylines in an episode of *Offshore* are heavy or conflictual. The episode containing the funeral of Per Guldbrandson is, I believe, one of the most sombre episodes of any soap opera I have ever seen. This sombreness is also intensified by the general *mise-en-scène*, with shots of dimly-lit, narrow corridors on the rig, of dark interiors, particularly in the Torgersens' house, with often very striking use of chiaroscuro, and a soundtrack which at times sounds like an ancient lament. This is the aspect of *Offshore* which is most accurately prefigured by the first section of the opening sequence. Each episode also closes with a view of the rig shrouded in mist as night descends.

Soap opera, like television in general, has come late to Norway. It was originally clearly marked by a desire to avoid criticisms of 'American-ness' and to link into what was seen as a more 'British' style of 'realist' ongoing drama. But, as pointed out earlier, 'Britishness' has to be understood here in the very broad sense of 'non-glamourous'. In fact, while there had been very large audiences for the glamourous American soap *Dynasty* in Norway in the 1980s – even though interest did fade towards the end (Gripsrud, 1995: 101–3) – there was little enduring interest in *real* nitty-gritty British soap opera in the 1990s, as evidenced by the fact that *EastEnders* was taken off the air after a relatively short run there at the beginning of the decade. *I de beste familier* cannot be understood by reference to British soaps, but has to be seen within the framework of a complex set of discourses and practices occurring in Norway in and around 1994.

The new soaps have brought very different styles and very different moods with them. Both *De syv søstre* and *Offshore* relate to their Norwegian audience by dramatizing issues which are seen as both contemporary and relevant by that audience. As Jostein Gripsrud put it in a short interview in the issue of *VG* mentioned earlier (26 November 1996), 'Both serials take up issues which reflect Norway today, in the form of topics such as immigration, conflicts in the workplace, the battle of the sexes and various social problems.' Both explicitly problematize class differences and social tensions. For all the fact that *De syv søstre* and the Swedish soap *Tre Kronor* are written by the same two people, they are actually very different soaps. In *De syv søstre* society has not been flattened out into an undifferentiated middle-class. Class structures continue to be visible, materially present and important, and it is in its own way much darker and more hard-hitting than the Swedish production. In much the same way as the complex relationship between soap viewers and soap producers in the UK did not allow the teen soap *Hollyoaks* to survive as an out-and-out 'new-style' soap, but have gradually brought it into the orbit of the older soaps, so the expectations of the Norwegian audience has kept Norway's teen soap closer in spirit to its adult soap. The Frydenlands in *De syv søstre* are presented positively when they show solidarity and understanding, the Torgersens – Barbara in particular – are depicted as trivial and narrow-minded while the oil-rig workforce – both the drillers and the catering staff – carry most of the positive values of *Offshore*. The social-democratic vision appears to have maintained a strength in Norway which it has to some extent lost elsewhere (though this is not to suggest that it does not have opponents also in Norway). No doubt Norway's decision not to join the European Union is at least to some extent both an expression of and a contributory factor to that continuity.

Notes

1. The Norwegian language has two written conventions: *bokmål*, based largely on the dialects spoken in and around Oslo, and *nynorsk*, based on a number of west coast dialects. See Gripsrud (1995: 74) for a brief discussion of this issue. A more detailed analysis can be found in Trudgill (1983: 161–6).
2. This interesting piece of information was passed on to me by Roel Puijk of the Høgskolen i Lillehammer, co-ordinator of an international project analysing coverage of the Lillehammer Winter Olympics in a range of countries. For further information see Puijk (1997).

Portugal

Television in Portugal

Portugal's first television station, Radiotelevisão Portuguesa (RTP), went on air on 7 March 1957, and until 1974 was highly controlled by the dictatorship first of Salazar, and then of Marcello Caetano (Ferreira, 1992: 183–4). Its second channel, TV2, began broadcasting on Christmas Day 1968. Following the revolution of 25 April 1974, RTP was transformed into a public company with its directors appointed by the state. The licence fee, previously an important source of income for RTP, was scrapped by the government on 26 January 1991.

Legislation passed in 1991 allowed for the creation of private television companies in Portugal. The two which eventually emerged on 6 October 1992 and 20 February 1993 respectively (Cádima, 1996: 156) were SIC (Sociedade Independente de Comunicação), controlled by the Balsemão group set up by former Prime Minister Pinto Balsemão, and TVI (Tele-visão Independente) belonging to the Rádio Renascença group and linked with the Catholic Church. TVI is, to my knowledge, the only station to have had such official links in western Europe.

The 1990s have been a difficult period for RTP, which, along with the loss of licence revenues, has also found the competition of SIC, in partic-ular, very difficult to deal with. At the moment SIC is the market leader with around 48 per cent of the audience, RTP's Canal 1 takes around 34 per cent, TVI has in the region of 12 per cent and TV2 around 6 per cent.

Domestic *telenovelas* in Portugal

Portugal was the first European country to experience the Latin American *telenovela*, imported Brazilian products arriving there shortly after the 1974 revolution (Martín-Barbero, 1995: 283), and with productions such as *Gabriela* attracting huge audiences and triggering enormous debates in the media at large (Marques de Melo, 1995: 324). The large-scale presence of these Brazilian products in the Portuguese market is crucial for an understanding of the development of the domestic *telenovela* in Portugal since, contrary to what is frequently thought, the production values of these *telenovelas* are often very high (O'Donnell, 1996a). Indeed, cinematic production values have been standard in Brazilian *telenovelas* since *Beto Rockefeller* in 1969 (Lopez, 1995: 262). The structural influence of the Brazilian *telenovela* can be seen in such elements as the length of the Portuguese *telenovela* – in both countries the average number of episodes is now around 150–60 – and also in the use of song, which in both Brazilian and Portuguese productions is frequently foregrounded, filling the entire soundtrack for quite lengthy periods, and it is not uncommon for the songs subsequently to be sold on cassette or CD (this was the case in Portugal with Paco Bandeira's soundtrack for *Roseira Brava*, for example).

No doubt partly as a result of this early Brazilian influence, Portugal was also the first European country to produce *telenovelas* of its own, being some ten years ahead of its nearest 'rivals' in this field: Italy and Greece. The first Portuguese *telenovela* appeared in 1982, and a list of productions in the 1980s is as follows: *Vila Faia* (1982: 100 episodes), *Origens* (Origins) (1983: 120 episodes), *Chuva na Areia* (Rain on the Sand) (1985: 88 episodes) and *Palavras Cruzadas* (Crosswords) (1987: 120 episodes). I have no acquaintance with these early productions, though some are still being repeated on RTP even today.

Though the production of domestic *telenovelas* has continued in Portugal in the 1990s, it is important to point out that the most popular television serials continue to be Latin American, and overwhelmingly Brazilian, much to the annoyance of those involved in the production of the domestic *telenovelas* and to the annoyance of certain cultural élites within Portuguese society. Brazilian *telenovelas* have continued to be the most popular programmes even after the arrival of the two new commercial channels SIC and TVI. In fact, early attempts by SIC to break the dominance of RTP centred quite precisely on screening alternative peak-time Brazilian *telenovelas*. This strategy immediately began to close the gap on Canal 1, and since 1995, having signed an exclusive contract with the Brazilian giant TV Globo – the largest and most experienced producer of *telenovelas* in the world – thereby depriving RTP of its usual source of Brazilian productions, SIC has begun to dominate television ratings with its prime-time Brazilian offerings. First *Irmãos Coragem* (Brothers Courage) and then *A Próxima*

Vítima (The Next Victim) regularly scored over 20 per cent, a development which, as we shall see later, has had a considerable influence on the timing of Portugal's domestic *telenovelas*. SIC's subsequent imports such as *Explode Coração* (Explode Heart), *O Rei do Gado* (The King of the Cattle) and *A Indomada* (The Untamed) have continued to top the ratings.

After a five-year break, RTP's domestic production began again in the early 1990s when it became clear that the introduction of private channels was now unstoppable. These new *telenovelas* have been *Cinzas* (Ashes) (1992: 150 episodes), *A Banqueira do Povo* (The People's Banker) (1993: 130 episodes), *Verão Quente* (Hot Summer) (1993–4: 130 episodes), *Na Paz dos Anjos* (In the Peace of the Angels) (1994: 160 episodes), *Desencontros* (Mismatches) (1995: 150 episodes), *Roseira Brava* (Wild Rose) (1996: 130 episodes), *Primeiro Amor* (First Love) (1996: 130 episodes) and *Vidas de Sal* (Lives of Salt) (1996–7: 150 episodes). A new production entitled *Filhos do Vento* (Children of the Wind) (1997–8: 150 episodes) went on air recently, with *A Grande Aposta* (The Big Gamble) now in production. All of these *telenovelas* have been produced by Nicolau Breyner Productions (NBP) for RTP and screened on Canal 1.

Although I saw a small number of episodes of both *A Banqueira do Povo* and *Verão Quente* while they were actually showing, my real acquaintance with domestic Portuguese *telenovelas* dates from *Na Paz dos Anjos*. However, given the sheer number of these productions and the speed of their turnover (which is about twice as fast as the turnover of Catalan *telenovelas*, for example), and in view of the fact that I am inevitably more familiar with some than with others, I should like to concentrate, from different angles, on *Na Paz dos Anjos*, *Desencontros*, *Roseira Brava* and *Vidas de Sal*.

A humorous serial: Na Paz dos Anjos

Na Paz dos Anjos began in April 1994, and combined a traditional *telenovela* format with strong elements of comedy. It was set in the fictitious town of Riberia dos Anjos, and its main storyline, if indeed it can be called that, related to Sebastião Ribeiro and the miraculous microchip he had invented, and the various moves by others to gain possession of it (he threw it into the sea in the final episode, something which is very much in keeping with the serial as a whole). *Na Paz dos Anjos* combines elements of pastiche with self-parody. The *TV Guia Internacional* (April 1996) described it as follows: 'It seeks out the humour of the thirties and forties, of the films of Vasco Santana and António Silva, giving them an up-to-date form.'

Some of the plotlines are outrageous, the characters grimace and gesture in a manner which is positively camp, the sound effects are completely over the top – cymbals when something surprising is announced, castanets, drums, arpeggios and so on. Both the music and the gestures constantly undermine the content of the storylines: jaunty melodies accompany a mother begging her daughter to come home, business plans are discussed against a background of dance music and the like. And all this is mixed in with the kidnap of Sebastião and his fiancée Teresa, a sequence during which he is badly beaten up and she is threatened with sexual assault. In the midst of all this, one of the characters – an unnamed elderly gentleman who strolls around the town and plays absolutely no part in any of the storylines whatsoever – talks directly to camera at least once in every episode, commenting on events in Riberia dos Anjos and on how the relationships between its various inhabitants are developing. In the 50 or so serials I have analysed as part of this study, this is the only case I have found where one of the characters steps out of the diegetic world in this way during the actual narrative (see the chapter on German soaps, however, for a variation on this theme).

A cops-and-robbers serial: Desencontros

Desencontros, which began in January 1995, was a (relatively) fast-paced tale of both business and love intrigue with a strong crime-story plotline. Its four main characters – Emídio, Alfredo, André and Bernardo – were all detectives, and Emídio's death in a shoot-out was a major event in the narrative. Much of the action (or much of the talking, to be more precise) took place in the smoke-filled police station, and it featured murders – the investigation of the murder of the engineer Rafael Antunes was the major storyline, involving a large number of the characters – shoot-outs, kidnappings, money laundering, property speculation and diamond smuggling.

Desencontros was at the centre of a heated polemic in Portugal in the summer of 1995 when it was taken from its original peak-time slot of 20.45 and moved to 21.30. The reason for this was RTP's attempts to counter the success of SIC's peak-time Brazilian *telenovelas* as mentioned above. Having been cut off from its traditional supply from Globo, RTP decided to screen *A Idade da Loba* (The Age of the She-Wolf) in direct competition with SIC's *Irmãos Coragem* at 20.45, simply shunting its own product forward 45 minutes. Though officially a joint production between RTP and the Brazilian company Bandeirantes, *A Idade da Loba* was in fact very much a Brazilian-style production, set in Rio de Janeiro and featuring overwhelmingly Brazilian actors: it was quite rightly described as 'very Brazilian' by *TV 7 Dias* of 21–27 July 1995.

The ensuing polemic revolved around this demotion of a Portuguese product from its peak-time slot in favour of a Brazilian one. It was widely argued that the Portuguese products – *Desencontros* in particular – were of higher quality and that the actors were significantly better. As Moita Flores, one of the authors of *Desencontros* put it: 'The telenovela *Irmãos Coragem* has a couple of good actors which keep it going while the others are "hams" who probably couldn't even get work here, while it is perhaps the opposite in *Desencontros*' (*TV 7 Dias*, 21 July 1994).

A dynastic serial: Roseira Brava

Roseira Brava, which began screening in January 1996, broke new ground for both NBP and RTP by being Portugal's first resolutely rural *telenovela*. The Wild Rose of the title is in fact the name of a sprawling estate in the Alentejo, the region of Portugal to the east and south of Lisbon across the Tagus. The theme tune, which is the closest thing to a Spaghetti-Western theme tune of any European serial I have encountered – is played out over scenes of the rolling plains of the Alentejo, complete with gliding storks and galloping wild horses, all viewed through a slowly revolving wagon wheel. There are a considerable number of location shots in every episode filmed in and around the fictitious village of Santo Estêvão, the real village of Brinches close to the town of Serpa, itself situated between the city of Beja and the Spanish frontier.

Roseira Brava in fact offers a number of remarkable similarities with the Catalan production *Nissaga de poder* which went on the air around the same time (see page 166). I am not suggesting any influence of one production on the other – or indeed, any knowledge of those involved in one production of even the existence of the other – since there is absolutely nothing to suggest that this might be the case, but the similarities are nonetheless striking. Both are rural; both feature a sprawling estate which is the main source of work for the local population, producing vines in Catalonia and cork in Portugal, and whose handing down through the family line is a source of conflict; both involve murderously unscrupulous owners – Mateu Montsolís in Catalonia, Raul Navarro in Portugal – who will stop at nothing to get their own way and to get the woman they want, and who combine life in the country with business in the capital; both feature a young lawyer who decides to stay in the country rather than be tempted by the high life of the city. There are even coincidences of detail, such as the mysterious fires which threaten to destroy the estates, the competitors whose outlets are ruthlessly closed off and who subsequently die (though in different ways), the unacknowledged sons (though these are of vastly differing ages).

Despite the similarities, however, the symbolic worlds constructed by these two soaps are very different. While moral protagonism in *Nissaga de poder* lies clearly with a group of young technocrats who form an alliance with the agricultural workers against both the paternalistic old regime and the cut-throat, neo-liberal vanguard (see page 168), moral protagonism in *Roseira Brava* lies with Matilde Vilhena and those around her. Matilde is a good-looking but unglamorous woman in her mid-forties (she dresses in a low-key, down-on-the-farm way) who stands at the centre of all the major conflicts of the narrative. She is surrounded by individuals and groups with whom she is constantly contrasted, usually positively, though in different ways. Within the world of the village she contrasts both with the older peasant women who are very deferential, unmodern in their dress, and locked into a world of small-town gossip and religiosity. She contrasts with the brutal entrepreneurialism of Raul Navarro, who, like Fèlix Montsolís in *Nissaga de poder*, thinks nothing of firing workers whose families have worked on the estate for generations since he thinks it would be more profitable to turn it into a tourist complex (the old-style paternalist approach is represented in *Roseira Brava* by Raul's aunt Rita). She also contrasts strongly with the glamorous Lisbon young things who have been sucked into Raul's world of unfeeling business manoeuvering. In short, moral leadership does not lie in *Roseira Brava* with a group of young university graduates, but with a combative middle-aged woman in a small-town environment. She is not a flawless heroine, and commits more than one mistake as the story unfolds, but there is no doubt that she is the heroine of the piece.

A seaboard serial: Vidas de Sal

Vidas de Sal began in the second half of 1996 and continued into 1997. It is set in the fictitious village of Praia da Fé near the actual town of Sesimbra on the Bay of Setúbal, some twenty kilometres due south of Lisbon, views of which dominate the opening sequence. Praia da Fé is a fishing village, and the lives of the fishermen and their families and problems relating to fishing, not just on a Portuguese but also on an EU level, are an important part of the backdrop to the serial (a feature it shares with *Goenkale* in the Basque Country (see page 170)). There are frequent references to the difficulties caused to Portuguese fishermen by EU regulations: 'We know that the fact that our old-fashioned fishing methods make our fish more expensive than that of the Spaniards is incompatible with the progress of the country,' says one of the major characters in an episode towards the end of the production.

Despite this, however, *Vidas de Sal* is only partly about fishermen. The main character is Eugénia Reis, a woman in her 1970s (played by the same actress who played Rita Navarro in *Roseira Brava*). A widow, she has used her late husband's modest fortune to set up PescaRica, a company which eventually bought over the local fishermen, transforming them into its own fleet. The main conflict in *Vidas de Sal* is that between Eugénia and Vasco Tavares (played by Nicolau Breyner himself), the owner of the rival company FrigoPesca, though numerous other personal conflicts also arise to spice the mixture.

Though it had moments of high drama – the blockade erected by the fishermen to stop FrigoPesca's trucks reaching Praia de Fé was an interesting incident from many points of view – I personally found *Vidas de Sal* a less satisfying *telenovela* than *Desencontros* or *Roseira Brava*. These earlier productions were tautly written throughout, maintained a high level of dramatic energy until the end, and had strongly developed characters. *Vidas de Sal* seemed to me to run out of steam before it ran out of episodes, with dramatic interest being dispersed into numerous, at times rather frustrating, subplots as the ending approached.

Analysis

The Portuguese *telenovelas* made by Nicolau Breyner Produções for RTP are produced at breakneck speed. A 150-episode production is usually completed in around five months, at a rate of over one episode per day, and, unlike the Catalan productions, for example, the entire *telenovela* is 'in the can' before any of it goes on the air. In view of the extreme time pressures under which they are put together, it has to be said that the production values of these *telenovelas* are surprisingly high. The first episodes, in particular, are often very impressive. In fact, the opening three minutes of *Roseira Brava*, which recount, in compressed form, the trial of António Barbosa and his sentence of eight years in prison, are positively cinematic in quality, and this is the most stunning opening to any television serial I have ever seen. There are a number of fairly obvious reasons for this. One is the need for a particularly striking opening in order to instantly involve the viewer in a new production. The other is that these opening episodes are routinely shown in preview to the press before the production goes on air, and it is important for their production values to be high in order to ensure good reviews. It would be fair to say that the following episodes of *Roseira Brava* do not quite keep up this level of sophistication. However, even if the opening episodes represent peaks in production values, the general quality level of these products is much higher than is often thought.

In view of this, how is their relatively poor performance *vis-à-vis* the imported Brazilian product to be explained? The greater popularity of the imported *telenovelas* is beyond question. In fact the polemic surrounding the timing of *Desencontros* in the Portuguese press makes little sense since the audience figures for the period in question show that while SIC's Brazilian *telenovelas* averaged around 22 per cent and peaked at 24 per cent, *Desencontros* rarely exceeded 12 per cent. It was always, in fact, fractionally behind even *A Idade da Loba*, even if only by a few decimal points, but the combined total for the two Brazilian productions with which it was competing was in the region of 34 to 36 per cent, substantially in advance of the viewing figures for the domestic product.

Martín-Barbero argues – as do a number of other Latin American scholars – that the Latin American *telenovela* plays a fundamentally modernizing role in Latin American societies, through 'its capacity to make an archaic narrative the repository for propositions to modernize some dimensions of life. The evolution and diversification of the genre has gradually introduced new themes and perspectives ... the public's complicity with the genre is in part due to the soap opera's permeability to the transformations of modern life' (1995: 281). Brazilian *telenovelas* in particular have been at the forefront of this endeavour, due largely to their origin in the 1960s as an oppositional form of popular culture during Brazil's long military dictatorship. The Portuguese *telenovelas* have been slow to develop this kind of potential. The difference is clearly acknowledged in Portugal. For example, the president of the Portuguese Viewers' Association wrote in the newspaper *Público* on 22 October 1995:

As a rule, the *telenovelas* from our sister country [Brazil] carry laudable, and in some cases even progressive social, cultural and political values. In fact, Brazilian *telenovelas* frequently defend women's rights, promote the modernisation of family and intergenerational relationships; denounce racism; attack caciquism and political clientelism (and, on occasions, criticise fascism, particularly as regards the military dictatorship which was in power in Brazil between the sixties and the 1980s); they promote democracy and democratic procedures; they attack corruption; they fight against prejudice; in short, they champion culture, progress, freedom of thought, scientific points of view, the desire to know and transform the world, brotherhood and generosity. In this, let's face it, they distinguish themselves from the Portuguese *telenovelas*, which are usually conformist and conservative.

In a review of *A Próxima Vítima* published in the *Diário de Notícias* of 19 October 1995 Guilherme de Melo also spoke of an incident in which the character Sandro had explained his homosexuality to his mother, pointing out that it was not a question of choice, that he had been born different from most of his friends, and demanding the right to live his life that way. The journalist described this as 'a scene which, as far as the public at large is concerned, will have done more to promote understanding of this problem (?) than all the debates and discussions held until now'. This view of homosexuality contrasts strongly with that taken by *Na Paz dos Anjos*, for example, where the homosexual hairdresser Clo – portrayed as Brazilian! – was an out-and-out caricature.

It would be very difficult to describe *Na Paz dos Anjos* as being in any way progressive. In fact, when viewing this production the term 'post-modern' came insistently to mind. *Na Paz dos Anjos* is in many respects strongly reminiscent of the German soap opera *Gute Zeiten, Schlechte Zeiten* in its 1994 phase: outrageous storylines, self-parodying acting, slapstick comedy, laughable cliff-hangers, and so on (see page 63). However, given post-modernism's links with at least relatively widespread economic affluence and an intense mediatization of social relations, there appear to be more grounds for applying such a term to media products in Germany than there are in the case of a relatively underdeveloped country such as Portugal ... unless, that is, we assume that *Na Paz dos Anjos* was aimed precisely at that sector of Portuguese society which is itself relatively affluent and at home with the self-referential and self-mocking nature of this kind of media output.

Viewing figures for the earlier Portuguese *telenovelas* support this view of a more narrowly defined target audience. For example, though popular – it rated seventh in Canal 1's listings for 20 to 26 December 1993 with a 20.7 per cent share of the total possible audience (*TVMais*, 31 December 1993) – the 1993–4 production *Verão Quente* never in fact seriously challenged the peak-time Latin American products which at their height could attract almost half of the total *potential* audience in Portugal. By March 1994 it had dropped out of Canal 1's top ten (*TVMais*, 25 March 1994), its average audience share over the whole period of its broadcast being just over 13 per cent. Figures for *Na Paz dos Anjos* were, if anything, somewhat lower at 10.4 per cent (whereas *Gute Zeiten, Schlechte Zeiten*'s post-modern phase earned it a very substantial increase in viewers), and indeed it was moved around the schedules considerably, much to the frustration of the actors.

There does appear to have been something of a change in the domestic *telenovelas* since *Desencontros* with its rough-hewn policemen and its more realistic feel. This change was referred to by José Mendes in an article published in *Expresso* on 6 January 1996. Referring to the author of *Desencontros* he wrote:

Ever since Moita Flores tried to use his free time in the CID to write 'Desencontros' the production of Portuguese *telenovelas* has been forced to change completely. Policemen and villains showed on screen that if there was anything that bound them together it was trueness to life. It is this search for believable characters, in a story in which the spectator can recognise something of himself, which inspires and guides 'Roseira Brava' ... after 'Desencontros' the touchstone now is the idea that the Portuguese are not interested in epics from the year dot or family sagas about people who 'have lost everything' and spend their lives and all the episodes sighing for the good old times.

And indeed *Roseira Brava*, *Primeiro Amor* and *Vidas de Sal* have tackled economic and ultimately political issues which were given little space earlier on. They have also gone for real-life settings, and have moved out of Lisbon exploring more and more different parts of the country.

The current production *Filhos do Vento* is set in the Ribatejo, the region of Portugal to the north-east of Lisbon on both sides of the Tagus, and, in a move reminiscent of *Metsolat* in Finland (see page 52), it deals not just with the present but also with the recent past. It in fact has two time frames, the first in the 1970s and the second in the 1990s, and it constantly shifts

between the two, centering on two generations of two feuding families, the
Abrantes and the Vieiras. It was described in *TV Guia Internacional* (May
1997) as follows: ' "Filhos do Vento" is a telenovela which attempts to
examine the processes of change in the Ribatejo and, in a broader context,
to examine the transformations of contemporary Portuguese society', and
according to its author Moita Flores it will deal with 'the great problems of
our day-to-day lives, such as euthanasia, the donation of organs, the nature
of the relationship between the courts and the media, violence in the family,
the question of single mothers, issues related to abandoned children and the
possibility of them being adopted, and other current themes' (whatever
happened to unemployment, which is *the* 'great problem of our day-to-day
lives' for many people?).

But despite these changes the Portuguese *telenovelas* continue to address
a mainly middle-aged, conservative audience. It is not that there are no
younger characters in these *telenovelas* – in fact they can be quite numerous
– but they are somehow always narratively outgunned by the older ones. In
Desencontros it was Emídio, by far the youngest of the detectives, who was
killed off. And though there were a number of love stories in this production, the one which eventually dominated at the end was that between
Raquel Antunes and Miguel Serpa, in their early forties and fifties respectively. As explained above, the moral centre of gravity in *Roseira Brava* is
provided by the 45-year-old Matilde and, though to a lesser extent, by the
somewhat older António Barbosa, while in *Vidas de Sal* it lies with the even
older Eugénia and António, both in their 1970s. I am not, of course,
suggesting that moral protagonism can never be vested in older characters
in television serials (Ingeborg in the Danish soap *Landsbyen* is a case in point
(see page 43)): what I am saying is that these productions make little effort
to include the younger characters in the moral universe of the older ones, or
to provide them with a coherent one of their own, often leaving them
isolated and stranded in the narrative as a result.

And there is still an overwhelming sense of caution and constraint. In
Desencontros Ana Serpa is berated by her wealthy mother on account of her
relationship with Emídio, since the mother does not view Emídio as a
suitable type of person for her. A very similar situation cropped up in early
1997 in the Spanish production *Vidas cruzadas*. But while Patricia in *Vidas
cruzadas* defended her own choices and poured scorn on her mother's point
of view (see page 172), Ana bowed to her mother's pressure and broke with
Emídio, only going back to him shortly before he was killed. And when the
fishermen set up a barricade to defend their livelihoods in *Vidas de Sal*, they
were lectured by countless characters that this was not the way to do things,
that there were 'proper procedures to follow'. In fact the Portuguese
telenovelas seem much more at home with conservative, traditional values
than with progressive ones: even the fact that production is completed
before they are screened seems to reflect an absence of nerve. When

statements of progressive values appear, they seem to make these because they feel obliged to, rather than because, as is the case of the Brazilian *telenovelas*, they are an organic part of their relationship with their audience, but the popularity of the Brazilian products shows clearly what the popular Portuguese audience wants.

In an interview given in *TV 7 Dias* on 1 September 1995 the actor Virgílio Castelo (he appeared in both *Roseira Brava* and *Vidas de Sal*) described the audience of the Portuguese *telenovelas* as follows: 'Portugal is not the Third World and the Portuguese public is a demanding public . . . I think we are a very developed people on that level, even though we might not be on an economic level, or a political level, or a social level.' What exactly he means by 'the Portuguese public' is not immediately clear, and whether this public is 'demanding' or not is an ideological question, not an aesthetic one. What is certain is that the popular audience *is* demanding something different from the domestic products which are currently available, and RTP's *telenovelas* will not attract that popular audience until its demands are understood and met at levels which extend far beyond the boundaries of television culture. It may be useful here to quote from Gramsci's analysis of the cultural panic caused among Italian intellectuals in the early part of the twentieth century by the fact that the reading material most in demand among Italy's popular classes was neither Italian nor contemporary, but in fact consisted of nineteenth-century French *feuilleton*-type novels such as Eugène Sue's *Mystères de Paris* (this cultural panic had striking similarities not just with the current situation in Portugal, but also with the panics which arose in many western European countries in the 1980s as a result of the popularity of *Dallas* and its stablemates). Speaking of this phenomenon, Gramsci wrote (Forgacs, 1988: 365, 367):

But in fact neither a popular artistic literature nor a local production of 'popular' literatures exists because 'writers' and 'people' do not have the same conception of the world. In other words the feelings of the people are not lived by the writers as their own, nor do the writers have a 'national educative' function: they have not and do not set themselves the problem of elaborating popular feelings after having relived them and made them their own . . . if people like the novels of a hundred years ago, it means that their taste and ideology are precisely those of a hundred years ago . . .

What is the meaning of the fact that the Italian people prefer to read foreign writers? It means that they *undergo* the moral and intellectual hegemony of foreign intellectuals, that they feel more closely related to foreign intellectuals than to 'domestic' ones, that there is no national intellectual and moral bloc, either hierarchical or, still less, egalitarian. The intellectuals do not come from the people, even if by accident some of them have origins among the people. They do not feel tied to them (rhetoric apart), they do not know and sense their needs, aspirations and feelings. In relation to the people, they are something detached, without foundation, a caste and not an articulation with organic functions of the people themselves.

Paraphrasing Gramsci, if the Portuguese popular audiences like Brazilian *telenovelas*, it means that their taste and ideology are precisely those of the Brazilian *telenovelas*. If they prefer Brazilian *telenovelas* to the domestic ones, it means that the domestic ones are out of touch with the tastes and the ideology of the popular audience.

In the final scene of the final episode of *Vidas de Sal* Eugénia Reis and Mestre António, both in their seventies, meet at the end of a long breakwater stretching out into the sea. 'Am I very late?' she asks. 'Forty years, Eugénia,' he replies, as the camera slowly zooms out and they gradually shrink to become indistinguishable dots seen from a distance of about a mile. And indeed, the Portuguese *telenovelas* produced so far have been living in the past and refusing stubbornly to catch up with the present other than in the most superficial ways and as a result continue to find themselves at some distance from society as a whole: as the *TV Guia Internacional* wrote of *Filhos do Vento* (January 1997): '"Filhos do Vento" looks to the past with one idea always in mind. We are always much more what we were than what we think we are.' The mass *telenovela* audience in Portugal is clearly asking for a more modern product and, I believe, a more modern society: indeed, political institutions in Portugal are increasingly under pressure from an ever more critical public (Braga da Cruz, 1995). Political resistance to those demands is accompanied by the cultural resistance of the domestic serial. Perhaps *Filhos do Vento* will represent a serious step forward. Only time will tell.

Postscript

The latest Brazilian *telenovela*, *A Indomada*, began on SIC in the last week of April 1997 and quickly went to the top of the viewing figures with audience shares of around 24 to 25 per cent, or some 2,126,000 viewers. In the same week *Filhos do Vento*'s shares were around 13 to 14 per cent, some 1,291,000 viewers, and it was placed nineteenth in the ratings.

Spain

Television in Spain

Spain's first television channel, the state-owned Televisión de España (TVE), started broadcasting on 28 October 1956. Funding from advertising was introduced in 1958, and, alone among European countries, Spain has never levied a television licence fee since. The second channel, TVE2, was introduced in September 1965, both stations being closely controlled by the state during the long Franco dictatorship. Following Franco's death in 1975 and the transition to a democratic system over the following two years, Spanish Television was given an entirely new statute in December 1978. This did not, however, completely abolish political influence in the running of the company: the members of the board of governors are still elected by the Spanish parliament, and the director general is appointed for a five-year term by the government in office.

In the 1980s the monopoly status of TVE was undermined from two different directions. The first of these was the appearance of regional television stations in a number of Spain's new Autonomous Communities, first Basque Television (ETB) in 1982, followed by the first Catalan channel TV3 in 1983, Televisión de Galicia (broadcasting in Galician) in 1985, and Canal Sur in Andalusia, Telemadrid in Madrid and Canal 9 in Valencia (broadcasting in Catalan), all in 1989. During the same period both ETB and Catalan Television went on to add second channels in their respective Communities. These regional channels, which have their own programming and purchasing policies, can attract very sizeable audiences, and are often the most popular channels in their particular Community, particularly where they broadcast in a language other than Castilian. In 1989 they joined together to form FORTA (the Federation of Autonomous Radio and

Television Organizations) in order to increase their collective strength.

The second major change was the arrival of the commercial national stations Antena 3, Canal + and Telecinco, set up following a complicated bidding process in 1989, and going on air in 1990 (Mateo and Corbella, 1992: 201–2). Antena 3 is a generalist channel very much in the style of TVE1 (now restyled as 'La Primera', TVE2 having become 'La Dos'), which it is now seriously challenging as the most viewed channel in Spain. Canal + is – like its sister French company – a subscription channel specializing in films whose programmes are encrypted. Telecinco – sometimes referred to as 'Tele Teta' ('Boobs TV') in view of its profusion of scantily-clad game hostesses – concentrates mostly on 'entertainment', from tumultuous game shows to often highly confrontational 'reality shows'. In recent years its market share has grown to over 20 per cent, and it attracts a primarily younger audience.

Domestic soaps and *telenovelas* in Spain

The main form of television serial in Spain in the 1980s was the Latin American *telenovela*, which made its first appearance in January 1986 with the Mexican production *Los ricos también lloran* (The Rich Also Cry). These were enormously successful in the late 1980s, with the Venezuelan *Cristal* attracting the second highest viewership of any programme by the time it ended in November 1990 (Villagrasa, 1992: 399). So great was their popularity that they became standard elements of Spanish conversation. As Villagrasa points out (415–16):

For the first time in the history of Spanish television, an afternoon soap was beating all the peak hour programmes. It also gained one of the most loyal followings among television programmes. *Cristal* and its leading actors became something of a social phenomenon stretching into all walks of life, even into political speeches on the state of the country.

The daily audience for *telenovelas* in the late 1980s was estimated by former presenter Pilar Gómez Miranda at between nine and twelve million (Roura, 1993: 74).

Though the initial craze for Latin American *telenovelas* in Spain has to some extent subsided, the mid-afternoon offering on TVE1 still attracts a large and faithful, mainly female, viewership (Roura, 1993: 16): for example, over five million people watched *Kassandra* in March 1994 (*La Vanguardia*, 13 March 1994). As *El País* points out (4 February 1994), 'these "housewives" provide the television companies with a faithful audience and juicy advertising contracts'.

Spain's earliest attempts at *telenovela* production all involved joint ventures with established Latin American producers. Success was not guaranteed. Villagrasa speaks of a joint production between Televisión Española, the Brazilian company TV Globo and the Swiss company RSI for a *telenovela* of 170 episodes each lasting 45 minutes (1992: 380). Unfortunately, no name is given for this production, and I have been unable to find any evidence that such a project was ever completed or put on air. A second production which he mentions, *El oro y el barro* (Gold and Mud), a 110-hour joint Spanish-Argentinian venture announced with a tremendous fanfare of publicity in Spain in 1992, was shown to disappointing audience ratings that year on Antena 3 (*El País*, 4 February 1994). More recent productions have been slightly more successful. *Déjate querer* (Let Yourself be Loved), Telecinco's prime-time *telenovela* shown in 1994, was a joint Spanish-Argentinian production, and Antena 3 continued to be active in this field, undertaking two further joint productions with South American producers: *Amor de papel* (Paper Love) with Venevisión of Venezuela and *El desprecio* (Scorn) with Radio Caracas, also of Venezuela, both of which were eventually screened.

Domestic production in Spain's Autonomous Communities

In the first half of the 1990s, the real success stories in television serial production in Spain were not to be found at the level of all-Spanish television, but in the television stations of the Autonomies, as the following will make clear.

Catalonia

A trail-blazing serial: Poble Nou

The first truly domestic *telenovela* to be produced in Spain was a Catalan production, appearing on TV3, and it was very much a *telenovela* with a difference. It was entitled *Poble Nou*, and was broadcast on a five-day-a-week basis throughout 1994 with a break in July and August, going out at 16.35 during what is known in Spain as the 'sobremesa' (or 'sobretaula' in Catalonia), the mid-to-late-afternoon period which, due to Spaniards' different eating times, constitutes a kind of secondary or even parallel prime-time. *Poble Nou* was entirely in Catalan, was not sub-titled, and was unavailable elsewhere in Spain. The title means quite literally 'New People', but Poblenou is also a district of Barcelona: the opening sequence flies over the newly-built waterfront Olympic Village before veering onto the much older Poblenou district, straddling Barcelona's main thoroughfare, the Avinguda Diagonal.

Like the Welsh-language soap *Pobol y Cwm* in Wales and the Gaelic soap *Machair* in Scotland (see pp. 193 and 201), *Poble Nou*'s aim was as much linguistic as televisual. It was seen as a central element in the official campaign to normalize the use of Catalan as the language of everyday life in Catalonia (during the Franco regime, as is well known, the public use of Catalan had been banned): indeed, the final credits of each episode included the names of its two 'language advisers'. This aspect of the programme attracted a certain amount of criticism, since it would in fact be quite difficult to find at least a public environment in Barcelona where everyone spoke Catalan quite so exclusively: Barcelona is the Catalan city where the percentage of Catalan speakers is lowest, at around 65 per cent (Atkinson, 1997), and Castilian is quite widely heard in public places. These criticisms were, of course, more common in the Castilian-language press. For example, the Barcelona daily *La Vanguardia* of 13 March 1994 ironized on how takes had to be re-shot because actors had used Spanish expressions instead of Catalan ones.

Despite this, by March 1994 *Poble Nou*'s audience had grown to 700,000 (a 33 per cent audience share), making TV3 the most watched channel in Catalonia from 15.35 to 16.00. In the words of the Catalan-language daily *Avui* (15 March 1994), *Poble Nou* was 'one step away from becoming a sociological phenomenon'. Its final episode in December 1994 was watched by over one-and-a-half million people (*El Temps*, 16 January 1995), the kind of audience normally only achieved in Catalonia by football matches between Barcelona and Real Madrid.

Dealing as it does with the day-to-day lives of a group of ordinary people living in Poblenou, *Poble Nou* clearly owed a debt to earlier Catalan productions such as *La Granja* (The Shop). But its thematic links with *EastEnders* – a soap which enjoys considerable success in Catalonia (but is not screened elsewhere in Spain) – were also obvious and in fact acknowledged: indeed *Poble Nou* took over *EastEnders*' previous time-slot. In *Poble Nou* people are quite literally seen working at the kitchen sink and carrying out other equally mundane tasks. *Poble Nou* is in fact something of a hybrid between a soap and a *telenovela*: in the words of the Valencian magazine *El Temps* (9 May 1994), it represented a cocktail made up with 'a little bit of *EastEnders*, a measure of *Neighbours*, a dash of Brazilian and Venezuelan *telenovelas*, and the appropriate amount of *La Granja*'.

Poble Nou centred on the various members of the Aiguader family (who learn in the opening episode that they have won the lottery). It has a kind of main storyline, provided by the fight by the inhabitants of Poblenou against dishonest architect Eudald Balcells who had initially offered them flats in the Olympic Village if they agreed to their existing houses being knocked down for redevelopment, but then tried to palm them off with flats on the outskirts of Barcelona instead, putting the flats in the Olympic Village on general sale: in fact the story of this struggle provided the material for a parallel storyline, that of a best-selling book – itself called *Poble Nou* – written by Anna Aiguader. However, this story is surrounded by a much larger group of parallel stories than would normally be found in a *telenovela*, and as the story proceeded there were breast cancers, drugs, murders, AIDS, scurrilous business dealings and so on. *Poble Nou* was originally scheduled to run for 120 episodes, and an ending had already been written for the final episode. However, due to its enormous success, the decision was taken to add another 70 episodes. The result of this was that the scriptwriters had to abandon their original ending and in mid-1994 still did not know how the serial would finish (*El Temps*, 9 May 1994). In the end the specially-extended final episode of *Poble Nou* was extremely positive and optimistic, with virtually all the problems raised in the preceding narrative resolved.

As clearly demonstrated by an audience analysis carried out when the fortieth episode was being screened, *Poble Nou* made the *telenovela* respectable viewing for a wide cross-section of Catalan society (including men), many of whom continued to have reservations of various kinds regarding the imported products. As *El Temps* of 9 May 1994 put it:

This study brought out a fundamental difference between *Poble Nou* and all previously known television serials: the viewers were not ashamed to admit that they followed it faithfully. If being hooked on a *telenovela* used to be almost a private vice, it has now become a new reason for being with other people, to such an extent that . . . many of those interviewed thought that not watching *Poble Nou* could isolate you from many conversations and from the population at large.

It set itself a clearly modernizing mission. As the chief writer Josep Maria Benet i Jornet (one of Catalonia's leading contemporary dramatists) put it in *El Temps* (9 May 1994):

We have a progressive view of society and human relationships . . . and we try to put these liberal values across through our characters' stories. We show a woman who is capable of living without having to depend on her husband, a homosexual couple who are not disapproved of and who behave like any other couple, a boy and a girl who go and live together without anyone making a fuss . . . we are doing this deliberately.

As reported in the same issue of *El Temps*, these views aroused discomfort in Opus Dei and public condemnation from the Archbishopric of Barcelona – no doubt a very positive outcome as far as the producers were concerned.

However, this *telenovela* also played a clear nation-building role within Catalonia – the role which, according to Columbian theorist Martín-Barbero (1987: 179) the Latin American *radionovela* and its successor the *telenovela* also play there. According to the same article in *El Temps*, the Head of Drama of TV3 had set one of the aims of the programme as follows:

it had to be a product for all ages, one which would bring together in front of the screen the grandmother and the grandson, who normally don't watch television together ... it had to try to identify with the majority of its audience by creating lower-middle-class characters as its starting point.

Poble Nou is a televisual contribution to that sense of 'convivència' ('living together') which is so essential to Catalan national identity (O'Donnell and León Solís, 1994). It contains working-class characters who earn their living working in supermarkets and pubs (but not in factories), while the very rich people to be found in the American supersoaps and some of the Latin American *telenovelas* are nowhere to be seen: the 'enemy' in *Poble Nou* is a municipal architect. Though its audience clearly included Castilian-speakers (*El Temps*, 22 May 1995), this Catalan-language *telenovela* attempted to create a sense of community in which language is an important factor. As the credits rolled on the final episode of *Poble Nou* in December 1994, the viewers were left looking at a caption superimposed on a night-time view of the Rambla de Poblenou which read 'We've come a long distance. And it has been made possible by you who are watching us. Thank you and goodbye.'

Following its completion on TV3, *Poble Nou* was sold to Antena 3 where it began screening in spring 1995. It was beamed throughout Spain in a dubbed version from 19.45 to 20.30 every weekday evening under the new title *Los mejores años* (The Best Years), but to nothing like the kind of audience shares it achieved in Catalonia (the dubbing was done, incidentally, by the original actors).

A spin-off serial: La Rosa

So great was the success of *Poble Nou* that it gave rise to a 29-episode spin-off entitled *La Rosa*, which started screening in October 1995. *La Rosa* was also written by Josep Maria Benet i Jornet and it centred on the mother, Rosa Aiguader, who had been the central character of *Poble Nou*. In this spin-off, Rosa, having left Antònio, moves together with her daughter Anna and her son Martí to Manresa, north-east of Barcelona, where she opens a bookshop. The opening sequence consists of a long aerial view not just of this charming Catalan city, but also of the spiralling rock formations of Montserrat, only a few miles distant from Manresa and the site of a famous monastery. In fact, 30 million pesetas was contributed to the budget of *La Rosa* by the town hall and various business organizations in Manresa, which allowed a much higher percentage of outside shots than in *Poble Nou*, some of them clearly designed to attract visitors. *La Rosa* went out once a week on Sundays, as opposed to *Poble Nou*'s five-day-a-week regime, and it quickly became the most popular Sunday programme in Catalonia, attracting an average of 800,000 viewers per episode (*El Temps*, 6 November 1995). *La*

Rosa differed from *Poble Nou* in at least one respect – in the character of Alfonso Duarte. Whereas *Poble Nou* had been 100 per cent Catalan, this Madrid lawyer, who had come to Manresa ten years before the beginning of the narrative following the death of his wife, normally spoke Catalan but would occasionally switch to Castilian in moments of high tension.

There were many adventures in *La Rosa*. They started with the disappearance of Anna's husband Jaume in Zaire (after having been presumed dead in a plane crash), but many of them centred on the brutish Francesc Raurell, who would not only rape Anna, but would also set fire to the bookshop in an attempt to force Rosa to move out so that he could sell the property to developers. However, like *Poble Nou*, *La Rosa* had a very optimistic ending with Anna being reunited with her husband and having her new book accepted by a Barcelona publisher, Martí patching up his differences with his girlfriend Clàudia despite the distracting attentions of the man-eating Llum and competition from the amiable but un-worldly-wise Jofre, and Rosa finally agreeing to marry Alfonso after many hesitations and uncertainties.

A tragic serial: Secrets de família

Poble Nou was immediately followed on TV3 by a second Catalan-language *telenovela* called *Secrets de família* (Family Secrets), beginning in the first week of 1995. *Secrets de família* was set in Girona, to the north of Barcelona, and had numerous shots of famous landmarks in that city. Unlike *Poble Nou* it also contained one Castilian speaker, the doctor Enrique, who talks resolutely in Spanish while all around speak to each other and to him in Catalan. Another character, doctor Canals, spoke Catalan with a noticeable Valencian accent.

Secrets de família revolves around the lives of the members of the Riera family, and its world is a very dark world indeed. As the story unfolds we learn that, while Dolors and Albert Riera were students at Barcelona University in 1969, Albert and his brother Narcís had in fact played cards for Dolors, and that, on losing, Narcís had left for the United States where he has been ever since. The initial complication of the narrative is provided by Narcís's return from the States for a heart operation. Although he attempts to keep this secret from the rest of the family, the son Aleix, a doctor, discovers it through his medical contacts. A whole string of events are then put in motion which not only disinter the appalling tragedies of the past but also unleash new tragedies in the present as Dolors's marriage with Albert disintegrates as she finds herself once again drawn to Narcís, and the latter's second wife Laura falls to her death over a cliff near their house at Port de la Selva.

Secrets de família was certainly a popular production, reaching audiences of almost 840,000 in October 1995, an audience share of 27.7 per cent (*El*

Temps, 2 October 1995). Nonetheless, it never quite matched the runaway success of *Poble Nou*. Perhaps the novelty value had to some extent worn off, but the generally sombre mood may also have been less appealing. As a reviewer in *La Vanguardia* suggested (12 February 1995), 'How can I put it? "Poble Nou" was Mediterranean and "Secrets de família" seems Swedish. "Secrets de família" ... is tense, it's claustrophobic, it's like a fjord, it's Ibsen ... When all's said and done, what is lacking in "Secrets de família" is a sense of humour, the most serious of all the senses.' This is unfair, since there was a certain amount of humour in *Secrets de família*, relating mostly to Enrique and his various amorous conquests, but there can be no doubt that the dominant tone was tragic.

Secrets de família seems to me to be linked with and to derive from a second and very powerful strand of discourses of Catalan history and identity which simultaneously contradict and complement those which can be seen to be given narrative form in *Poble Nou* and its spin-off *La Rosa*. The world of *Secrets de família* is, to use a Spanish term, 'esperpentic'.[1] It is a world where nothing makes sense, where words and actions have been so radically dislocated from their conventional meanings that it becomes impossible to find a way out, let alone a way forward. It is a world where a man expresses his love for a woman by raping her or by attempting to blackmail her into having a relationship with him. It is a world where it is possible to 'win' a woman at a game of cards, and where people die under mysterious circumstances which are never fully cleared up. It is above all a world where the past utterly overwhelms the present and destroys the future under the guise of 'destiny'. If *Poble Nou* represents the modern, dynamic, forward-looking face of Catalonia, *Secrets de família* can be seen on at least one level to express its continuing struggle with the burden of the past, very specifically the Francoist past (the original rape and game of cards take place during the Franco era). I am not suggesting that it was the intention of the author to present *Secrets de família* as a kind of allegory of Catalonia in this way (following a long conversation with her about *Secrets de família* I have no reason to believe that this is the case), but I am saying that these two converging discourses – of a modern, forward-looking country carrying the millstone of an alien and dictatorial past around its neck – are clearly present in Catalan culture, and that they can, at least partly, explain the simultaneous popularity of such different cultural products as *Poble Nou* and *Secrets de família*.

A Catalan Falcon Crest? Nissaga de poder

Nissaga de poder (Lineage of Power) followed shortly after the completion of *Secrets de família*. Like *Poble Nou* it also goes out during the 'sobretaula' every day from 15.30 to 16.10 and, at the time of writing, it is just entering its third season, making it the longest-running Catalan serial ever. It is

written by Josep Maria Benet i Jornet, who had also been responsible for
Poble Nou and *La Rosa*. It is set in the vine-growing area of Alt Penedès
between Barcelona and Tarragona where the Catalan champagne *cava* is
produced, and the programme's sponsors, in fact, include a number of *cava*
producers as well as business and tourist organizations in the town of
Vilafranca del Penedès. The opening sequence is a long aerial shot of
expansive vineyards with their accompanying dwellings, sheds and out-
houses. The bulk of the action takes place in the village of Santa Eulàlia del
Penedès, though some scenes also take place in Vilafranca and some in
Barcelona. After a slowish start, due in part to missing the traditional start-
of-season date of early January, *Nissaga de poder* now attracts audiences of
around 700,000. It is usually the second most-viewed programme in
Catalonia, sometimes the first, and very rarely lower than third.

Nissaga de poder is based on three families, by far the most important of
which is the landowning Montsolís family whose wealth dates back to the
eighteenth century. The current head of the family is Mateu Montsolís,
who lives in the ancestral mansion with the other members of his family.
Also living on the estate is Mateu's younger brother Raimon. Following a
tradition still current in the Catalan countryside, the oldest son inherits the
bulk of the land in order to keep the estate intact. The estate has therefore
passed from the grandfather Fèlix Montsolís to Mateu, and will be passed
on by him to his oldest son, Fèlix, by-passing Raimon altogether. Although
Raimon could not, by any stretch of the imagination, be described as poor,
he has very little land and produces craft wines using traditional small-scale
methods. The second family is that of Maurici Castro, head of production
of the Montsolís *cava*, while the third is that of the *masovers* (roughly 'tenant
farmers') Tomàs and Assumpció, who have also brought up the now almost
30-year-old Eduard, widely believed in the village to be the son of Mateu
Montsolís and Àngels Estivills, whom Mateu actually murders at the
beginning of the narrative, making it look like suicide.

Family relationships are very complicated in *Nissaga de poder*. As the
narrative unfolds we learn that Eduard is actually the son of Mateu and his
sister Eulàlia, who had had an incestuous relationship before his marriage
(the death of Àngels Estivills is the direct result of her threat to make this
information public). Later, Eulàlia also has a relationship with her nephew
and Mateu's son Fèlix.

Nissaga de poder clearly differs from its predecessors in a number of ways.
The first is that the social level of the characters seems much higher than
anything seen before. Secondly, it is one of a relatively small number of
European television serials to specifically feature conflicts between employers and workers, and even strikes. There are three different models of
industrial relations present. One is that represented by Mateu Montsolís
who, though (quite literally) murderously ruthless in both his personal and
business affairs, maintains an old-style paternalistic relationship with his

workforce, a relationship with strong Francoist overtones. His son Fèlix, aided and abetted by his friend Amadeu whom he met in the United States, is a clear representative of the neo-liberal strategy, seeing workers merely as another form of disposable capital to be hired and fired at will. The third group has both an older and a younger generation. The older generation consists of Conrad Agulló who, in the period immediately following the Spanish Civil War, had helped the Montsolís family by lending them machinery when their harvest had been ruined by flooding, and also by Raimon with his small-scale operations, his traditional wines and his respect for local traditions. The main representatives of the younger generation are Mateu's son Gabriel who, to his father's fury, decides to pursue a career as a labour lawyer in order to help the socially disadvantaged, and Eduard.

This third group represent a vision of society based on solidarity and mutual respect with a human dimension lacking in the other two. The youngsters are not 'working-class heroes' in any stereotypical sense. They are all university-educated (a lawyer, an accountant, a university lecturer and an oenologist), but they line up clearly with the agricultural workers in the face of reaction, both old and new: Gabriel even causes a family schism by representing the workers against his father. The distribution of moral protagonism in the narrative makes it quite clear that this group, though not economically dominant and, at least initially, by no means the most powerful, is where the moral centre of the *telenovela* lies.

The Basque Country

A small-town soap: Goenkale

The Basque Country (or Euskadi, as it is known in Basque) is now also enjoying its own highly successful Basque-language soap. Entitled *Goenkale* (High Road), it was launched in October 1994 and is shown five days a week on ETB1, going out at 22.00. It costs around two million pesetas per episode (*Egin*, 8 June 1995) and, unlike its Catalan counterparts, it is a genuine soap, running continually except for a summer break, and has no intention of ever coming to an end. The Director-General of Basque Television was quoted as saying that *Goenkale* would not repeat the mistake of *Poble Nou* by being taken off the air after a highly successful year, but would be more like '*Coronation Street*, which after twenty years of screening still has a faithful audience' (*Hika*, August 1995).

Goenkale is produced by the independent production company Pausoka for ETB, and is far and away the most-watched Basque-language programme ever produced, initially attracting around half a million viewers, though this would later fall to around 400,000. It has, in fact, acquired the kind of status in the Basque Country which *Poble Nou* acquired in

Catalonia, becoming, like it, a 'social phenomenon' (*El Diario Vasco*, 19 February 1995) – so much so that, in the early part of 1995, a study was carried out by Sociology Faculty of the Universidad del País Vasco and Basque Television to investigate the factors of its success in order that these might be applied to future Basque-language productions by ETB.

As in the case of the Catalan soaps, *Goenkale*'s objectives are also at least partly linguistic, and indeed its producers had studied the production methods of the Welsh soap *Pobol y Cwm*. One of *Goenkale*'s clear objectives was to strengthen the position of the Basque language (or Euskera) in Euskadi since it, like Catalan in Catalonia, was banned from public use throughout the Franco regime: in fact the position of Euskera in Euskadi is much less encouraging than that of Catalan in Catalonia, being spoken by around 20 per cent of the population, and for all its popularity *Goenkale* has fewer viewers in Euskadi than Spanish-language programmes such as the sit-com *Farmacia de guardia* (*El Diario Vasco*, 7 November 1994). This caused, for example, problems in finding actors to play the parts of the older characters, while casting for the younger ones was quite straightforward (*El País*, 4 October 1994), and indeed the bulk of the viewers, some 65 per cent, are aged between 14 and 24 (*Egin*, 30 March 1995). The style of Basque chosen is deliberately neutral, not based on any particular dialect, and is self-consciously simple and non-prosey. Referring to the *ikastolas*, special schools in Euskadi where Euskera is the medium of education, a journalist in the Spanish-language Basque newspaper *Deia* wrote (8 June 1995): '*Goenkale* is, if you'll allow me to say so, doing as much for Euskera as the ikastolas. With one of the largest audiences on ETB1 ... many people are learning Euskera as a matter of urgency in order to be able to know what the dialogues between Satur and Eusebio are about. And since it's children and young people who are working the remote control, those die-hards who still refer to *vascuence* [the Francoist term for the Basque language] have no choice but to go to bed in order to avoid a family schism.'

Alas, I myself know no Euskera whatsoever, and although I have 'seen' (quite literally) perhaps half a dozen episodes of this production, I am not really able to analyse it in any particular detail. What follows is mostly gleaned from articles on *Goenkale* taken from the Castilian-language press of Euskadi.

Goenkale is set in the fictitious coastal town of Arralde (location shooting is done in the actual town of Getaria) with around 10,000 inhabitants, and it deals with the lives of the members of the Lasa family. Like most soaps it had a fairly dramatic opening, centering on the resentments and jealousies caused by the inheritance left by the matriarch of the family. A short summary of forthcoming episodes in *El Diario Vasco* of 7 March 1995 shows roughly what is involved: 'Will Carlos survive? Will Joxemari overcome his addiction to alcohol? Will the town come to terms with Jon Ander's homosexuality? Is Teresa completely above board?' But it is not just about family relationships. Neighbours often meet to discuss matters germane to life in a fishing town such as conflicts over anchovy catches and the like. And in the second season beginning in October 1995 attention shifted somewhat to the future of the town itself, whether it would continue to be a traditional fishing town or whether it should become a tourist resort.

It is widely felt in Euskadi that *Goenkale* is very close to 'real life'. Thus the actor Mikel Laskurain, who plays the part of Puskas, suggested that the programme 'shows people the way they are here. *Goenkale* reflects the day-to-day life of any town in Euskal Herria and not as happens in the American series where everyone is rich' (*El Diario Vasco*, 19 February 1995) – a claim very similar to that made for the Norwegian soap *I de beste familier*, for example (see page 142). The study carried out by the Universidad del País Vasco mentioned earlier also confirmed this view among *Goenkale*'s viewers. Nonetheless, it is quite clear that certain aspects of Basque society are conspicuous by their absence. The most obvious is any reference to the ETA, an organization committed to winning an independent Basque Country through armed struggle. Xabier Puerta, the 'creator' of *Goenkale*, is very aware of this absence, and in a rather uncomfortable interview published in *Hika* (August 1995) stressed that this was not of his choosing:

We are making this product for – so to speak – a specific client, ETB, which has its own rules of conduct. Consequently, in order for this product to maintain its place in the schedules and not find itself in difficulties, it has, for example, to sideline the political element. We are writing in a society with powerful political conflicts and confrontations, but none of that can appear in *Goenkale*.

He offered a similar reason for the fact that *Goenkale* is entirely in Euskera, something which is even less likely than finding an exclusively Catalan-speaking community in Barcelona: 'This is a product which is being made for ETB1 and so it is in Euskera ... in ETB1 we are obliged to do everything in Euskera.' He also recognized that, in order to reach the longevity of *Coronation Street*, *Goenkale* would have to broaden its canvas:

The prospect of it becoming a *Coronation Street* has also been one of the reasons why ... we have decided to take the story a little bit out of the purely family-based nucleus of the Lasas and give greater importance to the town of Arralde. Arralde can come up with more stories to tell over 5, 6 or 7 years than the Lasa family on its own, although it will still be present at the centre of the narrative.

This is as clear a statement as any of the simultaneously constraining and enabling power of genre, several other examples of which can be found elsewhere in this book.

Andalucía-Madrid

In January 1997 a new *telenovela* entitled *Vidas cruzadas* (Crossed Lives) was launched simultaneously by Telemadrid and Canal Sur, these being respectively the regional channels of the Autonomous Communities of Madrid and Andalusia. The original idea for the narrative came from the Madrid production company Zeppelin TV. However, since the bulk of expertise in the production of *telenovelas* is now to be found in Catalonia, the producers approached TV3 which is now heavily involved in this joint venture in various ways. Not only do they provide most of the production team, they also provide most of the production facilities, with perhaps as much as two-thirds of the scenes being shot in the Esplugues studios in Barcelona. Moreover, Maria Mercè Roca, who had written the storyline for *Secrets de família*, was called in to refine and streamline Zeppelin's original ideas. She simplified the original narrative a great deal, making it much more manageable in its overall ramifications.

Vidas cruzadas has proved rather more popular in Andalucía than in Madrid. This is partly a question of scheduling. In Madrid it goes out at 16.00, in other words *after* the 'sobremesa' when people are already returning to work, whereas in Andalucía it goes out in evening prime time at 20.00. But in general the Andalusian storylines are much more highly developed than the others. Not only are there many outside shots of Montoro, the town in which these storylines are set, and of down-town Córdoba, there are also location shots of the fields of olive trees and the mills and a general feeling of out-and-aboutness and open air. The characters also speak with instantly recognizable Andalusian accents. By contrast, with the exception of the inevitably very brief establishing shots, there are no outside shots in the Madrid storylines at all (hardly surprising, since they are filmed in Barcelona), and there is little, linguistically or otherwise, to give real depth to this apparent setting.

Vidas cruzadas is a tale of three families, and it has certain structural similarities – apparently entirely coincidental – with the *Sons and Daughters–Verbotene Liebe–Skilda världar* family of soaps (see pp. 70 and 183). The wealthiest of the three families are the Riberas, based in Madrid, and owners of a chain of four-star hotels throughout Spain. Also based in Madrid are the Vidal family who own a restaurant called Casa Nieves. The third family, the Úbedas, are based in Montoro near Córdoba in Andalucía where they grow olives and have their own mill for the production of olive oil. The links between these three families are Laura Vidal and Antonio Úbeda since, unbeknown to everyone, they are the illegitimate children of Julio Ribera, and had been placed in an orphanage shortly after their birth, with Laura being adopted almost immediately by José and Nieves Vidal, and Antonio being adopted much later at the age of twelve by Cosme and Aurora Úbeda. At the beginning of the narrative Julio Ribera commits suicide, first altering his will to include his illegitimate children as well as his legitimate children Patricia and Sergio. This sets the narrative in motion, bringing all the parties into contact with each other, and triggering desperate machinations by the older members of the Ribera family to prevent the twins from claiming their share of the inheritance.

Like *Nissaga de poder*, *Vidas cruzadas* is, on certain levels, a fairly glamorous production, and not just in terms of the lifestyle of some of its characters. The Andalusian actresses in particular are very beautiful, with the character of Ana, Antonio's former wife, being played by a former Miss Spain, the impressively huffy Eva Pedraza (something of a trend, since a former Miss Sweden, Petra Hultgren, had appeared in the Swedish soap *Vänner och fiender* in October 1996 (see page 184)). As in *Nissaga de poder*, *Vidas cruzadas* also sets up worlds of competing, indeed contradictory values. The baddies are undoubtedly the older Riberas, who are positively vicious and grasping in their attempts to block the twins' rights to their inheritance. They are selfish and unfeeling, and utterly unscrupulous. The four Ribero children occupy very much the moral high ground in this tale, as the legitimate children Patricia and Sergio defend their newly-found siblings' rights and help them by hiding their father's new will so that it cannot be destroyed by their mother. Their moral protagonism is expressed in other ways too. For example, Patricia is having a relationship with the South American barman Nelson and wants to move in with him. Her mother is horrified at this prospect, not just because Nelson is a mere barman ('barmen don't have names,' she points out, 'they're simply staff') but also because he is black. 'You should go out with someone from our class,' she shrieks at Patricia. 'The class of people you are talking of make me sick,' she replies. The good guys also include José and Nieves Vidal, honest folks whose main concern in life is the well-being of their children, and the Úbedas, seen as decent small business people fighting the might of international (and less than respectable) capital.

A domestic Spanish soap

The obstacles in the way of producing a state-wide *telenovela* or soap in Spain were always going to be considerable, given that the experiments of the all-Spanish channels in joint productions with Latin American producers had known only limited success. At least part of the problem is that the Latin American productions are seen irredeemably as women's products in Spain. For example, Assumpta Roura insists throughout her study of *telenovelas* in Spain that their audience is uniquely female (1993: 71):

The producers and scriptwriters of these series work in the conscious knowledge that the end consumer is exclusively female. The fact that a small male group might in the end be added to that audience is merely an anecdotal detail both for the producers and for the female consumers.

This view is widely shared in Spain. As *El País* puts it (4 February 1994) in typically scornful language: 'They are a refuge for housewives and souls in a permanent state of tearfulness', while Haro Tecglen, television reviewer for the same newspaper, parodies the dominant terms of this debate as follows (Roura, 1993: 34):

> The programmers aim them at women who are preferably a bit stupid, living in emotional vacuums, not working, convinced that they are giving more than they get, whose level of education is average to low, who are passive and subordinate. This is what their researchers and their audience analyses say.

While views such as these are simply not correct for Latin America, where *telenovelas* can attract audience shares of between 70 and 90 per cent (López, 1995: 260), there is, beneath the offensive chauvinist rhetoric, an element of truth in that the bulk of their viewers in Spain are indeed women. The afternoon *telenovelas* offered by La Primera are preceded by useful tips for housewives and mothers supplied by Irma Soriano, who addresses her audience unequivocally as 'vosotras' ('you') or 'nosotras' ('we'), using the feminine forms of the pronouns.

Not only do the Catalan and Basque *telenovelas* come out strongly against this gender bias (although figures show quite clearly that their audiences are also predominantly female), they also come out against what they see as a uniquely Latin American – and therefore un-European – penchant for melodrama. Josep Maria Benet persisted in his plans for *Poble Nou* despite hostile criticisms from a Brazilian scriptwriter who saw little prospect of success for such an unmelodramatic serial (*El Temps*, 9 September 1994), while a similar position was adopted by Xavier Puerta in relation to *Goenkale* (*Hika*, August 1995):

> Before starting production we took advice from professionals involved in these kinds of audiovisual productions and they all told us to stick closely to the norms of pure melodrama, pointing out that a *telenovela* could not depart from the norms of this genre and that our idea of going for a multi-genre production and not sticking to melodrama as the only option was madness. We did not accept that advice and things have gone well.

As in the case of Catalonia, this has been important in presenting Euskadi not just as modern, but as European. As an article on *Goenkale* in *El Diario Vasco* put it (15 October 1994):

> It is, or it wants to be, a *telenovela*, although on the basis of what we have seen it is not anything like the Venezuelan, Brazilian or Mexican versions. It's more

European, which is also good: it's already known that our mentality, no matter how much some people might insist to the contrary, has nothing to do with the Latin American mentality.

An all-Spanish soap or *telenovela* would not only have to cope with the various 'nationalities' within Spain – not an impossible task, as the popularity of *EastEnders* in Scotland shows (see page 196) – but would have to break radically with the viewing patterns of the past and gamble on calling into existence a 'modern' and 'European' audience on an all-Spanish scale. This has been easier in Communities such as Catalonia and Euskadi because these attributes – 'modernity' and 'Europeanness' – are high-profile elements of the kinds of national identities being forged there in specific contrast to what is simultaneously presented as a more old-fashioned and even backward 'Spanish' identity. The continuing grip of the Latin American *telenovelas* in the early 1990s made the chances of success for such a venture seem rather slim. However, it is undoubtedly the case that the popularity of the Latin American product has waned to some extent, a development which eventually opened up a space for an all-Spanish *telenovela* in late 1996.

Stories of everyday life? El súper

On 6 September 1996 Telecinco launched *El súper: historias de todos los días* (The Supermarket: Stories of Everyday Life), the first truly domestic, all-Spain, daily serial. So far, 215 episodes have been shown, and another 200 have been commissioned. Since the plan is to continue the production for as long as demand holds up, *El súper* is in fact more of a soap than a *telenovela*. It goes out every weekday at 19.15, and dominates that slot with an audience share of 32.3 per cent – some 2,572,000 viewers, 30 per cent of whom are men (Telecinco's own data).

El súper's genealogy is in fact rather similar to that of *Vidas cruzadas*, in that it, too, is produced by Zepellin TV with production expertise coming from Catalonia, and at the moment of writing its four scriptwriters are also Catalan. Its narrative is also reminiscent in many ways of that of *Vidas cruzadas*, though it lacks the latter's geographical diversity, since *El súper* is set entirely in Madrid. It, too, features an upper-class family, the Bernals (a very Catalan name), in this case the owners of a chain of supermarkets as opposed to hotels, and it includes a number of unacknowledged or unknown children who are either unexpectedly acknowledged or turn up out of the blue.

El súper's extended title is really rather misleading from a number of points of view. First, very little of the action actually takes place in the supermarket (though there is usually at least one visit there per episode).

Secondly, although the production is described in Telecinco's own literature as 'a slice of life', the conflicts and machinations which make up most of the storylines could not really be described as conforming to the 'everyday life' of the bulk of this programme's viewers. There are a number of petty bourgeois characters, but the bulk of the interest lies clearly with the upper-class group.

Moral protagonism is, however, shared out rather more widely. The 'goodies' not only include the Bernal daughters Mayka and Julia, whose ecological products are seen as combining good business with good health for the population at large (an increasingly frequent symbology in European soaps (see page 44)), but also the goodhearted Asunción and Eugenio (the adoptive parents of the previously unacknowledged Julia, who run a bar), and also Santiago (played by Chisco Amado, who had appeared earlier in the Catalan production *Secrets de família* in the role of the doctor Enrique), who accepts a job as a manager at the supermarket in order to help Julia and Mayka unseat Julia's unscrupulous ex-husband Alfonso. When Santiago's young son Luis visits him at the supermarket the following conversation takes place:

L: So, you're the boss of the supermarket.
S: No, Luis.
L: But you give the others orders.
S: I'm the manager. It's not a question of giving orders, but of organizing the work well.
L: So, who's the boss?
S: Well, Alfonso. He's the managing director of the whole chain of supermarkets. He organizes all the work in the supermarkets.
L: But you're the boss in this one. If you say something to one of the checkout assistants they've got to obey you, don't they?
S: Things don't work that way, Luis. Being in charge doesn't mean telling people to do things, whatever comes into your head. No, being the boss is a big responsibility, you know.

[*Fernando comes in*]

L: Is Fernando your boss?
F: Look, Luis, I usually say that the supermarket is like a big boat, you know. The person who's steering is important, but if the rowers don't do their work, whoosh, the boat sinks.

This conversation can usefully be compared with that taken from the Flemish soap *Familie* (see page 37) and the Italian soap *Un posto al sole* (see page 122). It is a simple expression of the social-democratic consensus and shared responsibilities, and is very 'Catalan' in spirit (I return to this point below). The bad guys in these *telenovelas* are those who do not abide by these rules, and who are driven by egotism and greed. In *El súper* these are Alfonso and Miguel's low-life companions from his previous existence.

Analysis

The origins of the domestic television serial in Spain are clearly 'regional' rather than national in nature. However, Catalonia, Euskadi and Andalucía are in a somewhat different position from most of the other Autonomous Communities in Spain. They belong to that group of Communities which are deemed in the terms of the Spanish Constitution to constitute 'historic nationalities' in their own right. There are four such Communities, the fourth being Galicia, a region which, despite very modest resources, also attempted to produce its own mini-*telenovela*, entitled *Compostela, sol e lúa* (Compostela, Sun and Moon), and screened there in March 1994 in three one-and-a-half-hour-long episodes. It elicited relatively little response from the Galician viewing public, but it nonetheless stresses the link between domestic *telenovela* production and the question of 'nationality' in Spain. And as I bring this chapter to a close (June 1997) I have just discovered that there is also a Catalan-language[2] *telenovela* in the Autonomous Community of Valencia entitled *A flor de pell* (On Edge) which has been running since late 1996. I have been unable to see any episodes of this production (though its unattractive timing – 12 noon – suggests that it is not a major crowd-puller there).

The timing of these serials is also almost certainly not coincidental. *Poble Nou* appeared at a point in recent Spanish history when Catalonia, and to a lesser extent, Euskadi had moved very much to centre stage in the political arena. Around this time the governing Spanish Socialist Party (PSOE) found itself in a minority in central government and required the support of other parliamentary groups to keep it afloat. This support was provided on an issue-by-issue basis by the Catalan and Basque nationalist parties (both rather conservative in outlook) in return for certain concessions to the Communities in terms of allowing them a greater say in managing their own finances and running their own affairs (following the defeat of the PSOE in 1996, a similar agreement was entered into with its successor, the conservative Partido Popular). This was also a period of intense controversy over the language policy being followed in Catalonia. The Catalan government has, however, stood firm on its commitment to strengthening the position of the Catalan language in Catalan society. Prior to the advent of the Catalan serials, figures showed quite clearly that, not only did most Catalans read more Castilian-language newspapers than Catalan-language ones, they also watched more Castilian-language television than they did Catalan-language television (O'Donnell and León Solís, 1994). The Catalan serials have at least partly reversed that trend, since they are now among the most viewed programmes in Catalonia when they are on the air.

Given the rather different linguistic situation in Euskadi, it is unlikely that *Goenkale* will ever match the pull of the Catalan productions, but its success in attracting viewers to a product in Euskera has been by any standards astonishing. However, these serials are not just about the language of their respective Communities, they are also about strengthening notions of national identity within these Communities. They all make a quite conscious attempt to appeal to an audience beyond such barriers as age and class, and in the Catalan case *Nissaga de poder* has also introduced that other fundamental axis of national identity – historical time. The dynastic Montsolís family takes Catalan national identity back into the history of this lineage, back beyond the Franco regime and into the mists of the past.

A further striking feature of these Spanish productions is the frequency with which the theme of inheritance is raised. It provided the opening drama of *Goenkale*, has been absolutely central to *Nissaga de poder*, *El súper* and *Vidas cruzadas*, and has also surfaced in important ways in both *La Rosa* and *Secrets de família*. It has been accompanied by a positive profusion of unacknowledged children fighting for their rights. This seems to me to be – and something quite similar can be found in a number of Portuguese *telenovelas*, for what I would argue are roughly similar reasons – a narrative enactment of the struggle of Spain's younger generations to demand their rights to a modern and participatory society from a dictatorial and self-seeking past, part of which – the grasping and self-promoting part – is threatening to reappear in the neo-liberal future. The links between old-style paternalism and new-style individualism are clear in a number of these productions.

What these *telenovelas* have in common – and my relatively limited acquaintance with *Goenkale* suggests that this is also the case there – is their insistence on 'convivencia', a moral consensus built around living with others, accepting responsibility for others and taking their well-being into account in one's behaviour and general outlook on life. The attitude towards America is highly enlightening in this respect, and can be illuminatingly compared with how this country is presented in the Flemish and German soaps (see pages 37 and 84). In the Spanish soaps America appears as truly sinister: it is a dark country from which characters return suffering from illnesses, fleeing from tragedy or from where they bring drug addiction or the worst forms of managerial brutalism. It represents truly alien values. The moral consensus, on the other hand, is open to anyone irrespective of class origin, but its most emblematic heroes are clearly the traditional petit bourgeoisie.

With its emphasis on dialogue, negotiation and agreement, 'convivencia' is fundamentally social-democratic in outlook. The legacy left by the so-called 'Socialist Years' in Spain – the period of PSOE government lasting from 1982 to 1996 – is a complex and contradictory one, combining a substantial liberalization of the Spanish economy and the privatization of many previously state-owned companies (which has contributed to the highest rate of unemployment anywhere in Europe) with the foundations of a modern welfare state. While many Spaniards undoubtedly tired of the corruption and increasing inefficiency of the PSOE, the welfare state it has left behind it is something few are now prepared to give up or see watered down. The new Partido Popular government, for its part, has had to be rather more circumspect in its statements about its plans for the welfare state than it would like to be – a circumspection which has been increased by its agreements with and dependence on its Catalan and Basque partners. If 'convivència' is being kept at least minimally alive on a political level in this way, the *telenovelas* with their strong Catalan influence are now contributing to its survival on the cultural level too.

Postscript

I am reliably informed that a new once-a-week, family-based serial has now started in the Basque Country, though I have no detailed information regarding its contents.

Notes

1. The term 'esperpento' was coined by the Spanish writer Ramón del Valle-Inclán (1870–1936) who originally applied to it a series of plays he wrote in the 1920s and 1930s, based, in the words of the protagonists of one of these plays, on a 'systematically deformed aesthetic' where everything is seen as though in a distorting mirror: 'classic heroes reflected in concave mirrors produce the *esperpento*' (see Valbuena Prats, 1968: III, 529). However, the term is now used more widely to describe literary productions concentrating on the grotesque and the absurd.
2. There is currently an intense and, indeed, incredibly acrid debate in Valencia as to whether the language spoken by part of the population (Valencia has areas where only Castilian is spoken) is Catalan or a different language called Valencian. From a linguistic point of view this is a non-debate, rather similar to suggesting that the language spoken in Flanders is not Dutch, or that the language spoken in Austria is not German. Though it will earn me the opprobrium of certain sectors of the Valencian political spectrum, I will call this language Catalan. For further details see Stewart (1997).

Sweden

Television in Sweden

Sweden's first television channel, run by the Swedish Broadcasting Corporation (Sveriges Television, SVT), was officially introduced in 1956, a second public service channel being introduced in 1969 (Gustafsson, 1992: 208). Neither advertising nor direct sponsorship was allowed on either of these channels. A decision was taken by the Swedish parliament in 1991 to allow the introduction of a third advertising-financed terrestrial channel outside the structures of SVT. As a result of this the commercially-run channel, TV4, which prior to that had broadcast only by satellite, moved to terrestrial operations in March 1992, and is now the leading competitor to the two public service channels (Carlsson and Anshelm, 1995: 229).

Prior to that, commercial television had made its entry into the Swedish media market in 1987 with the arrival of the satellite channel TV3, followed by the Nordic channel in 1989. TV3, which is financed entirely by advertising and is beamed from London, had a daily audience share in Sweden in 1992 in the region of 25–40 per cent (Petersen, 1992: 619), but this has now dropped to below 10 per cent (Cronström and Höijer, 1996: 105). TV4 has remained closer in style to the public service channels, as indeed its licence conditions require it to do, though its programmes in general are aimed at a somewhat younger audience. The Nordic channel, now known as Kanal 5 (or Femman), combines a large number of (mostly American) soaps and series with talk-shows. Though SVT's commitment to its original public service brief remains strong, there is no doubt that it has been obliged to change both its style and content in response to the arrival of these new competitors (Hadenius, 1992).

Domestic Swedish soaps

Swedish film and TV critic Leif Furhammar suggests that the first televised soap-type serial in Sweden was *De lyckligt lottade* (The Fortunate Ones), produced in six episodes in 1976 by the Gothenburg section of SVT, a regional section which had a reputation for programmes taking a problem-oriented approach to the contemporary social scene (Furhammar, 1991: 325). It was not until the mid-1980s, however, that the long-running serial became an established part of Swedish televisual output. The first such production was *Lösa förbindelser* (Loose Connections), broadcast in 30 episodes on a twice-a-week basis in 1985, and set in an artists' milieu in Stockholm. It attracted audiences of around three million – from a total population of around eight million – from all age ranges within Swedish society (*Röster i Radio TV*, no. 35, 1985).

Lösa förbindelser was followed in 1987–8 by the 48-episode production *Goda grannar* (Good Neighbours). Set in an apartment block, it attracted a large audience, particularly among older viewers (Ross, 1994: 243). The third soap of the 1980s was *Varuhuset* (The Department Store), a 60-episode serial broadcast in 1987–8, set in a department store and featuring everyone from the upper-class owners to the canteen staff and warehousemen. It became something of a classic in Sweden, winning audience shares of over 60 per cent (Collin, 1994: 39). It has been reshown in its entirety several times (most recently in 1996) and has also been exported to a number of other Scandinavian countries.

A Swedish production from the end of the 1980s which came close to a soap format was *Svenska hjärtan* (Swedish Hearts), dealing with the lives of the inhabitants of a group of terraced houses just outside Gothenburg, 24 episodes of which were broadcast between 1987 and 1989. Although the author, Carin Mannheimer, took the view that length was not compatible with quality and stated publicly that she did not want her production to continue (Kainz, 1989: 13), a third set of six episodes was in fact broadcast six years later at the end of 1995.

Other notable long-running productions were *Det var då* (It Was Then), a 24-episode historical serial broadcast in 1989 and 1990 covering the twelve years between 1958 and 1970, and *Tre kärleker* (Three Loves), sixteen episodes of which were broadcast in 1989 and 1991, dealing with the members of a farming family during the Second World War. For further information on all these productions, see O'Donnell (1996b).

The once-a-week soaps

An offshore soap: Destination Nordsjön

The first new soap of the 1990s was the 30-part *Destination Nordsjön* (Destination North Sea), screened in 1990 on the newly established TV4 which was still restricted to satellite operations at the time and covered only part of the country. It was set on an oil rig in the North Sea and dealt with the lives of the helicopter crews in particular. Given TV4's relatively restricted reach, *Destination Nordsjön* could not match the drawing power of SVT's soaps, though it was considered successful enough to be repeated by TV4 in early 1994.

A yuppie soap: Storstad

After a three-year break from soap production, SVT returned to the genre in 1991 – the year in which the go-ahead was given for a new terrestrial channel – with *Storstad* (Big City), a 58-episode production described by the monthly magazine *Månadsjournalen* (no. 4, 1994) as a 'yuppie soap'. It was, like all previous SVT soaps, set in Stockholm, and dealt with the lives of different groups of people from varying social milieux, one of these being the immigrant Benucci family (who occasionally speak Italian subtitled in Swedish), following the tradition of the Spanish immigrant Carlos in *Varuhuset*. *Storstad* was also the first Swedish soap to introduce a sizeable group of teenagers in truly important roles.

Though it became one of the longest-running Swedish soaps, *Storstad* went through a long process of decline – attracting both critical rejection and poor viewing figures (Gustafsson and Lovén, 1993: 8) – before finally being taken off the air at the beginning of 1992. The term 'yuppie drama' may be a little unfair, since only one of the groups featured belonged clearly to that group, but the description was not entirely without foundation. *Storstad* was the story of isolated family groupings, unable to form an organic community despite their geographical proximity in the same district of Stockholm. Contact between the various groups who figured in the narrative was often minimal or non-existent: indeed, they were in a sense overwhelmed by the impersonality of the Big City of the title. Occasionally the characters would pass each other in the street with only the viewer able to make any kind of link between them, a very unusual narrative technique for a soap opera, since this genre seldom self-consciously signals its complicity with the viewer in this way. In a remarkable change of style, the opening shots of each episode, which initially featured different groups of people going about their (at times rather proletarian) business in different parts of Stockholm, were eventually replaced towards the end of the serial with a computer graphic of a 'virtual city', consisting of featureless blocks of brown and green. The sense of alienation was complete.

A soap adrift: Rederiet

Storstad was followed in 1992 by *Rederiet* (literally The Shipping Line, though officially translated as High Seas), which has proved to be by far the most successful and long-running Swedish soap of all time: its one hundredth episode on 11 January 1996 could reasonably be described as something of a mini national event, with heavy coverage in all the national dailies and on television, and the production of a special commemorative brochure by SVT. The bulk of the action takes place on a ferry sailing between Stockholm and Åland, a group of Swedish-speaking islands lying just off the coast of Finland. However, *Rederiet* continues the tradition of *Varuhuset* by including characters from a wide range of social backgrounds, from the wealthy owners of the line (the Dahlén family) to the men and women working in the ship's engine room and canteen, in particular the working-class Sjögren family. *Rederiet* attracts 30 per cent of all female and 21 per cent of all male viewers (Gustafsson and Lovén, 1994: 20). A repeat of the episode shown at 20.00 on SVT1 is screened on SVT2 on Fridays at 23.25 and Mondays at 17.00, giving the programme a total weekly audience of some 2.2 million, a figure which compares with audiences of 150,000 for the American daytime serial *The Bold and the Beautiful*, shown on Kanal 5 (Jiretorn, 1994: 11).

There is an obvious thematic and narrative continuity between *Varuhuset* and *Rederiet*: indeed, this was deliberately sought by the head of Kanal 1 Drama when the serial was launched (Gustafsson and Lovén, 1993: 8). Again the influence of a more 'European'-style 'social realism' is apparent. As the serial has proceeded now for over five years, the storylines have been notably characterized by criminality and corruption on a very large scale and the patriarchal structures of the Dahlén company have begun to look increasingly out of date: this has taken the form, on a narrative level, of the fissuring and dispersal of the family itself, and of the return of Reidar Dahlén's glamorous granddaughter (the glamour is not incidental) from the Wharton Business School in America to introduce a new management style into the company. Reidar's loss of control of the board to the unethical Pehr Silver is symptomatic of the changes afoot.

A small-town soap: Tre Kronor

The arrival of the 'new' terrestrial channel TV4 in 1992 inevitably brought changes to the Swedish soap scene. TV4 managed something of a *coup* by tempting Peter Emmanuel Falck – who had been involved in one capacity or another in almost all previous Swedish soaps up to and including *Rederiet* – to join them in the production of their new soap *Tre Kronor* (Three Crowns), a title which in Sweden is closely linked with sport, and in particular ice hockey, this being the name of the national ice hockey team. *Tre Kronor* in some ways breaks new ground for Swedish soaps, and in other ways continues some of the previously tried and tested formulae. It is the first soap to be set outside Stockholm – in the small town of Mälarviken – giving it a notably more 'suburban' feel than its predecessors, and it continues one of the lines of *Storstad* by having a large number of characters in their teens (these are almost entirely absent in *Rederiet*). Like *Storstad* it also features an immigrant family – in this case the black–African Sali family. *Tre Kronor* immediately became very successful, achieving audiences of around 1.8 million, a share of around 22 per cent.

The new daily soaps

A re-versioned soap: Skilda världar

On 23 September 1996 TV4 began screening Sweden's first-ever five-day-a-week soap, entitled *Skilda världar* (Separate Worlds). However, what nobody mentioned – neither TV4 nor any of the newspaper articles that I was personally able to read – was that this Grundy production is in fact (or at least was originally) a Swedish rewrite of the German Grundy production *Verbotene Liebe* (see page 70), with which it shares a common ancestry in the Australian soap *Sons and Daughters*. The early episodes of *Skilda världar* in particular are very close reworkings of the German model: some of the lines are actually taken verbatim from the German soap. *Skilda världar* was guaranteed a minimum of 140 episodes, which it completed, achieving average audiences of 1.35 million, a very respectable score. It was off the air for some time, but screening of a further 200 episodes began in Autumn 1997.

Despite the enormous structural similarities between the Swedish and the German production, however, there *are* differences. In the Swedish soap the aristocratic German von Anstetten family has become the merely upper-class (though still seriously rich) Bovallius family, while the middle-class Brandner family has become the working-class Toivonen family (Finnish names like Toivonen have a traditional working-class resonance in Sweden, while names like Bovallius are stereotypically upper-crust). The Toivonens live in a single-storey, flat-roofed terrace house in Uppsala, some 60 kilometres north-west of Stockholm, and while Arno Brandner owns a construction company, Matti Toivonen (and later Daniel) merely work in one, and both are seen in their hard hats walking along scaffolds, shifting planks and the like. They are, in fact, closer in terms of class position to the original Australian Palmer family. And in small but significant ways things are in general terms less glamourous and less glossy. Sandra Bovallius, in particular, is cast in much less of a film-star mould than Julia in *Verbotene Liebe*, and somehow there is rather more warmth all round. Matti, though burning on a short fuse and at times alienating his children, is less of a control freak than Arno, and has, in particular, an affectionate relationship with his daughter Stina. Even Rebecka Bovallius, described by *Expressen* as 'a treacherous upper-class mother [who] will be a truly horrible nightmare for all teenage girls', and who is undoubtedly scheming and manipulative, frequently displays a sense of humour which is nowhere to be found in *Verbotene Liebe*. In fact, as the serial has rolled on the class differences – as also happened in the German soap – have become less important as the relationships between the various characters have moved to centre stage: while *Verbotene Liebe*'s opening sequence stresses the class differences between the two families, *Skilda världar*'s opening sequence consists entirely of extreme close-up shots of the faces of the protagonists, each accompanied by his or her name.

Tales of everyday life: Vänner och fiender

A little over a month after the launch of *Skilda världar*, the satellite channel TV3 began its own five-day-a-week soap entitled *Vänner och fiender* (Friends and Enemies): the first episode, a 'special', lasting an hour, went out on 21 October 1996, subsequent 30-minute episodes being screened at 19.30. *Vänner och fiender* is an entirely domestic production, made for TV3 by the Jarowskij production company which transformed part of a former factory site in the town of Hallstahammar near Västerås (some 80 kilometres west of Stockholm) into an enormous set for this soap, a set which has come to be known as 'Hollyhammar' (the economic importance of this development for the region is not without importance, since Hallstahammar is an officially designated area of priority treatment with an unemployment rate of 16 per cent, and EU financing has been made available for the project which provides between 50 and 60 jobs to the local community). There are fifteen different locations on the set, one of which is a street along which – in a manner reminiscent of *Lindenstraße* (see page 55) – buses drive from time to time during filming, stopping to let passengers off and on. Following a technique which is, to the best of my knowledge, unique among European soaps, the scenes are shot chronologically. In other words, the first scene is filmed first, the second second, and so on until the end. Following this method, filming proceeds at the truly astonishing rate of two episodes per day.

Before production began, much was made in the Swedish tabloid press of the fact that Petra Hultgren, Miss Sweden 1995, had accepted a leading part in this soap (a 'lead' followed later by Eva Pedraza in Spain (see page 172)), and indeed she would later be briefly joined by former Swedish Miss World and Bond Girl Mary Stavin. Before viewing *Vänner och fiender* I rather expected a fairly glamorous soap. In fact it is a very *un*glamorous soap; one of the most unglamorous soaps showing anywhere in continental Europe.

Vänner och fiender is set in the fictitious small town of Erikshamn, described by the station announcers as being 'somewhere in Sweden'. There are two main family groups, the Åqvists and the Sundins, and various other more free-standing characters. Of all the soaps I have watched in the course of this study *Vänner och fiender* is by some distance the most discomfiting. People are simply caught in dispiriting situations beyond their control and are (sometimes intentionally, often unintentionally) horrible to each other in minutely banal and debilitatingly unspectacular ways. And all of this is reinforced by the uniquely unsettling production style of this soap. Virtually everything is shot using a steadycam. As a result almost all shots are accompanied by small but constantly perceptible peripheral movements. Outside shots abound since they are technically quite straightforward in the enormous purpose-built set, and they too are often characterized by considerable camera movement, the almost total absence of a fixed field of vision contributing to the slow but inexorable fragmentation of any sense of solidity. Dialogues at times verge on the incoherent (this has the unusual effect of highlighting how polished the dialogues of most seemingly 'naturalistic' soap operas actually are), the characters talk over each other, they look past the person they are talking to, they mumble and chew their words, conversations at times appear to be going nowhere at all. *Vänner och fiender*'s episodes don't end on cliffhangers, they simply peter out.

The last few lines of *Vänner och fiender*'s title song (it enjoyed considerable success when released as a single by Swedish group Together) goes as follows: 'There comes a time / in our lives / we have to dare / to tell the truth'. The 'truth' *Vänner och fiender* is telling is an awkward and uncomfortable one. It is the nightmare of the everyday, of people trying to hoover around others who cannot be bothered to lift their feet (a scene involving Madde and Niclas), of relationships which come apart at the seams – at all points in the age spectrum – because people are so taken up in their own lives that others have become invisible. Technical quality in this soap can be variable, but in its own off-beat, unconventional way *Vänner och fiender* exerts a horrifying fascination.

In April 1997 *Vänner och fiender* provided two juicy stories for the Swedish tabloids. The first concerned the outbreak of a 'soap war'. The original contract between TV3 and Jarowskij was for 170 episodes. These in fact proved very popular, pulling in audiences of around half a million, an extremely good score for TV3: in fact episodes of *Vänner och fiender* were always among TV3's top ten programmes for any week. In April, however, a dispute broke out between the two parties regarding the cost of continuing the soap. TV3 announced that it was cancelling *Vänner och fiender* and in response Jarowskij offered the serial to TV3's main competitor, Kanal 5. To this TV3 reacted by announcing that it would sue Jarowskij for 50 million kronor (approximately £5,000,000) if a single episode was shown on Kanal 5. The second piece of news, not at all unrelated to the first, was the announcement that Petra Hultgren was leaving the soap to move over to TV3's planned new hospital soap *Vita lögner* (White Lies) – it has not yet appeared – and that she would be replaced by Sara Alström who until then had played the role of the glamorous Lina Dahlén in *Rederiet*. The current situation is that *Vänner och fiender* will indeed continue on Kanal 5 in the Autumn (see postscript).

Analysis

The trajectory of Swedish television serials since the mid-1970s has followed a clear downwards curve both as regards the social milieu in which the action is set and as regards the age of the characters featured. There has also been a slow but steady dispersal in terms of location. This trajectory has accompanied – and to some extent reflected – the erosion of old-style social democracy as a political ideology in Sweden, a country in which the Social Democrats were long seen as the historic guardians of the so-called 'Swedish model'.

Furhammar (1992: 98) described *Goda grannar* as follows: 'It was fairly reminiscent of Swedish cinema in the 1930s when it was at its most *folkhem*-like and cosy.' And indeed *Goda grannar* can be seen as a symbolic representation of the *folkhem* (literally 'people's home', also known as the 'Swedish model'), a typically Scandinavian social-democratic political concept of a somewhat paternalistic state which accepted private enterprise but provided a highly developed welfare state and ensured more of a balance of power between employers and workers than is now fashionable, even in Sweden. As Swedish ethnologist Jonas Frykman puts it (1993: 163):

Throughout Europe in the inter-war period various states were faced with the move from old hierarchies, privileges and class societies to societies for all. The idea of the *Folkhem* was the Swedish variant of that transformation. Other countries would bring more restrictive models to bear. In a good home there were to be no more barriers, equality should reign, people's worth was to be judged by their inherent qualities, not their inherited advantages or social handicaps.

The concept of the *folkhem* is often used in Sweden in connection with soaps, even now, and both *Goda grannar* and *Varuhuset* can be seen as manifestations of different representations of the *folkhem*, since the concept of the *folkhem* signifies on at least two levels within Swedish society. One of these is the level of practice, or what might be called *Realpolitik*, where it represents a specific set of social, political and economic structures ensuring a greater balance of power between the different classes in Swedish society, a greater level of welfare for all, and a reduction in social tensions and conflicts. This is the type of *folkhem* to be found in *Varuhuset*, with its different classes and its social hierarchies whose fates are all bound together in the same communal enterprise. The second level of signification of the *folkhem* operates more precisely on the level of discourse – the vision of a utopian village-like society co-extensive with Swedish society as a whole, a symbolic reworking of the mythical Swedish 'Medelby' ('Average Town') of the 1940s (Frykman, 1993: 120). This is the level of *folkhem* manifest in *Goda grannar*. What is most striking about both productions, however, is the extent to which the original meanings of the *folkhem* are clearly falling apart.

In *Goda grannar* the patriarchal owner of the block of flats, Bror Öster, is ill and unable to run his affairs in the old-style, kindly-paternalistic manner. He hands over everyday administration of the building to the up-and-coming Pierre, who bullies the tenants financially and gets involved in property speculation with dealer Lars Westberg. These are clearly yuppies in the making, and are linked into the spirit of the times. As Ross (1994: 244) points out, 'Pierre is an unattractive person who represents the wheeler-dealer economy of the eighties.' In *Goda grannar* the building of the *folkhem* may still be standing, but the patriarchal protection has gone, and a process of disintegration of the internal fabric appears to be already underway, under attack from hostile forces from outside. *Varuhuset*, for its part, featured a whole range of social and economic conflicts: power struggles among owners and managers, career clashes among upwardly-mobile members of staff, commercial espionage, and a growing amount of criminal activity.

In fact, these two productions must be seen against the background of political change within Swedish society at the time. After almost four decades of uninterrupted power, the Social Democrats lost the elections of 1976 and were replaced by a Conservative (or to use Swedish terminology 'bourgeois') government from 1976 to 1982. During the long period of Social Democratic ascendancy, the two levels of signification of the *folkhem* – discourse and practice, vision and *Realpolitik* – held together, since it was believed that the social, economic and political structures set in place by the Social Democrats were in fact realizing the *folkhem* within Swedish society. As the Social Democratic era drew to a close, it was accompanied by a growing crisis of belief in that particular conjunction. In the political and social changes which followed, the two sides of the *folkhem* concept became unstuck and drifted apart, and each started to disintegrate in its own way. This is the process reflected in *Goda grannar* and *Varuhuset*, and it could also be seen in the popularity of the American supersoaps during the same period. As Michael Forsman puts it in his analysis of the 1980s: 'Soon almost half the population was watching "Dallas", while the culture pages in the newspapers discussed the "Dallasification of Sweden", which on a deeper level probably caught something of the onset of the erosion of the Swedish model, and I don't just mean within TV' (*Svenska Dagbladet*, 7 May 1996).

Storstad, the last soap to be produced while the public service monopoly remained intact and the last to be broadcast before the second electoral defeat of the Social Democrats in 1991, continues the theme of dispersal, both narrative and ideological, when compared with both *Varuhuset* and *Goda grannar*. As opposed to the organic societies of *Varuhuset* or *Goda grannar*, we are presented here with individualized groups each pursuing their own limited goals. If in the new neo-liberal era there is, as a famous champion of this ideology put it, 'no such thing as society', *Storstad* gives this televisual form.

Following the second formation of a 'bourgeois' government for the second time in fifteen years in 1991, a mock obituary in the tabloid *Aftonbladet* in June 1992 officially announced the death of the social-democratic *folkhem*. Tongue-in-cheek, perhaps, but this obituary reflected a clear feeling abroad in Swedish society at the time that the death sentence of the *folkhem* had already been written. These strains were clearly visible in *Rederiet* from the start: the opening scene of the first episode showed the company's offices being attacked by protesters opposing the building of a new ferry terminal in Stockholm.

The physical difference in the locations of *Varuhuset* and *Rederiet* – a department store which endlessly recycles its own tensions but remains standing, versus a ferry line where characters are constantly on the move, and move in and out of the narrative in a variety of ways (including falling/being pushed overboard) – is not coincidental. *Rederiet* is at one and the same time more claustrophobic and – in all senses of the phrase – more 'at sea' than *Varuhuset*. Lars Collin may describe a scene in episode 59 as an 'everyday drama from the *folkhem*' (1994: 38), but after over 100 episodes there is little of the *folkhem* left now: *Rederiet* represents both the implosion of the discursive *folkhem* and the abandonment of the socio-political one. It is adrift in a way in which more tightly location-bound serials (by far the majority group in Europe) are not: and while there were many contacts between the ship and land in the early episodes, as Bergendahl *et al.* point out in their study of the serial, 'the links between what happens on board the Freja and what happens on land are by and large broken and towards the end the series contains two worlds which are separated from each other' (1992: 31).

Rederiet's narrative shows the gravitational pull of social and ideological collapse. It traces a narrative descent from the *folkhem* – in both senses – of the inter-war period and after to the individualizing liberalism of the 1980s and 1990s: the ship is a mini-society adrift and left to its own devices, powerless to influence the decisions governing its existence taken in a distant location from which it is entirely cut off, a situation which Michael Forsman sees as a curiously appropriate metaphor of contemporary Sweden (*Svenska Dagbladet*, 7 May 1996): 'Moreover one could take the view that a floating consumer complex, within, yet quite cut off from, the elements, where all are fighting for their own survival, is a quite telling picture of Sweden today.' The long and nightmarish period during which the psycho-pathic and murderous Viggo Strieber was the captain of the ship was the expression of a social dystopia which ended only with his death at the end of the Spring 1995 season.

Tre Kronor to some extent represents, within the narrative-cum-ideological framework posited above, a certain regrouping of the Swedish soap. The edgy aimlessness of *Rederiet* with its frightening collection of amoral (Silver), psychotic (Désirée) and psychopathic characters (Viggo) – to mention only some of the more recent – is replaced by the life of a relatively stable small community which lacks the compactness of *Varuhuset* and *Goda grannar* but is not dwarfed by a large, anonymous conurbation as in *Storstad*. It is outside Stockholm, is somewhat remote, but is not adrift as in *Rederiet*. While there are distinct family groups as in *Storstad*, they are all linked with each other – mostly, though not exclusively, through the activities of their younger members – and a sense of shared destinies is maintained (in fact they all live in the same street). The social flattening-out is re-established and strengthened in a largely undifferentiated middle-class, and is accompanied by an almost total absence of serious economic issues. This is a new political utopia – full of personal problems, of course (such problems are part of the 'pleasure' of soaps) – but a utopia all the same, since it occurs at a time when the internal divisions within Swedish society are becoming *clearer*, not less distinct. As Michael Forsman puts it (*Svenska Dagbladet*, 7 May 1996): 'economic and life-style stratification is making Swedish society more and more difficult to grasp as a whole'. This is the new neo-liberal, re-ideologized *folkhem*, compressed and flattened out, and far from the political and economic realities of Swedish life.

The regrouping adumbrated by *Tre Kronor* is now reaching *Rederiet* as well. Towards the end of the Spring 1996 season three of its best-known middle-aged women characters were written out – causing a lively debate in the Swedish press and on Swedish television, including a phone-in to the head scriptwriter, and statements by the Ombudsman for Sexual Equality – leaving only one female character over 40 in the entire *dramatis personae* (a highly reduced age-range compared with *Tre Kronor* with its adolescents and sexagenarians). In their stead came a 28-year-old model and television presenter, Anna Järphammar, who featured among the list of 'Sweden's sexiest women' drawn up by a well-known men's clothing shop: together with Reidar's granddaughter Lina she would substantially increase the glamour factor in the soap. The writers argued that the narrative potential of the characters who had been written out had been exhausted, and that they were intending to introduce two new 'middle-aged' women characters (aged 38 and 41 respectively) in the Autumn season, but the process of rejuvenating and glamorizing the cast of the programme seems clear. The pitch at the younger audience is apparent. It is unlikely that *Rederiet* will ever lose the edginess of its constant business plotting and scheming, but it remains to be seen whether it will become more superficial – more ludic, even? – and less challenging as the old guard are slowly removed – even Reidar Dahlén must eventually go – and a new and more glamorous generation with a different set of values climbs on board.

The new daily soaps, for their part, provide a new utopian and dystopian vision of the new 'classless' society. The emphasis on class differences in the early episodes of *Skilda världar* will no doubt prove to have been very much a dramatic device as it was in *Verbotene Liebe*, and I expect them to diminish in importance (a process which has already begun). Like its German model *Skilda världar* will then, no doubt, become a narrative universe where good-looking people fall in and out of love with each other in an endless merry-go-round; all very pleasant to look at, but continuing the unchalleng-ing approach of *Tre Kronor*. *Vänner och fiender* has isolated the dystopian elements of *Rederiet* and removed them to 'somewhere in Sweden', a somewhere recognizable only in its absence of solidarity and its links to nowhere: unlike *Rederiet* it never reaches land.

The soap opera landscape in Sweden has changed enormously since the early 1990s. *Rederiet* is now over twice as long as the previously longest-running soap (*Varuhuset*), *Tre Kronor* shows absolutely no signs of coming to an end in the foreseeable future (announcements of its demise in December 1996 proved exaggerated), and the new daily soaps seem strong enough to continue. The sinking of the ferry *Estonia* in 1994, with the loss of over 900 lives, was a critical moment for *Rederiet* – there was serious talk in the press of the serial being unable to continue after this disaster – but it survived and, despite intermittent criticism for lack of quality and realism, it seems set to continue indefinitely. The ambivalent nature of the early Swedish soaps was, to some extent, part of a much larger process of dissolution within Swedish society as a whole. While some regrouping of the Swedish soaps was obvious around 1994–5, it is less clear that Swedish society has regrouped quite so convincingly. *Rederiet*'s endlessly questing dystopia and *Tre Kronor*'s endlessly circling utopia may be two poles of this larger social crisis, replaying the disintegration of the two poles of the *folkhem*, while the new soaps narrativize the same dispersal. Seen from this point of view the Swedish soaps offer a stereoscopic vision of society which has yet to come into focus. Whatever the case, all the narratives look set to run for some considerable time to come, and to tell their own tales of the disintegration and re-formation of the 'Swedish model'.

Postscript

TV3's attempts to gain an injunction preventing Kanal 5 from screening *Vänner och fiender* were unsuccessful. On Monday 8 September 1997 both channels started screening different episodes of the soap at the same time, TV3 showing the first of its 33 remaining unscreened episodes, and Kanal 5 the first of its 170 new ones, with the character of Madde being played by a different actress on each channel. This is, to the best of my knowledge, the first time anything like this has ever happened. Sixty-one per cent of viewers watched the Kanal 5 version, and 39 per cent the TV3 version, though the total viewership, 340,000, was somewhat down on the previous season's score.

The United Kingdom

Television in the United Kingdom

The United Kingdom has the most long-established television system in Europe, with nationwide broadcasting well into its stride by the early 1950s (Alvarado *et al.*: 1992). It is also the European country with the longest-standing commercial television network, with the Independent Television Company (ITV) – a network of regional television stations – beginning operations in 1955. The BBC introduced its new minority-viewing channel, BBC2, in April 1964, with Channel 4, a state-sponsored corporation which derives the bulk of its financing from advertising, beginning operations in 1982, and quickly acquiring a reputation for innovative programming. Following a White Paper in 1989, the franchises for the ITV broadcasting areas were awarded through a bidding process, coming into force on 1 January 1993 and valid for ten years.

Satellite television arrived in the UK in February 1989 with Rupert Murdoch's Sky television, which would eventually merge in 1990 with the rival British Satellite Broadcasting (BSB), producing BSkyB (see Chippindale and Franks, 1991). Satellite television has, however, been slow to take off in the UK, current penetration, including cable, being around 30 per cent of television households. The current market shares in the UK are as follows: BBC1, 33.4 per cent; BBC2, 11.9 per cent; ITV, 32.7 per cent; Channel 4, 10.3 per cent; satellite 11.6 per cent.

The UK's fifth terrestrial channel, Channel 5, went on stream officially on 30 March 1997. It is aimed fairly and squarely at a younger market – its programme director, Dawn Airey, is reported to have said that she won't be making shows for anyone over 40 – and it describes itself as simultaneously 'modern and mainstream'. Its initial target is a 5 per cent market share.

Domestic UK soaps

The UK, and England in particular, has the longest tradition of soap operas in Europe, with almost a dozen productions (some admittedly rather short-lived) dating from the early 1950s. The most important of these are listed below, and further analysis of them can be found in Brunsdon (1981), Buckingham (1987), Buckman (1984), Crofts (1995), Dyer (1981), Geraghty (1991; 1995), Griffiths (1995), Hobson (1983), Kilborn (1992), Kingsley (1988), Liebes and Livingstone (1992) and Silj (1988).

Coronation Street (1960–), now showing four episodes a week on ITV, is currently the longest-running programme in Europe. It is set in a suburb of Manchester and its average audience for the Autumn of 1996 was 15.5 million, though on any given day it can often score over 17 million, and it can occasionally peak at over 20 million (its greatest audience of all time was 29 million on 8 December 1989). ITV's second soap was the long-running *Crossroads* (1964–88), set in a motel near Birmingham. *Emmerdale Farm* (1972–), also shown on ITV, changed its name in the early 1990s to *Emmerdale*. Set in the Yorkshire dales, it is the most rustic of the UK soaps. Its average audience for the Autumn 1996 season was 11.8 million, though it can occasionally be as high as 13 million.

Channel 4's first soap, *Brookside* (1982–), is set on a suburban housing estate in Liverpool and often deals with difficult and highly contentious issues. It is usually Channel 4's most popular programme, with average audiences in the Autumn 1996 season being four million, though it has occasionally reached eight million.

The BBC's most successful soap so far is *EastEnders* (1985–). It is currently the most popular programme in the UK, with average audiences in Autumn 1996 of 15.7 million, though it can peak at over 18 million. It is set in the fictitious borough of Walford in London, and deals with the lives of a variety of people living in Albert Square. Its most viewed episode occurred on Christmas Day 1986 and was watched by 31.1 million people.

Beyond these UK soaps there is also a daily Welsh-language soap, *Pobol y Cwm* (People of the Valley) (1974–) which, since 1988, has been the only soap in Europe – perhaps anywhere – to be shot on the day it is broadcast, and a once-a-week Scottish soap, *Take the High Road* (1979–), which changed its name to *High Road* in 1993. Set on the picturesque banks of Loch Lomond, *High Road*'s most striking feature is that it is spoken almost entirely in Standard English (albeit with Scottish accents), while Standard English is a form of speech routinely ignored by the overwhelming majority of the Scottish population as far as everyday communication is concerned. But *High Road* speaks the language of its audience. With its scenic setting and predominantly middle-aged cast it provides a rural idyll for middle-aged, well-educated Scots living in the residential areas of the central belt.

It has never really gripped the popular imagination, and has consistently attracted fewer viewers than *EastEnders* (Kingsley, 1988: 425)

No account of the complexity of the soap opera phenomenon in the United Kingdom would be complete without some mention of the two imported Australian soaps *Neighbours* and *Home and Away*. *Neighbours* was the first to arrive in 1986, followed by *Home and Away* in 1988. Their initial viewing figures were astonishing, with *Neighbours* reaching over sixteen million in January 1988. Though they have remained popular in their early evening spot, particularly among younger audiences, there has been a slow process of attrition, with audiences for both now between seven and eight million, and for the first time they seem set to fall out of the list of the 50 most popular programmes in the UK.

The 1990s have not been a particularly easy time for new British soaps. It is not difficult to see why. The hold of the four main soaps on the public imagination is so great that any new soap more or less automatically runs the risk of simply repeating their appeal, or of finding a niche which is so exotic as to be doomed to minority viewing. More or less directly as a result of this, of the four new soaps which have appeared in the 1990s on British terrestrial television, two have failed, and a third has had to manoeuvre considerably to stay afloat.

An exotic soap: Eldorado

The BBC soap *Eldorado* started on 6 July 1992 and lasted almost exactly one year, on a twice-a-week basis, coming to an end on 9 July 1993. Quite exceptionally for a British soap, it was set not in Britain, but in a tourist complex in Spain. While the title sequences of all British soaps have always given some indication of the setting, *Eldorado*'s title sequence consisted of a computer-generated sun shining above a computer-generated sea, the sun eventually becoming the 'o' of the title *Eldorado* (the end of the title sequence of the Italian soap *Un posto al sole* is not dissimilar (see page 116)). *Eldorado* was an expensive production, since the BBC had a complex built specifically for this purpose in Coín, on the Costa del Sol, at a cost of £1.5 million, with total start-up costs reportedly approaching ten million pounds.

Hostile mainstream criticism of soap operas in the UK is still regular and widespread, but it is probably true to say that no other British soap has ever been exposed to the levels of scorn suffered by *Eldorado*. Everything was attacked: the bizarreness of the location, the characterization, unconvincing to the point of stereotype, even the accents of the non-British characters were the subject of derision. The producers of *Eldorado* did take these early criticisms to heart and made a number of changes. The narrative focus moved away from the setting and more on to the characters, the characterization itself was improved, the storylines improved, and so on, all resulting in a recovery of viewing figures from just under three million to around 7–8 million. Unfortunately for *Eldorado*, however, the BBC's charter was up for renewal, questions of 'quality' were very much in the air, and the soap looked like an easy scapegoat. It was axed by the new BBC1 Controller, Alan Yentob, only weeks after he took up his post.

Eldorado enjoys a continuing ghostly existence in the British media as an ongoing object of fun. The impression it has left behind most indelibly is one of a curiously alien production that viewers could not really relate to. As a reviewer in the *Observer* (17 April 1994) put it:

The insoluble problem, however, was its internationalism. However well-intentioned . . . it ran aground on British audiences' preference for soaps that are rooted in distinct, knowable locations. These may bear little resemblance to reality . . . but nonetheless, they are convincing and satisfying enough for us to participate in the shared fantasy of the fiction.

Eldorado was doomed because it was nowhere, a fact signalled by its credit sequence which, shunning the maps and exteriors used by all other soaps, favoured an abstracted, place-less image of sea and sun. Its multi-lingual paella of personnel hardly helped the situation. Brits-in-Spain might have stood a chance of being the basis for a workable soap, but to hurl sundry Danes, Swedes, Germans and French at the audience was to severely over-estimate the Euro-tolerance of the viewing millions.

In fact, the 'whereness' of a soap is a complicated business. Anyone watching *EastEnders* for any length of time, for example, will quickly conclude that, despite the map of London with which it opens, this soap is not in fact *in* London, any more than *Brookside* is *in* Liverpool, the various scenes of Liverpool with which it starts notwithstanding. It is quite possible to watch both these soaps for months on end not only without seeing but indeed without hearing about any part of the city in which they are supposedly set. In fact, on those few occasions when the action moves elsewhere – when the youngsters in *EastEnders* went to spend the September Weekend in Blackpool, for example, or when Max and Susanna Farnam in *Brookside* went to the south of France – the viewers saw incalculably more of these settings than they ever see of either London or Liverpool. In fact the supposed location of these soaps is carried overwhelmingly by the dialects which the bulk of their characters speak: cockney in *EastEnders*, scouse in *Brookside*. But these dialects operate primarily as *sociolects* in these productions. In other words, *EastEnders* and *Brookside* are not in a *geographical* space but in a socio-economic one – in an identifiable sector of the socio-economic spectrum of British society strongly identified in the collective imagination with certain dialects and accents – cockney and scouse, for example – but definitely not with others (Oxbridge accents or Received Pronunciation). It is this factor which explains the strong identification of the Scottish audience with these two soaps, even though they are geographically 'elsewhere', while they find it much more difficult to take to *Emmerdale*, whose sense of place is much more highly developed, with numerous shots of the Yorkshire Dales.

Seen from this point of view, *Eldorado*'s mistake was not just to be geographically misplaced – though this was undoubtedly a factor – its main problem was that it was socio-economically misplaced. It was not so much the villas that seemed alien as the lifestyle of those who occupied them. British soaps occupy a clearly definable space in British public culture. Survival is not guaranteed within it, but it is certainly not possible outside it.

A *yuppie soap:* Castles

In 1995 the BBC tried yet again to launch a new soap. Entitled *Castles*, it first went on air in a special hour-long episode at the end of May, before moving on to a twice-a-week basis at 20.30 in the first week of June, and it dealt with the lives of three generations of the Castles family. The (grand)-parents are James and Margaret Castle, who live in a large and lavishly decorated house in North London: the opening sequence consists of the camera moving slowly over a range of photographs mounted in gilt-edged frames showing various family groupings. As a piano plays a somewhat mournful melody in the background, the sequence ends with a view of the family name spelled out in stained glass above the front door – a detail which is quite sufficient on its own to identify both the relative spending power and the middle-class tastes of the family in question.

James Castle, whose accent suggests an Irish origin – and consequently, in the mythology of regional accents of the British Isles, a probably humble origin – is the owner of a large building supplies company, and is a man of means. The first episode opens dramatically, in a way quite reminiscent of the German soap *Jede Menge Leben* (see page 76), with James admitting, during a surprise birthday party for his wife, that he has, in fact, being having an affair for some time with another woman, the somewhat younger Christine Henshaw. The main difference with the German soap is that everything is taking place twenty years later. While Dorothee Berger celebrates her fortieth birthday at the beginning of *Jede Menge Leben*, Margaret Castle is celebrating her sixtieth birthday, their children are in their thirties, and their grandchildren are the same age as the children in the German soap.

Castles makes a rather obvious attempt to avoid certain of the stereotypes which might well be mobilized around such a situation, but in fact ends up falling somewhat predictably into others: the joyless deflation of the misbehaving husband revealed, the angular dignity of the wronged wife, the studied nobility of the 'other woman', the clucking concern of the daughters-in-law, the emotional ineptitude of the sons who have no idea how to respond in such a situation. And this is all compounded by the inescapable yuppiness of the decor, both material and linguistic. The plummy Home Counties accents of the characters immediately put *Castles* out on a limb in relation to other British soaps (not even *Eldorado* was this orotund). And everything else fits in: the pubs they drink in, what they drink, the way they drink it, the furniture they have at home, even their hairstyles. The caricature is at times so overwhelming that it is difficult to believe it is not deliberate. When Philip Castle argues with his son Paul about whether the latter should go to university, comparing him unfavourably with his older brother David, their conversation goes as follows:

Philip: Anyway, you couldn't follow in your brother's footsteps even if you wanted to. David is a very intelligent young man and he has worked very hard to get where he has.

Paul: 'Oh gosh,' he said, stung by his father's words. 'You watch, I'll show you. I'll go to university as well so they can be as proud of me.' Come on.

'Oh dear,' he said. And when the boozy brother, Matthew, complete with baggy brown cords and dangling grey cardigan, resigns his job as a schoolteacher to the astonishment of his partner, Alison, it is in order to, as he puts it, 'write a novel dealing ironically with British society as we approach the end of the second millennium ... but don't worry, it'll have lashings of sex.'

For someone like myself, who comes from the rather more egalitarian public culture of Scotland, characters such as these come over as somehow alien and unsympathetic even when they are trying to be nice. They look like the beached whales of the Thatcherite era, lacking sufficient self-knowledge to realize that the (at least rhetorical) tide has gone out leaving them morally high and dry. They are the overgrown teenagers of liberal individualism, narcissistic at a point in their lives where most people are too busy to be their own audience, on stage even when they are at home, ritualized into noise and posture as a substitute for feeling, incapable of expressing solidarity because no one has ever shown them the script. Creatures from another planet, indeed. But the fate of *Castles* shows that such a view is by no means a Scottish prerogative. *Castles* is undoubtedly the BBC's most spectacularly unsuccessful soap to date, failing completely to generate or hold a viable viewership. Falling from an initial 7.7 million to around three million, it moved backwards in the schedules, going from 20.30 on Tuesdays and Thursdays to 19.00 on Sundays and Mondays, and disappeared after only 24 episodes on 20 August, even though a continuation had originally been planned (in fact £100,000 had already been spent commissioning new scripts). In the end, *Castles* was unable to live down its rounded BBC-English vowels and all they stand for.

A teen soap: Hollyoaks

Channel 4's second soap opera, entitled *Hollyoaks*, first went on air on
Monday 23 October 1995 at 18.30, on a once-a-week basis. The Produced by the
Mersey TV company of Phil Redmond, the doyen of British soap writers –
he created *Brookside* and the very popular children's soaps *Grange Hill* and
Byker Grove and has also been involved with *Emmerdale* – it was the first
domestic soap to be deliberately aimed at a teenage market. It was,
therefore, part of a quite different strategy from that pursued by all earlier
British soaps. As an article in *Broadcast* (16 February 1996) put it:

Mersey TV's Phil Redmond, executive producer of *Hollyoaks*, sees the arrival of
the niche soap as inevitable. 'The idea of targeted soaps is perfectly feasible as TV
audiences fragment,' he says. 'There's not been a need for it yet as terrestrial
broadcasters have a dominant position in the market. But I can see a time when
there's a legitimate need for a soap regularly targeting 20-year-olds, 30-year-olds or
whatever . . . Soaps with a small audience and the right demographic will bring in
more money than a soap with a broad audience and the wrong demographic,' he
argues.

But *Hollyoaks* was also different from the traditional soaps in other ways. I
still vividly remember watching the early episodes with a sinking feeling as
teenage fashion victims called each other on their mobile phones from street
corners in the douce city of Chester or ran off counterfeit pop concert
tickets on the colour laser printers in their rooms. Where, I thought, was
such a programme going to find an audience that would stick? Subsequent
events were to prove me both wrong and right. Wrong in that not only did
Hollyoaks continue – it currently attracts an audience of around three
million: minor league when compared with the classic soaps, but quite
reasonable for Channel 4 – but it actually went on to a twice-a-week basis
(Mondays and Thursdays) from September 1996. Right in that it has
changed a considerable amount in the intervening period.

Hollyoaks was originally based on seven teenagers, all of whom appear in
the opening sequence in either individual or group shots in a band of film
which runs up the left side of the screen. As is now the norm for teen soaps
in Europe (and beyond), they are all very good-looking: in fact, Jeremy
Edwards, the actor who plays Kurt Benson, was a former Armani model. As
the *Guardian* (2 October 1995) put it:

The seven stars of *Hollyoaks* are good looking, bright eyed and cheerful, the sort of
youngsters whose mothers made sure they went to the dentist. On screen they tend
to fix up their all-important social lives by mobile phone. And the boys, when they
are not strumming guitars, ride out to meet their mates on flash motor bikes, doing
'wheelies' on the way.

But as well as the good looks, in the early life of the soap it was all, despite the mildly proletarian Jambo Bolton and Tony Hutchison, terribly twee. A number of the characters – most notably Kurt, Dawn Cunningham and Maddie Parker – had extremely polished accents, while Natasha Anderson's was positively cut-glass: not at all what one might expect of inhabitants of Chester (which is about fifteen miles south of Liverpool where *Brookside* is set). In fact, the absence of northern accents appears as one of the frequently asked questions (FAQs) in the *Hollyoaks* website, part of the answer being: 'As for their accents, it was more important that the actors fitted the image that Phil Redmond had in his mind when he created the characters than any specific regional accent.'

I was not alone in feeling that this choice of milieu might be the programme's fatal flaw. As a very hostile review in the *Sunday Times* of 29 October 1995 – immediately after the first episode – put it:

With *Hollyoaks*, his new television series, Phil Redmond is deliberately targeting a youth audience. Big mistake.

The show's Achilles heel will be the same one that did for *Eldorado*. The characters are all middle-class with Prozac smiles, far too pleased with themselves and with no common history. The British will take as many airbrushed Australian and Californian soaps as are made, but we want our homegrown soaps to be realistic. We want our soap stars miserable and squabbling in the mire with the rest of us.

The choice of Chester as a location seemed to confirm this overall impression, as did the name *Hollyoaks*, redolent of the small and cosy middle-class housing developments which are springing up all over Britain and which invariably have names containing terms like Grove or Coppice or Bank and the names of trees such as Birch or Larch or Elms or similar. This point was made also by the *Guardian* (2 October 1995):

Hollyoaks is supposed to be a mythical and affluent suburb of Chester, deemed by social trends reports to be a pleasant part of middle England, where urban squalor and restrictions to walking around the streets with friends at night do not apply.

The storylines were to deliberately avoid any suggestion of being issue-led (an 'accusation' frequently levelled against *Brookside*). As Lucinda Whiteley, Channel 4's commissioning editor for children's programmes, put it:

Hollyoaks is not meant to be grim. It does not take as a starting point that the youth of today are all into drugs or crime. It is meant to explore other parts of teenage life: like oh God, will I ever get a boyfriend? Or why doesn't my hair ever look right? (*Guardian*, 2 October 1995).

And indeed, in the early part of its life, the soap stuck to this view with remarkable tenacity. Combined with this, the treatment was all very positive and upbeat. 'Now to a place where it's all happening,' trilled the station announcer introducing the first episode of *Hollyoaks*, adding at the end of the second: 'Next week, wake up to the latest battle between the sexes ... deception, fraud, any tactic goes ... high spirits on *Hollyoaks*, 6.30, next Monday on 4.'

Hollyoaks did not, however, adhere to this approach in the longer term. It is not difficult to see why. From a narrative point of view it was a non-starter. Teenagers do indeed agonize over their hair and whether or not they are attractive enough to the opposite sex, but the dramatic potential of bad-hair days is frankly limited, and there is only so often the relationship carousel can go round in a soap with a relatively limited number of characters. In fact quite remarkable changes were to take place in this soap after its first run of 26 episodes. The most striking sign of these changes was the dramatic writing out of Natasha. At the end of the first series two of the young male characters, Dermot Ashton and Rob Hawthorn, spiked her drink with drugs during a party, causing her death. This single change simultaneously altered the whole feel of the soap – since Natasha had been by far the most la-di-da character – and introduced those issues which were not supposed to be part of the soap's appeal. As Phil Redmond said in an interview reproduced on the *Hollyoaks* website:

I want people to sympathise with Natasha. She's the victim of something she knows nothing about so it is entirely different from, say, the other recent and high profile drug deaths. Ours is a story where a teenager who has never been into drugs is brought into contact with them through no fault of her own. Natasha's case is an appalling tragedy which the *Hollyoaks* cast and, I hope, the viewers will be debating.

And other changes occurred. The various sets of parents became much more important, as did the younger children who also started to feature more regularly in storylines, and even began to appear in the title sequence. Northern accents (Jude Cunningham's is quite noticeable) – or at least less burnished accents – began to be more in evidence. The new owner of the local pub was even Scottish.

In the meantime the 'battle of the sexes' lost some of its rougher edges, and the over-the-top laddism and Girl Power bravura of the early episodes has tended to disappear. The upbeat atmosphere has simultaneously become rather more downbeat as a more problematizing approach has begun to emerge. For example, a recent storyline introduced the 'issue' of teenage pregnancies, while another featured the problems of dyslexia, and one of the more peripheral younger characters, the disc jockey Bazz FM, came out as a homosexual. But even the occupations have changed. Kurt briefly got a job in his father's warehouse before signing up – amazingly – as a worker on a building site. Tony became a small business man running a failing video shop and a sandwich supply service. This is all very different from the *Hollyoaks* of just over a year before: more complex, more differentiated, more problem-oriented, less affluent, less smug. *Hollyoaks* is not, and never will be, *EastEnders*, but it has moved much more clearly into the field of classic British soap opera in a way which could not have been predicted at the outset.

Despite this, *Hollyoaks* continues to be different from other British soaps in a number of ways. The most obvious of these is the quite widespread use of extradiegetic music, which has never featured in any way in any British soap. The absence of music is not a stylistic but a *structural* difference between British and other soaps, and derives from the now long-standing 'slice of life' discourse (Jordan, 1981: 27) which accompanied the earliest British soaps: the vague idea that, somehow or other, the camera just happened to be there recording what was going on. Alone of British soaps *Hollyoaks* also plays with narrative time, using freeze frames, speeding the film up, or displaying what Metz would have called 'episodic sequences': 'a symbolic summary of stages in an implied chronological development, usually entailing a compression of time' (Stam *et al.*, 1992: 41). *Hollyoaks* is also the only British soap to 'quote', for example, using the music from *Mission Impossible*, *The Good, the Bad and the Ugly* and even *Psycho*, or taking off well-known adverts.

Hollyoaks' trajectory from smart-assed, teen-yuppie soap to something much more down-market and sober shows where the real centre of gravity of British soaps lies. The pull is so great that nothing wanting to be taken seriously as a soap can possibly resist: resistance means spinning off into oblivion (*Castles*) or crashing into the sun (*Eldorado*). *Hollyoaks'* greatest merit is, perhaps, that it has managed to retain its sense of difference, originality and sense of humour even as it has been pulled into the orbit of giant planets such as *EastEnders* and *Coronation Street*. In many senses it remains unique. It will need to in order to face down the forthcoming challenge from Channel 5.

A Gaelic soap: Machair

The first episode of *Machair*, Scotland's first ever Gaelic-language soap, went on air on Wednesday, 6 January 1993 at 18.30 (the Gaelic term 'machair' refers to the grass-covered part of a sandy beach above the high-water line: such a feature usually appears as a still before and after the commercial break in the middle of each episode). It was both produced and broadcast throughout central Scotland by the then Scottish Television company, or STV (which has since changed its name to Scottish), and was also broadcast in the north by Grampian, these two companies being those whose ITV franchise area contains native Gaelic speakers. *Machair* is broadcast with English subtitles for its non-Gaelic-speaking viewers, of which I am one.

Machair must be seen – in fact, only makes sense when seen – within the broader framework of Gaelic and Gaelic-language programming policy in Scotland in the late 1980s and early 1990s. Gaelic is a Celtic language closely related to Irish Gaelic and more distantly related to Welsh and Breton. According to the 1991 UK census, it is spoken (with varying degrees of competence) by some 65,000 people in Scotland, less than 1.5 per cent of the total population. Gaelic-speaking communities in the traditional sense of the word are now almost entirely limited to the Western Isles (mostly the northern part of Skye, Lewis and Harris, Uist and Barra). There are over 12,000 Gaelic speakers in Glasgow, but they are dispersed around the various suburbs, and maintain to some extent artificial communities through clubs, associations, weekend Gaelic-medium schools and so on (see Cormack, 1993, for further details).

In December 1989 the Thatcher government announced that it would allocate £8 million (later increased to £9.5 million) within the framework of its forthcoming Broadcasting Act to set up a Gaelic Television Fund whose aim would be to increase the amount of Gaelic-language television in Scotland from 100 to 300 hours per year, starting in 1993. The fund was to be administered by the Comataidh Telebhisein Gàidhlig (Gaelic Television Committee), or CTG, whose offices are now located in Stornoway on Lewis. When STV bid – unopposed – for a renewal of its ITV franchise in 1991, its proposal contained a specific commitment to produce 200 hours of Gaelic-language programming, including a soap opera. *Machair* was the result of that commitment.

Prior to its launch, it is probably fair to say that there was a certain amount of scepticism in at least some sections of the Lowland press about the arrival of this Gaelic soap: indeed, some journalists referred to it dismissively as *Gaeldorado*. In the event, however, its audience pull surpassed all expectations. Average audiences for the first season were 451,000, while the second episode was watched by no fewer than 516,000 viewers – almost eight times more people than there are Gaelic speakers in the country. It averaged a 28% audience share in the Grampian area (with 40% for the final episode of the first season) and 20% in central Scotland: very healthy – indeed, in some senses, quite remarkable – figures given the general dislike of subtitled programmes in Scotland and the UK as a whole.

Press reaction following the earliest episodes also proved to be very positive, with comments such as 'Telly's first Gaelic soap got the thumbs up from viewers last night' (*Daily Record*, 7 January 1993) or 'Move over, *Eldorado* – Scotland's new Gaelic soap is a clear winner with TV viewers' (*Sunday Mail*, 10 January 1993). *Scotland on Sunday*, Scotland's best-selling quality Sunday newspaper, was particularly complimentary. Its reviewer, former TV presenter Kenneth Roy, wrote:

Machair, the new Gaelic soap opera, is a credit to the company and a smack in the face for those of us, myself included, who were doubtful whether all that Gaelic broadcasting money would do much for the future of the language ... It is professionally produced, well-written, serious in purpose, and captures the essential atmosphere of the Hebrides fairly convincingly (10 January 1993).

(The comments reproduced above are taken from Cormack, 1994, who provides a comprehensive review of press reaction at the time.)

Machair is set in the Hebridean island of Lewis off the north-west coast of Scotland, and much of the action takes place in a fictitious further education college called Bradan Mòr specializing in business and media education. The filming is done on location, and *Machair* has among the highest, if not *the* highest, proportion of outside shots of any soap anywhere in Europe (the CTG spent one-third of its entire available budget on the first season of *Machair*). The stunning Hebridean scenery, whose lochs and mountains are constantly in view, is at least part of the attraction of the programme for urbanized Lowland Scots such as myself.

Machair is the only current European soap I am aware of where there is actual tension between the opening and closing sequences and the rest of the programme. *Machair* is the only British soap to have a title song (sung at the end of each episode, not the beginning). It is sung in Gaelic and develops a nostalgic coming-home theme. Its opening lines are as follows: 'It's long since I went to the city / I had to make my living there / But the machair always drew me / Seed of marram, my people's bloom.' The tempo is slow, and the melody is plaintive and elegiac, played out over brooding, crepuscular Hebridean landscapes. In fact this theme song – undoubtedly the most haunting theme song of any European soap – belongs squarely within a discourse which is well-known in Scotland: that of the Celtic Twilight (Chapman, 1978: 102–6), a discourse of ancient laments in an unknown language lost in the mists of time (the opening theme music, with its bodhrans and ethereal female voices, also belongs, though in a less developed manner, to the same discourse).

Machair's narratives, however, come out strongly against these kinds of associative ties. In the college, in particular, Gaelic is seen as the medium through which the students learn and acquire skills in business studies and computing, speculate on the stock market, do market analyses, draw up business plans and produce brochures using pagemaking software on their AppleMacs. The youthfulness of the characters – they dress like students anywhere else in Scotland, listen to the same kinds of music, follow the same football teams and so on – is also important in this respect. As Rhoda Macdonald (1994: 4), Scottish's Head of Gaelic Programmes, put it in a lecture given in the Sabhal Mòr college:

What *Machair* did and still does is make Gaelic look viable and alive ... It shows the language being used by young people for whom it is a vital part of the future and not, as has been the case, only about the past.

In *Machair* Gaelic is seen as fully integrated into, and equal to the demands of, contemporary Scottish life. The characters can be seen shopping in large, airy, well-stocked supermarkets, and when Mairead has her baby she does so in the very modern-looking Western Isles Hospital in Stornoway.

Machair is, however, different. What makes it stand out from other British soaps is its rather unique sense of community. In particular, class is not a defining feature of *Machair*. In fact, the island community is the prime definer over and above even notions of Scottishness or Englishness. It would, nonetheless, be naive to suggest that class structures do not actually exist on the islands – a recent controversy centred on the attempt by the Chief of the Clan Macleod on Skye to charge two crofters £20,000 per annum for the use of a few yards of foreshore for their fish-farming operation. This is one of a number of related ways in which *Machair* is not, as Rhoda Macdonald once claimed, 'a reflection of present day reality' (1994: 4).

Machair has been, by any standards, the most successful Gaelic-language programme ever to be screened in Scotland. Until quite recently its future seemed assured. Both the Conservative and Labour parties made it clear that CTG funding would continue no matter who won the 1997 general election, and in September 1996 the CTG opened a £1.3 million studio in Stornoway, part of whose aim was to help overcome some of the production difficulties *Machair* had to contend with. As the *Herald* (19 September 1996) put it:

The complex . . . is part of an ambitious plan by the Gaelic Television Committee (CTG) to create a 'media village' which would attract more broadcasters to the Western Isles . . . The Glasgow-based commercial station [Scottish] will use the studio for at least 20 weeks a year. Ms Rhoda Macdonald, head of Gaelic at Scottish, said the new facility secured the future of *Machair* for at least the next three years.

However, an announcement by the CTG in January 1997 suggested that its future might be in some doubt since, rather than simply continuing to fund its existing commitments, the Committee decided to put all its programming requirements out to tender. As an article in the *Stornoway Gazette* (14 February 1997) put it:

From the end of this month Comataidh Telebhisein Gaidhlig will invite broadcasters to tender for all areas of television output. Current programmes will run their course – but if there is a preferred alternative bid for, say, another soap, then look out 'Machair'.

This was perhaps inevitable since *Machair* has not been able to hold onto its audience in the longer term. Perhaps the novelty value wore off, or perhaps – indeed a more likely explanation – scheduling it opposite *EastEnders* was

to throw it into a contest it could not possibly win. In any case, by the end
of the 1996 season its viewing figures had fallen to 165,000, around one-
third of its viewers three years earlier.

It would undoubtedly be possible to produce a cheaper soap than
Machair – such soaps abound taking Europe as a whole. It is not that
Machair is the UK's most expensive soap – its £77,000 per episode is some
distance behind *EastEnders*' £110,000 – but it is certainly the most expensive per viewer. However, what could not be reproduced so easily would be
Machair's 'goodwill' in the economic sense. It has built up a core following
not only among Gaels, but among a surprising number of Lowlanders many
of whom probably knew very little about island life before this programme
went on air, and its viewing figures have climbed back more recently to just
over 200,000 (*Scotland on Sunday*, 13 April 1997). As Rhoda Macdonald put
it on another occasion: 'Drama is the most popular form of television and it
has a spectral appeal. People aged 5 or 85 will watch drama. "Machair"
makes Gaelic viable' (1993: 16). *Machair*, however, may have to reposition
itself if it is to survive in the longer term.

A chaotic soap: Family Affairs

It was clear from the outset that the UK's fifth terrestrial channel, Channel
5, would inevitably include a soap in its portfolio of programmes. Given
Channel 5's initial commitment to a 'stripped and stranded' format, with
the same programmes occupying the same time-slot every day, it was also
clear that this soap would be the UK's first five-day-a-week soap of the
1990s. Early information suggested it would be a medical soap entitled
Lifeline, and would be a co-production with Grundy (*Broadcast*, 16 February 1996). Subsequent intelligence suggested a change of title to *Running
Wild* (*Broadcast*, 31 January 1997), though no details were available as to
content. The title was finally firmly announced as *Family Affairs*, a soap set
in Maidenhead (west of London) and based on three generations of the Hart
family. According to the *Herald* (11 February 1997) 'the makers of *Family
Affairs* allegedly chose the town because it was neutral commuter country
with none of the regionalized quirkiness of the temperamental Scousers in
Brookside . . . or the miserable urban decay of *EastEnders*'. It goes out daily
at 18.30, and therefore clashes on Mondays and Thursdays with *Hollyoaks*.

Corinne Hollingworth, the new channel's controller of drama, described
Family Affairs as follows in the *Independent* (17 February 1997):

The grandfather, Angus, is quite working class, a miner who manned the picket
lines and comes from the north . . . His son Chris is also from the north, but has
moved south. He is a builder who decided in the late Seventies to set up by himself,
and he and his wife Annie are lower middle class. But their children have had

education and they've moved up. Holly, 24, is a trainee lawyer. Her twin, Duncan, has opted out and is an entrepreneur who sets up music gigs. Their sister Melanie, 19, is our Spice Girl: she works in a shop and plays hard; she doesn't work hard and has a good time. The youngest son, Jamie, is 13 and still at school.

This all sounded like a rather depressing mixture of *Castles* and the early *Hollyoaks*, but in the event, *Family Affairs* – produced by Grundy and Thames Television for Channel 5 – proved to be a much more shrewdly pitched soap than such advance coverage suggested, with its wide range of accents – Geordie, Scouse and Scottish, as well as Home Counties – its chaotic and overcrowded petty bourgeois Hart household living constantly on the brink of bankruptcy, and its teenage daughter thrown out of her flat for being unable to pay her rent (someone somewhere had learned the lessons of the past). It attracted a first-night audience of 1.5 million, though this proved to be partly a curiosity-audience attracted by the actual Spice Girls opening the new channel. In the following weeks its audience quickly fell back to around half a million, though it has now climbed again to just under one million. Though low in comparison with the other terrestrial channels, this kind of audience is well within Channel 5's expectations given its very partial coverage of the UK as a whole – its target for the end of 1997 is a 5 per cent audience share (*Guardian*, 2 June 1997) – and *Family Affairs* will almost certainly run for some time to come.

Analysis

It is something of a commonplace in writing about British soaps – in both academic and journalistic writing, both within the UK and abroad – that these programmes are about the British working class. A few examples should suffice to show how widespread this view is:

Thus what is important about it [*Coronation Street*] – its central focus on working-class life and on strong female characters – is still held in the particular way of setting up ideas and images of the working class and women that are crystallised and given new life in *The Uses of Literacy*. (Dyer, 1981: 2)

Thus, for instance, unlike in other countries, in Great Britain the working class is the privileged protagonist of serial fiction and can recognise itself (but in the past tense, i.e. nostalgically) in minimalist and everyday stories such as those of *Coronation Street*. (Silj, 1988: 200)

Situated in a town in the north (!) [exclamation mark in original] of England, *Coronation Street* reflects the daily life of the people who live in the street of the title; these people belong almost exclusively to the working class with a few striving for upwards mobility. (Hayward, 1990: 151)

The world of Italian fiction is predominantly the world of the haute bourgeoisie, or at the very least a world of the well-to-do classes ... In any case this is hardly surprising: the powerful, the wealthy, the privileged are probably the subjects by choice of television narratives everywhere ... perhaps the only exception is British productions where working class environments are more frequently represented. (Buonanno, 1994: 177)

While soaps always have a tendency to deal with the everyday and the mundane even in their most extreme moments, in British soaps this emphasis on the quotidian is inevitably intertwined with issues of class and religion. The working class, as a specific group, not just as ordinary people, was represented in *Coronation Street* ... The majority of the characters [of *EastEnders* and *Brookside*] are working class and ... the audience is invited to understand the programmes from that class perspective. (Geraghty, 1995: 66–7)

We are dealing here [in the German soap *Lindenstraße*] with what is perhaps a specifically German narrowing of social reality to the representation of the middle class ... Things are rather different in Great Britain: there there are many serials which deal with the working class, for example, *Lindenstraße*'s model *Coronation Street*. (Jurga, 1995: 59)

Although some 'yuppies' crept into the square in the late 1980s, it is basically a working class area, with a strong cockney culture and values. (*Evening Times EastEnder Special*, 29 January 1997)

My own acquaintance with the early episodes of the UK's major soaps is limited to those which are available on commercial video or appear from time to time in 'specials' outlining the history of the soap. It is, therefore, relatively slight, and I would not want to generalize over much on what I have seen of those earlier periods. What I can say, however, on the basis of my reasonably consistent viewing of current British soaps over the past few years is that not only are the bulk of their characters not members of the British working class, but the British working class is in fact one of the great *absentees* of current British soaps. The overwhelming bulk of the characters who currently populate British soaps own garages, pubs, restaurants, hairdressing salons, second-hand car businesses, market stalls, hotels, pizzerias, electrical appliance stores, taxi businesses, building yards, travel agencies, home delivery services, video shops, fish-and-chip shops, whole-sale electrical businesses, freezer shops, bookmakers' businesses, beauty parlours, clothing factories, cafés, even farms. This is not by any stretch of the imagination the British working class. On the contrary, it is quite clearly and unequivocally the traditional petite bourgeoisie.

Jordan (1981: 31) already pointed to this contradiction some time ago. Talking of *Coronation Street* she says:

The programme has deployed a whole series of petty bourgeois characters ... Only Hilda Ogden of the long-standing characters is of the working class proper ... Yet by its insistence the programme manages so well to *seem* to be about the working class that even such obviously bourgeois characters as Mike Baldwin are seen as deviant members of the working class, rather than as members of another fraction.

If anything, the move in the 1990s has been towards the total removal of the relatively few genuine working-class characters there ever were. The proletarian Arthur Fowler has now disappeared entirely from *EastEnders*. Even *Brookside* – initially a kind of staging post for both the upwardly and the downwardly mobile – has lost the working-class characters and trade unionists (Geraghty, 1995: 73–4) which once made it quite distinctive. In view of all this, how is this 'seeming' to be about the working class of British soap operas achieved? It is due essentially to the fact that, although the characters belong economically to the petite bourgeoisie, in all other respects they have many of the traditional preoccupations of the working class and even *look* like members of the working class: in their very ordinary, at times rather grubby housing, their entirely unglamorous lifestyles, their run-of-the-mill clothes and the conspicuous absence of wealth. But it is carried, above all, by the traditionally proletarian resonance of the way they speak (the question of accents was specifically raised as an issue in the second episode of *Brookside* when Lucy Collins was bullied at school because of her 'upper-class' accent, and more recently a similar fate has befallen young Danny Simpson). In the political mythology of British dialectology, to speak with a cockney or a scouse or a Lancashire accent is to be working-class.

It might be argued that, from a narrative point of view, it is easier to work with characters who are 'around' rather than characters who are 'away' at work, but Scandinavian soaps such as *Rederiet* (see page 182) or *Offshore* (see page 141) show that it is perfectly possible to construct soaps which combine characters from a range of different social classes. The absence of the working class is neither a narrative necessity nor a coincidence. It has to do with the current balances of power within British society as a whole. Even if the characters in British soaps are 'of the classes immediately visible to the working classes (shopkeepers, say, or the two-man business)' (Jordan, 1981: 28), their economic circumstances – essentially the fact that they are self-employed – mean that a range of fundamental working-class concerns are seldom (if ever) raised. Since the departure of Bobby Grant from *Brookside* some years ago, the only other character in a current British soap who was a trade unionist was Eddie Grant, also in *Brookside*, in the mid-1990s. Since most are their own bosses, employer–employee conflicts are something of a rarity. Again with the exception of the strike in *Brookside* in the early 1980s, the relatively small number of other incidents I can think of over the years have all been related to Mike Baldwin and his small clothing factory in *Coronation Street*: but while there was an – admittedly low-key –

strike when he fired Hilda Ogden in June/July 1978 (Patterson and Stewart, 1981: 82), no one went on strike when he fired the pregnant Tricia Armstrong in December 1996.

The traditional petite bourgeoisie is without any doubt the least powerful and the least influential class in Britain today. It is, in fact, perhaps even more so than elsewhere in Europe, a class in terminal decline. The 1980s, however, saw a quite clear and rather determined attempt to alter the moral-political landscape of the UK. Part of the ideological push of Thatcherism was centred on a restructuring of what in Gramscian terms would be termed the 'historical bloc' (Forgacs, 1988: 195), in other words those classes and class fractions on whom moral and political leadership of society as a whole has been bestowed, the political, social and cultural structures which favour their promotion and perpetuation, and the complex set of discourses, practices and cultural and intellectual products which emerge as a result. The rhetoric of Thatcherism quite consciously and deliberately attributed moral and economic protagonism to those small businessmen – the class which enjoys narrative protagonism in the British soaps – whose celebratory self-enrichment (or 'wealth creation', in the official terms of the discourse) was going to cascade ever downwards and save the nation from collapse: as Phillips correctly points out in her analysis of the discourse of Thatcherism (1996: 212), 'enterprise' became one of the key words of Thatcherist rhetoric. However, the class which the practices of Thatcherism actually sought to co-opt into moral and economic leadership was not – indeed could not be – a rejuvenated and thrusting petite bourgeoisie, but the new professional and managerial middle classes of whom the yuppies were merely the more flamboyant representatives.

The economic strand of this strategy was forcefully pushed through by the Conservatives and areas of public life such as education and the National Health Service found themselves restructured along income-generating, profit-oriented, productivity-based lines, with the collapse of the miners' strike in 1984 effectively eliminating all serious resistance. However, the Thatcherite attempts to bestow consensually agreed qualities of *moral* leadership on these new middle classes – either in their own terms or through the symbolic mediation of the petite bourgeoisie – failed in the UK. Indeed, since the fall of Mrs Thatcher in 1991 the Conservatives – without significantly altering their political or economic practices – struggled more and more to find a new moral focus in the supposedly 'caring, sharing nineties', a failure which, amongst other things, almost certainly cost them the 1997 election. They failed because Thatcherism was unable to create a large enough nationwide constituency for such views beyond the south-east of England, and the bulk of the population outside that region refused to take the bait.

Both the launch of this strategy and its ultimate collapse were played out in *EastEnders* and *Brookside*. In 1987 the upwardly-mobile James Wilmott-

Brown (double-barrelled names have a mythology all of their own in the UK) opened the yuppie pub, the Dagmar, in *EastEnders*. His symbolic relationship with the other characters in the soap was made clear when he raped Kathy Beale, as a result of which Dennis Watts torched the Dagmar, burning it to the ground. In the meantime Jonathan and his yuppie friends – much derided by the other characters (Geraghty, 1995: 70) – have long since disappeared from *Brookside*. In neither case did any of the petit bourgeois characters aspire to the new values, which were invariably presented as alien. In fact, the displacement of selected aspects of working-class experience into (and the concomitant rejection of neo-liberal values from) the lives of petit bourgeois characters continues to be a defining feature of British soaps at this time: there is, of course, a very acute sense in which the isolated, embattled and inward-looking group of people who populate British soaps can be seen to represent the very real and widespread disarray of the British working class, particularly following the spectacular failure of the miners' strike. Geraghty (1995) explains in detail how the social, and ultimately, political issues raised by soaps such as *EastEnders* and *Brookside* are constantly deflected and contained by being placed firmly within the framework of the family. This is true, but they are also structurally diffused by the atomized, fragmented and unorganized class position of the protagonists. This is largely what gives British soaps their simultaneously progressive and conservative feel. If it is true, as writers such as Nairn (1988) and Anderson (1992) argue, that the dominant sections of the British ruling classes have, historically, shown little interest in incorporating the working class into a hegemonic project, that the British working class is in some sense 'elsewhere' in British society, then the leading soaps are at least part of that 'elsewhere'. *Coronation Street*'s roots are not really 'those of a Britain that exited with the last Labour government onto which has been grafted an ephemeral veneer of sitcom-esque jollity' (*Guardian*, 4 April 1994). It is set in a Britain which never was, and never will be, a country of publicans and shop owners where problems from the real world are taken in, reworked and reconfigured: they are transformed from political issues to personal ones, and dispersed into an unending flow of narrative. *EastEnders* and *Brookside* do essentially the same thing in their different ways. The result is both utopian and dystopian – an 'elsewhere' of endless talking where problems are constantly broken down into manageable pieces but never solved.

There is never any kind of clear-cut fit between the cultural output of a society as a whole and ideological realignments on a grand or even on a smaller scale. There are always slippages, overlaps and mismatches, temporal or otherwise. This accounts largely for the failure of both *Eldorado* and *Castles*. They derive ultimately from an ideological push which had already failed on the ground. They constructed narrative worlds into which working-class experience could not be displaced. They were unrecognizable to British soap opera viewers – geographically, linguistically, socially and morally. They failed to learn this lesson and died. *Hollyoaks* wised up in time and survived. *Family Affairs* has been shrewd enough to learn the lessons of the past.

But the search for new British soaps goes on, and there have been numerous false starts. While the financial return on a successful soap can be very considerable, start-up costs are high, and failure does not just mean a loss of revenue. There are significant ways in which the BBC has yet to recover from the fiasco of *Eldorado*. Rumours of new soaps abound. An ITV soap entitled *Quayside* and set in a rejuvenated part of Newcastle was announced for early 1997 (*Scotland on Sunday*, 20 October 1996) but has so far not appeared (at least not on network television). There has also been much talk of a new BBC soap to be called *The Lakes* and set in the Lake District in the north-west of England. The *Observer* (10 March 1996) wrote of it as follows:

The BBC thinks it has found the formula that will create Britain's next blockbuster TV soap – only it won't admit it. Television executives have been embarrassed so many times by hyping soap series which then flopped with the public that the word 'soap' has become almost taboo.

But if *The Lakes*, given the go-ahead last week by BBC1, is a success after its initial run, it will be turned into a long-running flagship serial drama – a soap, in plain English.

The new drama will be set in a hotel in the Lake District, reviving memories of one of the earliest TV soaps, *Crossroads* ... The programme-makers are hunting for a suitable location in the area, and are thought to be concentrating on Grasmere and Ambleside ... *The Lakes*, which will start shooting this summer, will be based partly in the hotel, with a mix of staff and guests, and partly in the local village.

So far, nothing has appeared. It is difficult to avoid concluding that the world of soap opera production in the UK is currently in some kind of crisis, with the viewers simply refusing to be taken in the direction that the stations want them to go. No doubt these negotiations between viewers and producers will continue, but there seems little likelihood of the current compromise position being disturbed in the short to medium term.

Postscript

On Sunday, 14 September 1997, *The Lakes* finally appeared, not as a soap, however, but as a mini-series consisting of four one-hour-and-fifty-minute episodes. The time for a new soap is clearly not yet ripe.

Some Interim Conclusions

Patterns and trends

When dealing with a potentially endless genre such as soap opera, any conclusions must, by definition, be interim ones. Moreover, space – quite literally – prevents me from developing a number of themes here that I would otherwise have liked to go into in some depth. Nonetheless, there are several general patterns and trends I would want to touch on, however briefly. These are areas in which my ideas are still to some extent fluid, and I will want to return to some of them in the future. In the meantime they may, of course, also be of interest to others.

Cultural defence: whose culture?

From the elevation of 1997 the cultural panics engendered in western Europe by the arrival of the American supersoaps in the 1980s can be seen much more clearly for what they were: aggressive reactions by the intellectual élites of the various countries concerned to their loss of control over the management of popular taste. While the notions of 'imperialism' and 'Americanization' were (and indeed still are) often foregrounded, they were, in reality, always secondary: the underlying rhetoric differed little from, for example, that of the 'culture and civilization' tradition in Great Britain as far back as the 1930s (Storey, 1993: 20–42), and has continued relatively unchanged into the 1990s, now using the new domestic soaps – particularly those showing on the commercial channels – as its target. The complaining groups were those who would, in Gramscian terms, be defined as the 'organic intellectuals' of the former status quo (Forgacs, 1988: 309), who, throughout western Europe, have traditionally aligned themselves over-whelmingly with the cultural conventions and values of the liberal bourgeoisie. And they had good reason to feel alarmed, since the oncoming neo-liberal advance is, in its populist discourses at least, scathingly anti-intellectual. Their defence of such aesthetic notions as 'quality', 'seriousness' and so on was in reality the defence of an ideology and its resultant social structures and practices which, to put it at its most basic, provided them with a social role and a livelihood. This group of people, like the social-democratic hegemony from which they emerged, are still very much on the defensive.

Nonetheless, it is clear that the domestic soap has supplanted the American soap as the main unit of consumption within that genre in the Europe of the 1990s. There are a few exceptions to the dominance of the domestic products. The popularity of *The Bold and the Beautiful* in Italy and, to a lesser extent, Finland is such an exception, as is (though involving a somewhat different set of relationships) the continuing domination of the Brazilian *telenovelas* in Portugal. But in general terms the domestic products reign supreme. This is the case even where there is 'outside' involvement of some kind, mostly as regards the various Grundy co-productions which have been analysed, but also in cases such as *De syv søstre* in Norway. So long as an original script is not simply being followed structurally, all such productions have quickly become entirely 'domestic'. Talking of such 'reversioned' soaps, Biltereyst (1992b: 537) wrote: 'It is a somewhat fright-ening thought that the danger of "globalization" does not only come from external imports, but may also be situated within the encoding of home-made programmes themselves.' Even assuming that 'globalization' as he understands it is actually taking place – itself a moot point (Ferguson, 1992) – and that it is somehow or other 'frightening', he has little to fear from these domesticated soaps.

It is, of course, important not to repeat the mistake of the 1980s in relation to these new soaps. At one point the American soaps appeared as though they were here to stay, more or less, for ever, but in the end they disappeared fairly quickly (because American audiences tired of them), and of course the new European soaps themselves likewise belong to a particular historic moment which may also pass, leading to their unexpected demise. I would personally expect some of the weaker soaps to disappear in the medium term, though the major soaps in each country look set to run for some time to come, and the *telenovela* traditions now established in Spain and Portugal show no immediate signs of faltering.

The new European domestic serials also continue a trend which was already apparent in the 1980s (Silj, 1988) and the early 1990s (Biltereyst, 1992): they do not export well. This is particularly the case if a 'language frontier' is concerned. There is a certain amount of exchange between the Nordic countries, in particular Sweden and Norway, which, apart from linguistic similarities, are divided by a relatively 'undramatic cultural frontier' and are 'politically, socially and culturally very close to each other' (Löfgren, 1993: 86) – with *Rederiet* having been shown in Norway for some years now in a prime-time slot on the commercial channel TV2. Denmark's *Landsbyen* has also been exported to Norway and Iceland. Apart from this, the only other exception of any note is *EastEnders*' relative popularity in Catalonia. Other experiments have been considerably less successful: *Marienhof* was shown for a brief period in Finland, as was *Rederiet* (which was originally co-financed by YLE and featured Finnish characters speaking Finnish), and *EastEnders* was shown for a brief period in Norway, but none was continued. And even exchanges between Scandinavian countries are not guaranteed success. In November 1996 TV3 Norway had to abandon its decision to screen the Swedish soap *Vänner och fiender* (which was reasonably successful in Sweden) when it managed to attract the derisory figure of between 15,000 and 26,000 viewers (*VG*, 26 November 1996). This, however, has not prevented the Swedish channels from buying in Norwegian soaps. As from autumn 1997 SVT2 will show *Offshore* and TV4 will show *De syv søstre*. It remains to be seen how successful they will be.

But even when there is a common language, state (or in some cases 'regional') boundaries can be so strong as to reduce the potential appeal of a 'foreign' soap. The most striking exception is the performance of the UK soaps – in particular *Coronation Street* – in Ireland, a situation which is quite unique. Apart from this, only *Lindenstraße*, which is shown in a prime-time slot in Austria, appears to run counter to this trend, and it is partly financed by ORF and features Austrian characters. As far as I am able to ascertain, there appears to be no appreciable audience at all in the Netherlands for the Flemish soap *Familie*, despite the fact that it is in Dutch, while *Goede Tijden, Slechte Tijden*, the Netherlands' most watched soap, is shown in Flanders on VTM at 12.30 in the afternoon. *Gute Zeiten, Schlechte Zeiten*, the most successful of Germany's new soaps with an audience of over five million there, appears to attract around only 120,000 viewers in Austria (*Neue Kronen-Zeitung*, 18 December 1995). In the UK, the Scottish soap *High Road*, which has a prime-time slot in Scotland, is shown in England in a mid-afternoon slot despite the fact that, although there are separate Scottish and English cultures which are in important ways different from each other, there is also a British culture in which both participate and to which both, in varying degrees, contribute.

The search for a pan-European soap has now been indefinitely postponed due to a serious lack of interest among viewers. Kilborn (1992: 112) talks of two pan-European projects, *Impact* and *Vintage*, which, to the best of my knowledge, never made it to the screen. The one which did – *Riviera* (see page 27) – flopped miserably. Other more 'international' soaps, such as the Dutch–Canadian–Argentinian *Foreign Affairs*, fared no better. These are experiments which are unlikely ever to be repeated.

However, to call the emergence of the new domestic soaps (and other domestic programmes) 'the new parochialism' (Tracey and Redal, 1995) seems to me to be wrong from a number of points of view. First, there was absolutely nothing *un*-parochial about *Dallas* and *Dynasty* and the other American soaps which swept through Europe in the 1980s. They did not create an international community of television viewers eager to discuss these programmes with members from other countries. Although the presence of these soaps in one country may have been important for their arrival in another – as in the case of Norway and Sweden, for example (Gripsrud, 1995) – they were consumed in splendid isolation in the different states and regions of Europe, with the outermost boundaries of Figure 1 (see page 11) remaining as impermeable as ever. Secondly, there is nothing 'new' about European audiences' preferences for domestic products. As Silj (1988) and others have shown, the domestic products were outperforming the imported ones even in the Europe of the 1980s. Thirdly, there is nothing necessarily 'parochial' about a preference for domestic cultural products. Schrøder argues that, when dealing with domestic products, viewers easily 'understand allusions to the common cultural heritage' (1988: 62), these allusions often being quite dense in soaps and *telenovelas*. This is quite correct, but as I hope to have shown in this book, they 'understand' a great deal more besides.

Realism: 'realist' or 'realistic'?

The notion of realism itself is – at least as far as academics are concerned – a relatively controversial one, as is shown by the fragmentation of the concept into more and more subdivisions: classic realism, social realism, empirical realism, documentary realism, psychological realism, emotional realism, neo-realism, even magical realism (this last formulation, invented by the Cuban writer Alejo Carpentier, is widely applied to a style of writing which flourished throughout Latin America in the 1950s and 1960s (see Valbuena Briones, 1969: 502)). There have been discussions of realism in relation to soaps in particular on a theoretical level (Jordan, 1981), or in relation to the production techniques used to give them their 'illusion of realness' (Barbatsis and Guy, 1991). In her analysis of *Coronation Street* Marion Jordan even suggests a category of 'soap opera realism', which seems to me a very circular appellation. The logical extension to this would be to have sit-com realism, science fiction realism, science fantasy realism and so on; and why not?

There is a copious literature on realism, and the concept itself has been the subject of quite high-profile exchanges of views in the *Screen* journal, one in the 1970s between Colin MacCabe and Colin McArthur (reprinted later as McArthur (1981) and MacCabe (1981a, 1981b)) and another in the

1990s between John Corner (1992) and Christopher Williams (1994). These debates are complex and at times ill-tempered. My own position is closest to that argued by John Corner, namely that any attempt to define 'realism' is an attempt to define the evanescent. As far as the present study is concerned I believe that such an attempt would be fruitless for at least three reasons:

1. My own view is that 'realism' should be seen as a nineteenth-century ideological-aesthetic movement with clear historical boundaries which are now closed. No one, I believe, would now *systematically* use notions such as 'impressionism' or 'expressionism' or even the early twentieth-century 'surrealism' in an attempt to define contemporary late-twentieth-century cultural output. And yet 'realism' lives on.

2. My own analysis – very briefly put – is that the increasing fragmentation of the concept derives inevitably from attempting to apply a nineteenth-century bourgeois aesthetic to areas of late-twentieth-century popular culture where it makes little sense, and where it can only be made to fit by breaking it down into smaller and smaller components with more and more restricted areas of applicability. 'Realism' as an ideological-aesthetic programme rose with the industrial bourgeoisies of the nineteenth century and was part of their attempt to express their domination of the material world through their culture. It involved a well-documented series of techniques mostly in the novel but also – though with somewhat different emphases – following Victor Hugo's Preface to *Cromwell* in 1827, on the stage. How (or even whether) it represented 'reality' is much less important than the fact there was some degree of agreement between authors and public that it did.

3. I have come across nothing in my researches to suggest that 'realism' in any of its academic meanings represents a primary demand from popular audiences in relation to soaps or *telenovelas* at all. 'Social realism' as it is understood in Great Britain is nowhere to be found in a number of the soaps analysed here, which has not prevented them from attracting sizeable audiences.

The English noun 'realism' has two meanings – an 'academic' one and a more 'everyday' one – which have resulted in two differentially derived adjectives, 'realist' and 'realistic', a situation which does not obtain in many other European languages where one adjective covers both meanings. Nonetheless, it is quite clear that the claim made for soaps and *telenovelas* by those responsible for producing and promoting them is that they are 'realistic' rather than 'realist'. The phrase 'slice of life' is actually used with some frequency, as are claims that they reflect 'the everyday life' of their viewers and that they will deal with 'highly topical' issues. Indeed, the level at which the *producers* are keen for the information presented by the soap to be 'realistic' in the sense that it is congruent with that provided by official and unofficial bodies of various kinds ('official realism'?) is precisely at the level of the metanarrative. Most of the soaps and *telenovelas* about which I have been able to acquire production details have groups of researchers whose job it is to make sure that the details of storylines dealing with what are at least potentially controversial issues have the *imprimatur* of some organization or body regarded as providing a reliable benchmark in relation to the issue in question. Indeed, in the UK episodes of soaps dealing with such issues will often be followed by the station announcer providing the address and phone number of the organization concerned.

As far as viewers of domestic soaps are concerned, however (and such audience research as is available does suggest that they tend to view their domestic soaps as 'realistic'), their requirements would seem to be as follows:

• Use of the national language, where appropriate in the 'regional' form of this language (Scottish English, Flemish, Valencian Catalan).
• Settings which are identifiably domestic in their architecture, interior decor, layout of streets, shops available, use of the national currency, car registration plates and so on, even in the colour and design of telephone and letter-boxes or the uniforms of the postmen and -women and of the police. These settings may be given 'real' names, but this does not in any sense guarantee the 'realness' of the locations appearing on the screen (in Germany *Lindenstraße* is filmed in Cologne and set in Munich, while *Marienhof* is filmed in Munich and set in Cologne).
• A lifestyle (including fashions, hairstyles, leisure activities, cuisine and so on) which is either close to theirs or at least shares certain key elements with theirs.

Beyond that, demands for any kind of 'realism' appear to be very small, particularly at the level of production values and of the micronarrative. Occasionally shaking walls, poor sound, extraneous noises (I have heard these), momentary losses of picture (I've seen this too), a total absence of outside shots, dialogues which are at times unconvincing, acting which can be less than inspirational, characters behaving 'out of character' or under-going complete changes of personality (sometimes aided by falling down stairs, being knocked on the head, etc.), changes of actors (at times quite dramatic), 'time leaps', anonymous settings, invented newspapers, extrava-gant storylines (resurrections, kidnaps, bizarre murders, incredible coincidences), all of these are breezily consumed by soap opera and *telenovela* viewers. The narrative worlds constructed by soaps are symbolic universes where elements chosen from a range of sources – of which the 'real' is only one – are mixed according to the internal and external needs of that universe as it emerges from the ongoing negotiations between pro-ducers and consumers, and not from any overriding need to somehow or other reproduce 'reality' faithfully or even present a particular version of it 'masterfully'.

Only this can explain widespread features of both soaps and *telenovelas* such as the following:

- The consistently heavy over-representation of emotionally 'available' characters. Particularly in the early stages of a soap or *telenovela* it is not unknown for no one in any age group to be in a stable relationship. Such few lasting relationships as there are are virtually all confined to the older age-group.
- The total absence of long-term unemployment (despite very high levels of unemployment in some of the countries where these programmes are shown) and of real poverty.
- The almost complete absence of the industrial working class and its near-total replacement primarily by the petite bourgeoisie and, though on a smaller scale, by the lumpenproletariat (only *Offshore* in Norway and, to a lesser extent, *Rederiet* in Sweden have main characters who are clearly industrial workers).
- The crowding of those in work into extremely small-scale jobs concentrated in retail, catering, fashion, fitness, advertising and, to a lesser extent, journalism. The scale is often so small that the work is actually carried out from home. Despite this, success seems guaranteed: cafés, restaurants and bars in particular are constantly packed. If this were actually the case this sector would be one of the most dynamic of European economies, whereas the reality is that most new catering outlets outside the big chains go bust.
- The sustained avoidance of virtually any reference to politics in the party-political sense. Political parties are hardly ever mentioned (*Landsbyen* in Denmark is the only exception to this), politicians are never named or else names are invented, overtly political issues dominating the headlines are studiously ignored.
- The ever-increasing trend towards glamour which can now be found almost everywhere, and of which the appearance of beauty queens and male models among the cast of these serials is only the most striking indication. This trend affects the young female characters in particular – even in the deepest Portuguese countryside they wash their hair every day with root-nourishing shampoo – but it is clearly extending to the older women too (many of whom routinely wear miniskirts well into their 1950s) and to male characters as well. Only the main UK soaps and those most directly inspired by them are to some extent resisting this trend.

None of these elements is compatible with even a 'realistic' construction of the narrative world.

- The first feature is a technical requirement of the micronarrative. Without a constant pool of emotionally available characters this level of the narrative would quickly stall (Bleicher, 1995: 45). As *Familie* shows, this need not necessarily constitute a 'tragic structure of feeling' (Ang, 1985: 68–72). Whether or not it is co-opted into such a structure of feeling depends entirely on what the serial does with it.

- The second element is partly a narrative and partly a discursive (and therefore partly an ideological) constraint. For all their endless nature, soaps are not ideally structured to deal with chronic situations. Their endless progression is predicated on a never-ending flow of small-scale local resolutions, and any problem which is too large or too intractable to solve in at least the medium term – not just unemployment – would eventually become counterproductive (however contradictory it might appear, one-off productions are structurally better suited to dealing with long-term problems). On the ideological level, unemployment and poverty are inconsistent with the generally 'empowering' discursive mode of soaps and *telenovelas*.

- The third and fourth features derive from an ingrained reluctance among cultural producers in bourgeois societies to ascribe any kind of protagonism whatsoever to the industrial proletariat (whose ascribed function is to behave 'responsibly'), by a desire to stress individual economic empowerment and to simultaneously efface corporate power, which is, of course, where the real economic muscle of contemporary western European societies lies.

- The fifth element is dictated by the serial's relationship with its audience. Despite the courage with which they will often tackle difficult social issues, soaps and *telenovelas* are extremely careful not to alienate any part of their audience by offending overtly political sensitivities.

- The final characteristic derives from the neo-liberal appropriation of 'glamour' and 'fun' and the increasing penetration of television serials by advertising and sponsorship.

I am not suggesting that soap opera and *telenovela* viewers are in any way unaware of the 'unrealistic' nature of the elements outlined above, or that complaints are not registered from time to time. What I am saying is that these elements are simply not critical to the pleasure viewers find in the serial itself. On the contrary, the level at which *viewers* are most critical is the level of the macronarrative, the level of the kind of society constructed by the serial and of the kind of values it defends. Mistakes at this level will almost always lead to a loss of popularity and, unless remedial action is taken, eventual collapse.

There is, in the final analysis, nothing particularly surprising about the relatively scant importance given by viewers to 'realism', emotional, psychological or otherwise. 'Realism' was simply not an issue for early nineteenth-century melodrama, for example, and it is at the level of the micronarrative that the debt of soaps and *telenovelas* to melodrama is most apparent. Melodrama itself grew out of a dramatic tradition in late eighteenth-century France in which the use of language was prohibited, which led to a reliance on exaggerated grimaces and gestures in order to communicate emotions to an often noisy public (Brooks, 1985: 56–80; Martín-Barbero, 1987: 124–32), a feature which can still be seen in most soaps today. In fact, the enduring inability to impose a 'realist' aesthetic on the population at large has been one of the major failures, in their own terms, of the bourgeois education systems which still exist in variously modified forms throughout Europe today. The secondary school students who sullenly wade their way through Balzac and Dickens and Galdós and Eça de Queirós will, once the compulsion of the education system has ceased, gleefully devour blockbusters and potboilers of the kind analysed in the USA by Radway (1984) – including Mills & Boon in the UK, 'Corín Tellado'-type novels in Spain, the various sub-genres of the Bastei-Heftchen in Germany, the so-called FLN literature in Sweden, Harlequin in its various spellings in a number of countries, and so on – where demands for 'realism' are as understated as they are for soaps and *telenovelas*. In fact, soaps and *telenovelas* seem to me to be at least partly a continuation in the bourgeois era of pre-bourgeois forms of narrative at times made more 'respectable' by being incorporated into the discourses and practices of 'social realism', 'psychological realism' and the like.

Gender models and life-cycles

Though the number of men watching soaps and *telenovelas* has undoubtedly increased – to the point where it can, at times, make up about a third of the viewership – there can be little doubt that the bulk of viewers continue to be women and girls – in some cases quite young girls. This has given rise to a very large literature relating to women – both as viewers and as characters – and soaps. Anyone wishing further information on this literature will find a very comprehensive bibliography in Brunsdon (1995).

Many of the already existing studies have concentrated on British or American soaps, and to a lesser extent Australian soaps. As far as Continental Europe is concerned, the only analyses I am aware of in this area relate to *Dallas*, and are provided by Ang (1985) for the Netherlands and Hjorth (1985) for Denmark. I would like here to deal very briefly with the new European soaps.

Are there gender-model patterns which can be seen to extend throughout the new European soap operas and *telenovelas*? Some can, in fact, be distinguished. Women in these productions, by and large, form groups which communicate internally on a much greater level of intimacy than their male counterparts. This is particularly obvious in the case of the younger women. In a number of cases young men with personal problems of one kind or another refuse to talk about them to other men (either of their own age or older), even when offers to listen sympathetically are made. Teenage boys in particular seem remarkably incompetent in this respect, whereas teenage girls are presented as much more expert both at talking to each other and at talking to their parents. Talking between adult men is often confrontational or based on formal or informal hierarchies of one kind or another. In a broad sense women's communities are seen as organic and men's as mechanical. This particular pattern both reflects and reproduces a well-established western discourse assigning women to a private sphere of language and intimacy and men to a public sphere of rhetoric and power. In very general terms, it can be said that women's collective private compe-tence is presented as positive, whereas men's individualizing public performance is often associated with destruction and even death.

Another quite obvious pattern is that physical violence and criminality are almost exclusively male preserves. Violence has in fact become quite common in soaps as more and more detective-type storylines – and indeed more and more policemen – have been introduced. But it is almost without exception carried out by men. The kind of physical violence carried out by women in *Brookside* appears to have no counterpart so far in continental Europe. There is, however, a gradient of acceptability as to the level of violence by men towards women which can actually be shown on screen, with the Scandinavian soaps being the most restrained and the Greek soaps the most graphic.

Other perhaps less obvious patterns can also be ascertained. Though women seldom reach the top positions of social and economic power available to men in certain soaps, this is not to say that power struggles do not exist among them. However, these can be very limited in scope (for example, struggles over who is in charge of the office), and the weapons used often conform to a stereotype of 'bitching' (smirks, pointed remarks, ill-concealed glee over small victories). While some male figures in positions of power can be either ruthless or downright crooks, others can on occasion be presented as honourable (if at times thoughtless). Again in very general terms, only men seem able to combine power with honour in this way. Uncomplicated power and femininity appear to be problematic. This discourse is of course not limited to soaps: it was (and continues to be) widely circulated in the UK in connection with Margaret Thatcher and, though officially frowned upon, enjoys a kind of subterranean existence in Norway in relation to Gro Harlem Brundtland. In this more complicated sense, soaps appear to be reproducing an essentially conservative patriarchal discourse of the functions of women in society.

As I watched hundreds of episodes of European soaps and *telenovelas* I became aware of what might be called a dominant life-cycle constructed by these serials in relation to men and women. I decided to experiment with this as a heuristic in order to try to pin down more closely the constructions of both men and women in these productions. Its broad outlines are as follows.

Babies and infants, though by no means absent, are *very* thin on the ground in European soaps (in fact, if the ratio of births to pregnancies in real life was anything like that in soaps the future of the human race would be in genuine jeapordy). When present, babies in particular are seen primarily as the business of the mother. Pre-teenage children are also rare. The girls – of whom Lillema in the Norwegian soap *I de beste familier* is the most striking example – are articulate and precocious. The boys – for example Oliver in *Gute Zeiten, Schlechte Zeiten* – are often associated with problems such as bullying at school.

Excepting these young children, characters fall into three main groups: (1) a 'youth' group involving older teenagers and people in their early twenties who are either not working or have only recently begun to work, and whose personal relationships have not yet settled in any sense; (2) a large group of people stretching from approximately their middle twenties to their 1950s and in some cases later, most of whom have relationships of some duration and usually some form of work: with the exception of the Italian soap *Un posto al sole*, virtually none of the women in this group are housewives; (3) an older generation of people who have retired and who in a number of cases own property which gives them a certain level of power over the other groups.

There are no teenagers at all in the Greek soaps. With this notable exception, as mentioned earlier, it is the younger women who provide much of the zest of European soaps, and they represent a modernizing force compared to which the young men often appear static and confused. Young women at times cope with violence and abuse, while the young men seem superficial and more interested in appearance than in substance. Given the demographic patterns of European soaps, it is difficult to understand why the theme of military service is so conspicuous by its absence. It receives a highly superficial treatment in *Gute Zeiten, Schlechte Zeiten* – where Heiko's 'Zivildienst' seems to last only a couple of months – and provides an entire plotline in *I de beste familier*, but is simply not raised as an issue elsewhere. This cannot be because of its lack of dramatic potential – the storyline in *I de beste familier* was in fact highly dramatic – nor because of its lack of interest for a young female audience. Perhaps by taking the viewer into an all-male world it would be incompatible with the narrative dynamics of soaps, which require members of both sexes for plot advancement. A *very* notable trend in European soaps – and in series in general – is the extension of this 'youth' group to include people in their late twenties and even early thirties who, despite their age, continue to behave in a way which is indistinguishable from that of the younger members of the group. It is a matter of record that, with increasing levels of economic insecurity, young Europeans are marrying later, but it is also much simpler to construct characters whose responsibilities extend little beyond themselves.

The middle group is by far the most complex. Here, the women, despite the clear superiority they have shown on a number of fronts before entering the world of work, find themselves faced with institutionalized (male) power and authority which they are more or less helpless to challenge. It is not that the men in this group are exclusively villainous: on the contrary, one finds thoughtful, considerate, and even positively soft-hearted men in European soaps. They simply enjoy certain advantages of which they often seem unaware. Successful challenges by women are often at the expense of personal relationships and the economic security they can bring, or in other cases women advance by becoming as manipulative and dishonest as the men around them. Occasionally men in this group seem able to survive as virtual dropouts in a way in which the women never could.

An indexical sign of women's weakened position during this stage is the frequency with which they appear physically confined to wheelchairs. There is virtually no European soap I have viewed which has not involved one or more women in a wheelchair at one point or another. Male characters can appear in wheelchairs, but much more infrequently (and are not necessarily diminished by this: in the Swedish soap *Tre Kronor* the teenage Klimax astonished everyone by fathering a child while confined to a wheelchair). Institutionalized male power is also indexically signalled by the increasing numbers of policemen among the established lists of characters, most of them carrying guns.

As regards the third group, in many European soaps there are no men of pensionable age. They are a missing generation. And when men of this third generation do appear, they often seem either out of touch or unconsciously destructive. They are past their 'sell-by' date. The older women, by contrast, are, with only a few exceptions, all still very much in possession of their faculties and often in central positions in regard to nurturing and advice. Not only that, they frequently own substantial amounts of property, which provides them with leverage of various kinds. While the young boys, and sometimes even the men in the middle group appear to live entirely for the present, the older women in particular provide a sense of historical continuity by linking past and present.

The general life-cycle constructed by European soaps – allowing for all kinds of local variations and individual exceptions which I am not able to go into here – is one in which women appear much more competent and dynamic than men and are indeed presented as in the ascendancy in their early lives and at the end of their lives, but where they are unable to make this greater competence count during the bulk of their lives where they have to face institutionalized power imbalances of various kinds. The discrimination inherent in this cycle is not only directed against women. Men often appear to have no function in it beyond the productive. While nurturing is presented as a life-long vocation, productivity appears to be related to the possession of labour power, and social value disappears when such labour power is lost. If this is the case, part of the discursive tangle of soap operas involves the problematizing of oppressive ideologies of manhood as well as of womanhood. But we must ask ourselves why women are 'rehabilitated' – and indeed allowed to own property and exercise a certain control – when both their reproductive capability has gone, and their ability to challenge men directly in the productive sphere has passed.

Seen from this point of view, the matriarchal figures of so many soaps may be an expression of the structural weakness of women in contemporary European societies rather than of their personal strength. They are allowed to be strong when their strength has been depoliticized and others are struggling as they struggled before. The disappearance of the men is irrelevant since the structures which gave them power as individuals remain in place. If soaps are a women's genre, their initial message may be flattering, but their ultimate message would appear to be survival in a battle where the other side's troops may disappear or retire injured but whose generals and heavy artillery always remain primed for action off-screen.

Soaps and society

Many of the new soaps studied in this book were launched by the newly emergent commercial channels of the late 1980s and early 1990s. The emergence of these channels itself was closely linked to the advance of neo-liberalism as an ideology and its related set of discourses and practices in western European countries. It might seem reasonable to expect that the soaps which appeared on these commercial channels would be generally favourable to the neo-liberal hegemony, while those offered by the older PSB channels would defend the former social-democratic hegemony since (with the obvious exceptions of Greece, Portugal and Spain) they arose during the period of its ascendancy and set themselves the task, in their various ways, of educating the working-classes into useful participation in that hegemony. This has not, of course, been unproblematically the case. Although a platonically 'pure' version of the neo-liberal ideology may exist in some textbook somewhere, its implementation in each country is highly conditioned and inflected by the prevailing political, economic, social and cultural conditions in that country at any particular moment in time and their respective and collective histories, and it is that particular balance of forces which has proved to be the most powerful shaping force in the new soaps and *telenovelas* in western Europe.

At one end of the spectrum of possible outcomes, the United Kingdom has seen the most resounding failure of any soap opera linked with the attempt to promote a neo-liberal hegemony by championing individualism and bestowing moral protagonism on the new middle-classes who would lead society forward to the new entrepreneurial-consumerist tomorrow. By any standards the collapse of *Eldorado* and, in particular, *Castles* was positively spectacular, and they represented costly failures for the BBC. I believe it is perfectly possible to argue that viewers switched off from *Castles* in a dry run of the way they would switch off from the Conservative government two years later. Soaps in Britain are the symbolic refuge of an embattled social-democratic worldview. *Hollyoaks* learned this lesson in time and survived. *Family Affairs* learned it in advance and seems to have achieved a solid enough base to continue.

At the other end of the spectrum lie the new German soaps. In their varying ways they both celebrate and construct an affluent and mostly younger middle-class consumer looking to pull society forward cheerfully in his or her wake. More than any other soaps the new German productions idealize the public sphere, particularly as far as their female characters are concerned: the public sphere is presented as an area of experience replete with opportunities for self-fulfilment, -advancement and leadership. It goes without saying that, even in a very affluent society such as Germany, the world of work in general does *not* offer guaranteed satisfaction and self-fulfilment to those who enter it. On the contrary, for both men and women – but in particular for immigrant women, who feature very little in these soaps – it can be an area of life characterized by unrewarding labour, low income and fatigue *in addition to* (rather than as an escape from) the ongoing responsibilities of home: in extreme cases it can be a site of degradation and even humiliation. Germany is the country with the greatest dichotomy in this respect. *Lindenstraße*, produced by a PSB station in a broad British tradition, both acknowledges and tackles the problems of German society, but the collapse of the 'public' *Jede Menge Leben* and the 'commercial' *So ist das Leben: die Wagenfelds*, together with the 'youthification' and glamorizing of *Marienhof* and the launch of *Verbotene Liebe* on the public service channel Das Erste show clearly where the centre of gravity of this particular soap-cum-social universe is moving.

In between these two extremes lie all kinds of permutations: the confident statement of top-down, social-democratic principle of the major Flemish soap *Familie*; the Norwegian soaps' principled stance against management aggression and official discrimination; the timid social-democratic suggestiveness of *Un posto al sole* in Italy; *Landsbyen*'s wistful nostalgia for more thoughtful times in Denmark; the uncelebratory defensiveness of the two main Dutch soaps *Goede Tijden, Slechte Tijden* and *Onderweg naar Morgen*; the awkward co-existence of the two strands of Swedish soaps, chronicling the disintegration of the *folkhem* but unable to work up much enthusiasm for the alternative; the unconvincing upward mobility of *Fair City* in Ireland, where the economic opportunities opened up by the 'tiger economy' allow erstwhile proles to open furniture-restoring workshops in lock-ups; and the epic rewriting of history as reconfigured entrepreneurial myth provided in Finland by *Puhtaat valkeat lakanat* and *Metsolat*.

In Portugal, Greece and Spain different histories have produced different kinds of societies and different serials. The Catalan *telenovelas* and others influenced by them struggle both to throw off a dictatorial past and repel the neo-liberal future, and attempt to construct an alliance capable of defending the values and gains of Spain's fledgling welfare state. Greece and Portugal are the two countries in Europe characterized by the most proprietorial attitude of those in power towards the state. During Cavaco Silva's ten-year period in office there were many references in Portugal to the emergence of the 'Orange State', orange being the colour of his party's official emblem. Many now feel that, since the victory of the Socialists in 1995, the state has merely changed from orange to pink (Robinson, 1997). The use of the state by Greek politicians as a source of grace and favour is a, by now, quite notorious element of the political structures of that country. The failure to develop the substance rather than the mechanics of a truly modern political system has resulted in a crisis of stasis which has also paralysed the television serials of these two countries. The Portuguese *telenovelas* address an intellectualizing sub-élite which appears to have opted out of any kind of modernizing mission in favour of élitism and privilege, leaving the way open to the satisfaction of popular tastes via imported products with a strongly modernizing message, and producing much the same kind of cultural panics as were visible elsewhere in Europe in relation to the American soaps of the 1980s. The Greek soaps remain utterly *sui generis*, allegorizing a society riven with internal tensions, largely closed in on itself, and lacking a feasible project for the future. It seems unlikely that either of these situations can continue indefinitely, and since *Desencontros* and, in particular, *Roseira Brava*, there are some small signs that the Portuguese productions are indeed changing.

Soaps and *telenovelas* remain unique indexes of the societies in which they are produced. Their endless presence, the constant need for renewal, the uninterrupted dialogue between producers and consumers, the toing and froing, the permanent negotiation over what is and what is not acceptable, give them an organic relationship with social and political trends, large and small. They are not so much 'in' the societies in question as 'of' them, their tangled roots stretching into the past and their ever-extending branches growing into the future. Their storylines may at times be trite and their dialogues may on occasions be trivial, but these serials are a dialect of the language of material power. Speakers become listeners and listeners become speakers in a constant interpenetration of roles. They are a form of popular democracy operating day in, day out, not just once every four or five years at the polls.

The social and human cost of the neo-liberal advance is there for all to see as throughout Europe job security diminishes, unemployment increases or is masked by permanent jobs being replaced by temporary, often low-paid ones; services of all kinds deteriorate, social tension rises, racism becomes more prevalent, people who cannot afford private medical treatment actually die because there are insufficient hospital beds, and it becomes impossible to visit any sizeable European town or city without being invited to purchase *The Big Issue* (UK), *Le Réverbère* (France), *El Farol* (Spain), *De Daklozenkrant* (Belgium), *miss* (Germany) or similar. And all this despite the fact that the countries of western Europe are among the wealthiest on earth.

It is not my intention to present the former social-democratic hegemony as some kind of paradise on Earth. Like any hegemony its function was to maintain the economically ruling class in its position of power through strategic alliances with, and concessions to, other groups, and it was marked by many weaknesses and imperfections and by frequent failures of courage and even goodwill among the politicians. It was inherently paternalistic and could often be arrogant and even arbitrary. It was characterized by a deep-seated aversion among its intellectuals to popular culture in all its manifestations. It is a place to which there can be, at least in its former manifestations, no return. Nonetheless, it did provide levels of support and security for ordinary people which are now under very real threat.

However imperfect the *practice* of social democracy may have been in certain respects, the journey towards a society which is interested in and pays greater attention to the needs of all its members cannot even begin until at least some of the basic *principles* of social democracy are rediscovered, revitalized and reasserted. And this study of European soaps shows clearly where these values are still alive and where they are still cherished. Almost without exception, the macronarratives of all the major soaps and *telenovelas* in most of the countries analysed – including Germany, where *Lindenstraße* continues to outperform the 'new' soaps by a factor of around 2 to 1 – promote the values of solidarity, caring for and about others, defending other people's rights, compromise and co-operation. In fact, these values are defended at all levels, at the micronarrative level of personal relationships and at the metanarrative level of topical issues as well as at the macronarrative, and those who wilfully break the rules are consistently presented as negative and destructive. Only the teen soaps celebrate individualism – 'teen' in the sense that they address an exclusively teen audience, or, as in the case of *Gute Zeiten, Schlechte Zeiten* in Germany, they continue to construct their audience as teenagers long after they have ceased to be teenagers in reality. But these are, in most cases, serials with very small viewerships and, if the experience of the Australian teen soaps is anything to go by, these soaps will remain 'forever young', they will not grow with their audience, and that audience will gradually move elsewhere, a process which is now well under way in the UK.

Throughout the great bulk of European soaps and *telenovelas*, greed and selfishness are *the* great sins, as are bullying and aggression. But these serials also come out against paternalism in all its forms, old and new. They create communities based on solidarity and sharing, but also communities which are open, participatory and democratic. Communities of this kind will not be possible in reality until the organic intellectuals of social democracy, be they academics, journalists, politicians or whatever, establish a meaningful contact with their only natural allies, the ordinary working people of European countries in general. And that will not happen until they develop a greater understanding of and a greater openness towards the vitalities and energies of popular culture rather than simply carping magisterially about its weakness and limitations (which undoubtedly exist), something they have, by and large, failed to do in the past. This is the challenge which lies ahead. This book hopes to have contributed, in however small a measure, to that process.

Bibliography

Allen, R.C. (1985) *Speaking of Soap Operas*, Chapel Hill and London: University of North Carolina Press.
Allen, R.C. (1989) 'Bursting bubbles: "soap opera", audiences, and the limits of genre', in E. Seiter, H. Borchers, G. Kreutzner and E.-M. Warth (eds), *Remote Control*, London: Routledge.
Allen, R.C. (1995) 'Introduction', in R.C. Allen (ed.), *To Be Continued . . . : Soap Operas Around the World*, London: Routledge.
Alvarado, M., Locksley, G. and Paskin, S. (1992) 'Great Britain', in A. Silj (ed.), *The New Television in Europe*, London: John Libbey.
Anderson, P. (1992) *English Questions*, London: Verso.
Ang, I. (1985) *Watching Dallas: Soap Opera and the Melodramatic Imagination*, London: Methuen.
Ang, I. (1991) *Desperately Seeking the Audience*, London: Routledge.
Atkinson, D. (1997) 'Attitudes towards language use in Catalonia: politics or sociolinguistics?', *International Journal of Iberian Studies*, 10(4).
Barbatsis, G. and Guy, Y. (1991) 'Analyzing meaning in form: soap opera's compositional construction of "realness"', *Journal of Broadcasting and Electronic Media*, 35(1).
Barthes, R. (1970) *S/Z*, Paris: Editions du Seuil.
Barthes, R. (1973) (Trans. A. Lavers) *Mythologies*, London: Granada.
Barthes, R. (1986) (Trans. R. Howard) 'From work to text', in *The Rustle of Language*, London: Basil Blackwell.
Bergendahl, H., Granlund, M. and Krutrök, S. (1992) *Rederiet: Analys av en svensk dramaserie*, Stockholm: JMK, Stockholm University.
Biltereyst, D. (1991) 'Resisting American hegemony: a comparative analysis of the reception of American and domestic fiction', *European Journal of Communication*, 6(4).
Biltereyst, D. (1992) 'Language and culture as ultimate barriers? An analysis of the circulation, consumption and popularity of fiction in small European countries', *European Journal of Communication*, 7(4).
Biltereyst, D. (1994) 'Stereotypes, kinetics and expression in US television fiction: a comparative textual analysis', paper presented at the Screen Conference, Glasgow.
Bleicher, J.K. (1995) 'Die *Lindenstraße* im Kontext deutscher Familienserien', in M. Jurga (ed.), *Lindenstraße: Produktion und Rezeption einer Erfolgsserie*, Opladen: Westdeutscher.

Bocca, G. (1990) *La disUNITÀ d'Italia*, Milan: Garzanti.

Braga da Cruz, M. (1995) *Instituições Políticas e Processos Sociais*, Venda Nova: Bertrand.

Brants, K. and McQuail, D. (1992) 'The Netherlands', in B.S. Østergaard (ed.), *The Media in Western Europe*, London: Sage.

Brooks, P. (1985) *The Melodramatic Imagination*, New York: Columbia University Press.

Brunsdon, C. (1981) '*Crossroads*: notes on soap opera', *Screen*, 22(4).

Brunsdon, C. (1995) 'The role of soap opera in the development of feminist television scholarship', in R.C. Allen (ed.), *To Be Continued . . . :Soap Operas Around the World*, London: Routledge.

Bryn, S. (1993) 'Coca-Cola Co. and the Olympic movement: sharing the same global vision?', in R. Puijk (ed.), *OL-94 og forskningen III*, Lillehammer: OL dokumentas-jonstjeneste.

Buckingham, D. (1987) *Public Secrets: EastEnders and Its Audience*, London: BFI.

Buckman, P. (1984) *All for Love: A Study in Soap Opera*, London: Secker and Warburg.

Buonanno, M. (1994) *Narrami o diva: studi sull'immaginario televisivo*, Naples: Liguori.

Butler, J.G. (1995) ' "I'm not a doctor, but I play one on TV": characters, actors and acting in television soap opera', in R.C. Allen (ed.), *To Be Continued . . . : Soap Operas Around the World*, London: Routledge.

Cádima, F.R. (1996) *História e Crítica da Comunicação*, Lisbon: Edições Século XXI.

Carlsson, U. and Anshelm, M. (1995) *Media Sverige 1995: Statistik och analys*, Gothenburg: Nordicom-Sverige.

Chanian, R. (1994) *La télévision de 1983 à 1993: Chronique des programmes et de leur public*, Paris: INA.

Chapman, M. (1978) *The Gaelic Vision in Scottish Culture*, London: Croom Helm.

Chippindale, P. and Franks, S. (1991) *Dished! The Rise and Fall of British Satellite Broadcasting*, London: Simon and Schuster.

Collin, L. (1994) 'Tystnad! Tvagning!', *Månadsjournal*, no. 4.

Cormack, M. (1993) 'Problems of minority language broadcasting: Gaelic in Scotland', *European Journal of Communication*, 8(1).

Cormack, M. (1994) 'Programming for cultural defence: the expansion of Gaelic television', *Scottish Affairs*, no. 6.

Corner, J. (1992) 'Presumption as theory: "realism" in television studies', *Screen*, 33(1).

Crofts, S. (1995) 'Global *Neighbours*?', in R.C. Allen (ed.), *To Be Continued . . . : Soap Operas Around the World*, London: Routledge.

Cronström, J. and Höijer, B. (1996) *En studie av våld i sex svenska TV-kanaler: 40 timmar i veckan*, Stockholm: Våldskildringsrådet.

Cunningham, S. and Jacka, E. (1996) *Australian Television and International Mediascapes*, Cambridge: Cambridge University Press.

Devereux, E. (1997) 'The theatre of reassurance? *Glenroe*, its audience and the coverage of social problems', in H.J. Kelly and B. O'Connor (eds), *Media Audiences in Ireland*, Dublin: University College Dublin Press.

Di Tota, M.F. (1997) 'Sporting success and political failure: sport as a metaphor for Italian politics', in R. Puijk (ed.), *Global Spotlight on Lillehammer*, London: John Libbey.

Dyer, R. (ed.) (1981) *Coronation Street*, London: BFI.

Earls, M. (1984) 'The Late Late Show: controversy and context', in M. McLoone and J. MacMahon (eds), *Television and Irish Society*, Dublin: RTE/IFI.

Eco, U. (1978) *Il superuomo di massa*, Milan: Bompiani.

Eco, U. (1981) *The Role of the Reader: Explorations in the Semiotics of Texts*, London: Hutchinson.

Eco, U. (1992) 'Overinterpreting texts', in S. Collini (ed.), *Interpretation and over-interpretation*, Cambridge: Cambridge University Press.

Fenati, B. and Rizza, N. (1992) 'Schedules and programmes on television in Italy', in A. Silj (ed.), *The New Television in Europe*, London: John Libbey.

Ferguson, M. (1992) 'Mythology about globalization', *European Journal of Communication*, 7(1).

Ferreira, J.H. (1992) 'Portugal', in B.S. Østergaard (ed.), *The Media in Western Europe*, London: Sage.

Feuer, J. (1984) 'Melodrama, serial form and television today', *Screen*, 25(1).

Fishman, J. (1991) *Reversing Language Shift*, Clevedon: Multilingual Matters.

Fiske, J. (1987) *Television Culture: Popular Pleasures and Politics*, London and New York: Methuen.

Forgacs, D. (1988) *A Gramsci Reader: Selected Writings 1916–1935*, London: Lawrence and Wishart.

Frey-Vor, G. (1995) 'Die Rezeption der *Lindenstraße* im Spiegel der angewandten Medienforschung', in M. Jurga (ed.), *Lindenstraße: Produktion und Rezeption einer Erfolgsserie*, Opladen: Westdeutscher Verlag.

Frykman, J. (1993) 'Nationella ord och handlingar', in B. Ehn, J. Frykman and O. Löfgren, *Försvenskningen av Sverige*, Stockholm: Natur och Kultur.

Furhammar, L. (1991) *Filmen i Sverige*, Stockholm: Wiken.

Furhammar, L. (1992) 'Hos Runåkers och Öhmans: Återblick på den svenska televisionens första tvåloperor', in *Rutmönster: Om TV*, Stockholm: Norstedts.

Geißendörfer, H.W. (1995) 'Lindenstraße: Die Dramaturgie der Endlosigkeit', in M. Jurga (ed.), *Lindenstraße: Produktion und Rezeption einer Erfolgsserie*, Opladen: Westdeutscher.

Geraghty, C. (1981) 'The continuous serial: a definition', in R. Dyer (ed.), *Coronation Street*, London: BFI.

Geraghty, C. (1991) *Women and Soap Opera: A Study of Prime Time Soap*, London: Polity.

Geraghty, C. (1995) 'Social issues and realist soaps: a study of British soaps in the 1980s/1990s', in R.C. Allen (ed.), *To Be Continued . . . : Soap Operas Around the World*, London: Routledge.

Gillespie, M. (1995) *Television, Ethnicity and Cultural Change*, London: Routledge.

González, R. (1995) 'Un savoir-faire latino-américain: la telenovela – les origines', in G. Schneier-Madanes (ed.), *L'Amérique latine et ses télévisions: Du local au mondial*, Paris: Anthropos/INA.

González, R.J. (1992) *El discurso televisivo: espectáculo de la posmodernidad*, Madrid: Catedra.

Griffiths, A. (1995) 'National and cultural identity in a Welsh-language soap opera', in R.C. Allen (ed.), *To Be Continued . . . : Soap Operas Around the World*, London: Routledge.

Gripsrud, J. (1995) *The Dynasty Years: Hollywood Television and Critical Media Studies*, London: Routledge.

Gustafsson, K.E. (1992) 'Sweden', in B.S. Østergaard (ed.), *The Media in Western Europe*, London: Sage.

Gustafsson, E. and Lovén, Å. (1993) *En produktionsstudie av TV-följetongen Rederiet*, Stockholm: JMK, Stockholm University.

Gustafsson, E. and Lovén, Å. (1994) *En receptionsstudie av Rederiets publik: kvinnor och män som TV-tittare*, Stockholm: JMK, Stockholm University.

Hadenius, S. (1992) 'Vulnerable values in a changing political and media system: the case of Sweden', in J.G. Blumler (ed.), *Television and the Public Interest: Vulnerable Values in West European Broadcasting*, London: Sage.

Halliwell, L. and Purser, P. (1982) *Halliwell's Television Companion*, London: Granada.

Hayward, S. (1990) 'Le feuilleton anglais: la querelle des anciens et des modernes "soap style" ', in R. Gardies (ed.), *Les Feuilletons télévisés européens*, Institut National de l'Audiovisuel.

Hellack, G. (1996) *Presse, Hörfunk und Fernsehen in der Bundesrepublik Deutschland*, Bonn: Inter Nationes.

Hietala, V. (1994) 'Finnish television today', in F. Bono and I. Bondeberg (eds), *Nordic Television: History, Politics and Aesthetics*, University of Copenhagen: Sekvens.

Hjorth, A. (1985) 'Kvinderne og *Dallas*', in R. Pittelkow (ed.), *Analyser af TV*, Copenhagen: Medusa.

Hobson, D. (1983) *Crossroads: The Drama of a Soap Opera*, London: Methuen.

Hoffman, M. (1992) 'Germany', in A. Silj (ed.), *The New Television in Europe*, London: John Libbey.

Jenny, E. (1992) 'Le dossier "Riviera" ', in R. Prédal (ed.), *Feuilletons et téléfilms français d'aujourd'hui*, Condé-sur-Noireau: Corlet-Télérama.

Jiretorn, E. (1994) *Glamour i vardagen: En innehålls- och receptionsanalys av såpoperan Glamour och dess tittare*, Stockholm: JMK, Stockholm University.

Jordan, M. (1981) 'Realism and convention', in R. Dyer (ed.), *Coronation Street*, London: BFI.

Jurga, M. (1995) 'Die *Lindenstraße* als kulturelles Forum', in M. Jurga (ed.), *Lindenstraße: Produktion und Rezeption einer Erfolgsserie*, Opladen: Westdeutscher.

Jurga, M. (ed.) (1995) *Lindenstraße: Produktion und Rezeption einer Erfolgsserie*, Opladen: Westdeutscher.

Kainz, G. (1989) *Svensk Tvålopera ... Finns det?*, Stockholm University: Institutionen för teater- och filmvetenskap.

Katz, E. and Liebes, T. (1990) *The Export of Meaning: Cross-Cultural Readings of Dallas*, New York: Oxford University Press.

Kelly, M. (1984) 'Twenty years of current affairs on RTE', in M. McLoone and J. MacMahon (eds), *Television and Irish Society*, Dublin: RTE/IFI.

Kelly, M. and Truetzschler, W. (1992) 'Ireland', in B. Østergaard (ed.), *The Media in Western Europe*, London: Sage.

Kilborn, R. (1992) *Television Soaps*, London: Batsford.

Kingsley, H. (1988) *Soap Box*, London: Methuen.

Liebes, T. and Livingstone, S.M. (1992) 'Mothers and lovers: managing women's role conflicts in American and British soap operas', in J.G. Blumler, J.M. McLeod and K.E. Rosengren (eds), *Comparatively Speaking: Communication and Culture across Space and Time*, London: Sage.

Löfgren, O. (1993) 'Nationella arenor', in B. Ehn, J. Frykman and O. Löfgren, *Försvenskningen av Sverige*, Stockholm: Natur och Kultur.

Lopez, A.M. (1995) 'Our welcomed guests', in R.C. Allen (ed.), *To Be Continued ... : Soap Operas Around the World*, London: Routledge.

López-Pumarejo, T. (1987) *Aproximación a la telenovela*, Madrid: Catedra.

Lotze, W. (1995) *Das amtliche Lindenstraßenbuch*, Frankfurt: Eichborn.

Lundby, K. and Futsæter, K.-A. (1993) *Flerkanalsamfunnet: Fra monopol til mangfold*, Oslo: Universitetsforlaget.

McArthur, C. (1981) 'Days of hope', in T. Bennet, S. Boyd-Bowman, C. Mercer and J. Woollacott (eds), *Popular Television and Film*, London: BFI.

MacCabe, C. (1981a) 'Realism and the cinema: notes on some Brechtian theses', in T. Bennet, S. Boyd-Bowman, C. Mercer and J. Woollacott (eds), *Popular Television and Film*, London: BFI.

MacCabe, C. (1981b) 'Days of hope: a response to Colin McArthur', in T. Bennet, S. Boyd-Bowman, C. Mercer and J. Woollacott (eds), *Popular Television and Film*, London: BFI.

MacDonald, R. (1993) 'Renaissance v. preservation', *Media Education Journal*, no. 14.

MacDonald, R. (1994) 'Gaelic renaissance versus Gaelic preservation', Sabhal Mòr lecture (unpublished).

McLoone, M. (1984) 'Strumpet city: the urban working class on Irish television', in M. McLoone and J. MacMahon (eds), *Television and Irish Society*, Dublin: RTE/IFI.

McLoone, M. and MacMahon, J. (eds) (1984) *Television and Irish Society*, Dublin: RTE/ IFI.

Marques de Melo, J. (1995) 'Development of the audiovisual industry in Brazil from importer to exporter of television programming', *Canadian Journal of Communication*, 20.

Martín-Barbero, J. (1987) *De los medios a las mediaciones: comunicación, cultura y hegemonía*, Barcelona: Gustavo Gili.

Martín-Barbero, J. (1995) 'Memory and form in the Latin American telenovela', in R.C. Allen (ed.), *To Be Continued . . . : Soap Operas Around the World*, London: Routledge.

Mateo, R. de and Corbella, J.M. (1992) 'Spain', in B.S. Østergaard (ed.), *The Media in Western Europe*, London: Sage.

Mazzoleni, G. (1992) 'Italy', in B. Østergaard (ed.), *The Media in Western Europe*, London: Sage.

Miller, D. (1995) 'The consumption of soap opera: *The Young and the Restless* and mass consumption in Trinidad', in R.C. Allen (ed.), *To Be Continued . . . : Soap Operas Around the World*, London: Routledge.

Mohr, P. and O'Donnell, H. (1996) 'The rise and rise of soap operas in Europe', *Scottish Communication Association Journal*, 2.

Morley, D. (1980) *The Nationwide Audience: Structure and Decoding*. London: BFI.

Murschetz, P. (1996) 'Transfrontier competition and the future of the ORF', *Intermedia*, 24(4).

Nairn, T. (1988) *The Enchanted Glass: Britain and Its Monarchy*, London: Radius.

Nieuwenhuis, A.J. (1992) 'Media policy in the Netherlands: beyond the market?', *European Journal of Communication*, 7(2).

O'Connor, B. (1990) *Soap and Sensibility: Audience Response to* Dallas *and* Glenroe, Dublin: RTE.

O'Donnell, H. (1994) 'Mapping the mythical: a geopolitics of national sporting stereotypes', *Discourse and Society*, 5(3).

O'Donnell, H. (1996a) 'From a Manichean universe to the kitchen sink: the *telenovela* in the Iberian peninsula', *International Journal of Iberian Studies*, 9(1).

O'Donnell, H. (1996b) 'From "People's Home" to "Home and Away": the growth and development of soap opera in Sweden', *Irish Communication Review*, no. 6.

O'Donnell, H. and León Solís, F. (1997) 'The Catalan Janus: discourses of national identity in the Catalan press', paper delivered at the First Scottish Conference of Catalan Studies, Strathclyde University.

Oltean, T. (1993) 'Series and seriality in media culture', *European Journal of Communication*, 8(1).

Ortiz, R. (1995) 'Un savoir-faire latino-américain: la telenovela – la fabrication', in G. Schneier-Madanes (ed.), *L'Amérique latine et ses télévisions: Du local au mondial*, Paris: Anthropos/INA.

Ortoleva, P. (1992) 'Private codes: commercial television in Italian society', in A. Silj (ed.), *The New Television in Europe*, London: John Libbey.

Østbye, H. (1992) 'Norway', in B.S. Østergaard (ed.), *The Media in Western Europe*, London: Sage.

Patterson, R. and Stewart, J. (1991) 'Street life', in R. Dyer (ed.), *Coronation Street*, London: BFI.

Pedersen, V. (1993) 'Soap, pin-up and burlesque: commercialisation and femininity in Danish television', *Nordicom*, 2.

Petersen, V. (1992) 'Commercial television in Scandinavia', in A. Silj (ed.), *The New Television in Europe*, London: John Libbey.

Petersen, V.G. and Siune, K. (1992) 'Denmark', in B.S. Østergaard (ed.), *The Media in Western Europe*, London: Sage.

Phillips, L. (1996) 'Rhetoric and the spread of the discourse of Thatcherism', *Discourse and Society*, 7(2).

Puijk, R. (ed.) (1997) *Global Spotlight on Lillehammer*, London: John Libbey.

Radway, J. (1984) *Reading the Romance: Women, Patriarchy, and Popular Literature*, Chapel Hill: University of North Carolina Press.

Robinson, R.A.H. (1997) 'Opposition parties and the premiership of Cavaco Silva', *International Journal of Iberian Studies*, 10(2).

Ross, S. (1994) 'Företagare i TV-fiktion', in H. De Geer (ed.), *Skapare, skojare och skurkar, företagaren i litteratur, film och konst*, Stockholm: Timbaro.

Ross, S. (1995) 'Makt och moral i fyra TV-serier: En publikstudie', paper presented at the 12th Nordic Conference on Mass Media Research, Helsingør.

Roura, A. (1993) *Telenovelas: pasiones de mujer*, Barcelona: Gedisa.

Schabedoth, E. (1995) 'Inhalt oder Form? Überlegungen zur Rezeptionsstruktur der *Lindenstraße*', in M. Jurga (ed.), Lindenstraße: *Produktion und Rezeption einer Erfolgsserie*, Opladen: Westdeutscher.

Schrøder, K. (1988) 'The pleasure of *Dynasty*: the weekly reconstruction of self-confidence', in P. Drummond and R. Patterson (eds), *Television and Its Audiences: International Research Perspectives*, London: BFI.

Sheehan, H. (1987) *Irish Television Drama: A Society and Its Stories*, Dublin: RTE.

Sheehan, H. (1993) 'Soap opera and social order: *Glenroe, Fair City* and contemporary Ireland', paper presented at the Imagining Ireland Conference, Irish Film Centre, Dublin.

Silj, A. (1988) *East of* Dallas: *The European Challenge to American Television*, London: BFI.

Silj, A. (1992) 'Domestic markets and the European market', in A. Silj (ed.), *The New Television in Europe*, London: John Libbey.

Stam, R., Burgoyne, R. and Flitterman-Lewis, S. (1992) *New Vocabularies in Film Semiotics: Structuralism, Post-Structuralism and Beyond*, London: Routledge.

Stern, L. (1978) 'Oedipal opera: *The Restless Years*', *Australian Journal of Screen Theory*, 4.

Stewart, M. (1997) 'Name wars: the case of *valencià*', *International Journal of Iberian Studies*, 9(3).

Storey, J. (1993) *An Introductory Guide to Cultural Theory and Popular Culture*, London: Harvester Wheatsheaf.

Tapper, H. (1992) 'Finland', in B.S. Østergaard (ed.), *The Media in Western Europe*, London: Sage.

Tracey, M. and Redal, W.W. (1995) 'The new parochialism: the triumph of the populist in the flow of international television', *Canadian Journal of Communication*, 20.

Trudgill, P. (1983) *Sociolinguistics: An Introduction to Language and Society* (rev. edn: 1st edn 1974), London: Penguin.

Tsagarousianou, R. and Sofos, S. (1993) 'The politics of identity: nationalism in contemporary Greece', in J. Amodia (ed.), *The Resurgence of Nationalist Movements in Europe*, Bradford Occasional Papers no. 12, Bradford: University of Bradford.

Tsaliki, L. (1995a) 'The media and the construction of an "imagined community": the role of media events on Greek television', *European Journal of Communication*, London: Sage.

Tsaliki, L. (1995b) 'Greek TV since deregulation', *Intermedia*, 23(5).

Valbuena Briones, A. (1969) *Literatura Hispanoamericana*, Barcelona: Gustavo Gili.

Valbuena Prats, A. (1968) *Historia de la Literatura Española*, Barcelona: Gustavo Gili.

Villagrasa, J.M. (1992) 'Spain: the emergence of commercial television', in A. Silj (ed.), *The New Television in Europe*, London: John Libbey.

Vogelgesang, W. (1995) 'Jugendliches Medien-Fantum: Die Anhänger der *Lindenstraße* im

Reigen medienvermittelter Jugendwelten', in M. Jurga (ed.), *Lindenstraße: Produktion und Rezeption einer Erfolgsserie*, Opladen: Westdeutscher.

Watson, I. (1997) 'A history of Irish language broadcasting: national ideology, commercial interest and minority rights', in M.J. Kelly and B. O'Connor (eds), *Media Audiences in Ireland*, Dublin: University College Dublin Press.

Williams, C. (1994) 'After the classic, the classical and ideology: the differences of realism', *Screen*, 35(3).

Wolf, M. (1994) 'Mass media: tra bulimia e anoressia', in P. Ginsborg (ed.), *Stato dell'Italia: Il balancio politico, economico, sociale e culturale di un paese che cambia*, Milan: Il Saggiatore.

Index of Names

Index of Programmes

Note on alphabetical order: definite and indefinite articles have been given at the start of entries.

Subject Index